APOSTLE C

MW01282804

LEADERSHIP
IN MOTION

Crisis! Essence! Purpose! Vision!

For book bulk purchase at special quantity discount for sales promotion, fund-raising, and educational needs, write to Harbor Lights Associates, Inc.
Email us at eldergemma@msn.com

Leadership in Motion
Copyright © 2014 by Gemma Valentine
Harbor Lights Associates, Inc.
P. O. Box 3273
McKinney, TX 75070

Printed in the U.S.A

For rights to publish in other languages please contact publisher.

Library of Congress Cataloging-in-Publication Data
Valentine, Gemma
Leadership in motion / Gemma Valentine . – 1st edition.

LCCN: 2014906180

1.Religion/Christianity/Leadership

ISBN:10:1497462401
ISBN-13:978-1497462403

Leaders are found in every sector of life. We have national leaders at various levels, community leaders, corporate leaders, church leaders and those who lead families. A leader is an instrument by which men and women clarify their own thoughts. Godly leaders provide a standard by which men and women measure themselves. When a trustworthy leader speaks, listeners judge their own beliefs according to what the person whom they respect is saying. A leader provides purpose and energy for life. Without vision and direction, people go through life discouraged and disillusioned. Leaders unite people. We were created with a need to belong and work together, but without leadership that will be impossible.

This book is dedicated to my husband John Adolphus Valentine, my daughters Nicole Reagan Valentine and Naomi Elizabeth Valentine Fayose, my father Emile Lazare and my mother Rhoda Naomi Lewis Lazare.

CONTENTS

Acknowledgments

Once again Apostle Gemma Valentine has blessed the Body of Christ with a thought provoking book. This is a must read for every minister who desires to understand the day and season the church is in. She provides balance and insight into the type of leadership necessary for this generation. It is truly an eye opener for many called into the ministry in these last days.

Apostle Bernadette Sylvester,
Divine Purpose Worship Reformation Center.

Many authors have written books on leadership for God's people, and we applaud them for their work. However, based on her experience being in ministry for many years, the author has written a book about God's leader for today's generation. In this book she gives the reader a look at leadership from a transformational point of view, which is leadership by example; while pointing out the problems that have surfaced among leaders, and the requirements for effective leadership for this present generation.

Network Participants,
Watchmen and Gatekeepers.

In this present season God is putting the spotlight on leadership in the Body of Christ. What qualifies a person to be a leader among men? And what qualities must a true leader possess? Apostle Valentine examines the essence of leadership, mainly because leaders have such influence over people, and people turn to their leaders for governance and direction.

Apostle John E. Wilson,
St John's Full Gospel Deliverance Church.

Introduction

Navigating through the changing landscape of ministry in the present generation has made me well aware that with the many reformation movements that have taken place in the Body of Christ, that if we, the leadership, are not in tune with the Holy Spirit we will miss the present moves of God and join the ranks of so many that are stuck in religiosity, ideologies, and misunderstanding. The hidden things of God can only come to us by revelation and we must have the wisdom and discernment to decipher the seasons and changes on the spiritual landscape, so we can relate, experience, and participate in present truth, like the men of the tribe of Issachar who knew what Israel ought to do.

There are many voices in Christendom vying for our attention and allegiance, and it will take courage for one to accept one's divine placement in this apostolic, prophetic age at a time when many leaders have lost their focus on eternity. Would you rather live long and have acceptance of man by conforming to the will of man and never achieve your divine destiny? Or would you rather live the life God ordained for you, and achieve your purpose with controversy and the critical disdain of others?

When the hand of God is on a person's life, and he or she has equivocally said yes to the summons and leading of the Holy Spirit, he or she has a responsibility to himself or herself to seek to know the will, mind and purpose of God for his or her life-long calling. Failure to do so may result in following the wrong voice with the wrong message and wrong motives; or he or she may face the ever present challenge of being stuck in an environment where there is no movement toward having a kingdom experience, upgrading to a new wine skin, receiving a new mantle, or entering a new dimension of grace and a new level of anointing prescribed by God.

There is also the hidden dangers that many of the chosen ones face, one of which is being raised in a spiritual environment, where there is a lack of mentorship and training conducive to raising the next generation of apostles, prophets, pastors, teachers and evangelists. If the headship leaders have not been given an allotment of apostolic or prophetic anointing and grace, how can they mentor, teach and train those in their congregation who may be called to that function in the Body of Christ? Most pastors suppress and condemn what they are not gifted in, instead of bringing in proven and qualified people to train and teach their congregation.

A mentorship program is vital for every young minister to learn the nuances of ministry. Everyone called to the ministry is not a pastor. Being called by God into ministry does not mean that a person has to start a church. There are souls out there that would never grace the doors of a church, but they will respond to someone in the market-place or someone engaged in field ministry whose calling is to the highways and hedges and not the four walls of the church.

It is essential that the minister in training knows that there is a period of time for development and maturity. When the natural seed is planted in fertile soil it experiences metamorphosis; the same rule applies to the spirit; there is a transitional change known as transformation, that all the sons of God have to experience to inherit their divine destiny. While many put all their focus on preaching, it is important that the minister in training or leader balance his or her focus on character development which is essential for longevity and the right impact on the society of believers. Honoring God is something we do with our lives, character, and our worship.

The lack of wisdom and understanding about one's personal call, and how to function in his or her divine calling, has caused many to give in to the pressures placed on them by people, who want them to take a position in ministry to which God did not call them. Then there are those restless ones whose anxiety has caused them to step out too soon to build a ministry without the necessary vision, skill or foundation. Every ministerial gift must have a foundation in the word of God, and should be trained in the rudiments and protocol of ministry. A relationship with Jesus Christ is established through seeking Him in prayer, studying the word, and intimacy with the Holy Spirit.

I recently listened to the testimony of an apostle who started a church and was having much difficulty with getting it off the ground. He moved the ministry to various locations hoping that people in those communities would attend his church, until finally he went before God to ask the most vital question, "What should I do?" God told him, "You are not to pastor a church."

He was walking in the grace of an itinerant ambassadorial apostle until someone he respected in ministry told him he should be a pastor; he agreed because his desire was to have a striving local church that could support the lifestyle he and his wife wanted. But that was not the will of God for his life. To be in God's will he had to revert to the specific nature of the call of God and the instructions given to him by the Spirit of God.

After Saul the son of Kish, of the tribe of Benjamin, was chosen by God to be the first king of Israel, he had to experience transformation before elevation. His spirit, mentality and emotions had to be transformed and elevated to the level of a governmental leader of a nation. The Prophet Samuel said to him, "Then the Spirit of God will fall on you, you will prophesy with them and be turned into another man! It happened as soon as he had turned his back to leave Samuel, God gave him another heart; and all those signs took place that day." (1 Samuel 10: 6, 9 –KJV, NIV, ASV).

The environment Saul was raised in did not facilitate the quality of grooming necessary to produce a king. When we first learned about Saul he was sent on an errand by his father to search for lost donkeys. Saul was not an aristocrat, he was not educated in the best schools of that period, he knew nothing about government or being the general of any army, but he was chosen by God.

God changed the man's heart and anointed him with the capability and presence to be a king above and beyond the level of the kings of the other nations around Israel, because Jehovah was his God; all Saul had to do was obey Jehovah and develop Godly character.

We are in a new day, there is a new move of the spirit, and a new generation of leaders is here. They have a different mindset and a different tone which will enable them to embrace this apostolic season. Leaders have to be a blessing if they want God's blessing. God wants leaders who have the heart to be a blessing in the community, and in the nation. We can no longer be narrow-minded and think about "my church, my people, and my ministry." We have to expand our thoughts to receive a kingdom mindset. God's kingdom rules over all. It is a kingdom anointing that will facilitate the breakthrough we need and desire.

As leaders we have to position ourselves for the future, the church needs able, powerful leaders, equipped with integrity, wisdom and truth, hating covetousness, and filled with the Holy Spirit. God is raising up an apostolic company that is kingdom-minded. The kingdom needs more than preachers, there is a need for builders, givers, intercessors, teachers, administrators, market place people that have resources, talents and gifts to align themselves with apostolic leaders like Nehemiah whose apostolic assignment was to rebuild the wall of the city.

The failures of many in leadership today are: [a] No precise word from God pertaining to their calling, mission, and purpose in the kingdom, [b] A lack of mentorship and training, [c] No knowledge of the ways of God or the fear of God, [d] Arrogance, ignorance, the spirit of entitlement, self-will, presumptuousness, jealousy, covetousness, pre-occupation with titles and labels, [e] Distracted by programs while spending less and less time in the presence of God, [f] Battle weariness. fighting battles God did not designate for them to fight, [g] Compromise, [h] Disobedience, [i] Impure heart and deviousness, [j] Using the word deceitfully, [k] Lack of power, lack of discernment, lack of prayer, and [l] Lack of vision, planning, and direction. Yet they are all asking the same question, why are there no miracles, signs and wonders taking place in the church?

The first Adam, as leader of mankind, released judgment; and every generation of man became a recipient of Adam's sin. However, Jesus as the second Adam came to release blessings, not to judge or condemn. When leaders fail to bless the people they release judgment; however, that judgment comes back to the leader when wounded people terminate their relationship with the house. The blessings leaders release also come back to them in the form of the favor of God. God's desire is for His people to be blessed.

True leaders with God's heart are empowered by God to bless the people of God. We are seeing the emergence of the supernatural, tangible power of God in this apostolic age. On one hand we see the old religious Adamic judgmental spirit of condemnation opposing what God is initiating. While on the other hand we see the heavens open and the blessings of the Lord being released upon God's people through authentic apostolic anointings and leadership.

We are in a season that demands fervent, effectual prayer to know the perfect will of God for our personal and corporate destiny. As the darkness of this world intensifies, the church has to intensify her prayer life to be powerful and effective. But too many leaders have been beaten down by the enemy, physically, mentally and emotionally, and they are engaging in meaningless warfare. They are majoring in minors, foolishness, unproductive deliberations about things that mean nothing to God, worrying about the things that the ungodly are pressured about, what to eat, what to drink, what to put on, how to pay the bills.

The admonition for today's leaders is this:
> "Be not conformed to this world but be transformed by the renewing of your mind, that you may prove what is the good, and acceptable and perfect will of God."
> -Romans 12: 2. KJV.

1. Crisis in Leadership

Government is a system of social control under which the right to make laws, and the right to enforce them is vested in a particular group in society we call the nation's leaders. There are many classifications of government. According to the classical formula, governments are distinguished by whether power is held by one man, a few, or a majority.

The basic law determining the form of government is called the constitution, which is fundamentally principles of government in a nation either implied in its laws, institutions, and customs, or embodied in one fundamental document or in several.

Modern governments perform many functions besides the traditional ones of providing internal and external security, order and justice. Most are involved in providing welfare services, regulating the economy, and establishing educational systems.

The extreme case of government regulation of every aspect of people's lives is totalitarianism. Totalitarianism is a modern autocratic government whereby the state is involved in all facets of society, including the daily life of its citizens. A totalitarian government seeks to control not only all economic and political matters, but attitudes, values and beliefs of its population, erasing the distinction between state and society. The citizen's duty to the state becomes the primary concern of the community, and the goal of the state is the replacement of existing ideologies in society with a constitution, and or religious dogma for a perfect society.

In the present and former decades of the twenty first century, many totalitarian governments have fallen and the society they were controlling erupted in anarchy against the attitudes, values and beliefs of their totalitarian government. All of these governments that have fallen had different ideological goals, such as communism and religious intolerance. Recently the governments that have fallen due to ideological beliefs were a religious totalitarian form of government that controlled and oppressed the people.

Biblical totalitarianism has more to do with personality, a term scholars call the cult of personality. A term implying the concentration of all power in a single charismatic leader who is deified. Many ancient societies such as Egypt had this form of totalitarianism. Along with other gods, Pharaoh, the king was deified.

It was never God's intent that His people, the nation of God, we know as the church, would be governed by a totalitarian form of government. When the children of Israel assembled at Sinai they entered into a covenant with Jehovah, the God of Abraham, Isaac and Jacob. He became their Lord and they became His people.

God gave them a constitution and laws to govern their society. Meanwhile the rest of the nations of the world indulged in the practice of idolatry in which they deified their leaders and worshipped a plethora of demonic gods. It was a law in the constitution of Israel that the nation of Israel must not have any other gods but Jehovah. He was the one and only God they were to worship.

This was the first nation of the world to practice a form of government known as theocracy. God chose leaders from among the people to teach society His laws. He raised up judges and eventually the people asked God for a king. Their kings were subject to the laws of Jehovah and when they turned away from Him to idolatry, they influenced the people to serve other demonic gods; for this sin the nation of Israel suffered hardship by the hands of their enemies. This was Jehovah's way of punishing them for their disobedience and disloyalty.

The New Testament dispensation brought change in the way God governed His people, standing between the Old and New Covenants is the cross. The cross symbolizes the fulfillment of the law and the prophets in Christ Jesus. He became the substitutionary sacrifice for the sins of mankind and the eternal High Priest who lives forever to make intercessions for His people.

He gave them a new constitution or a new covenant, which stated that His laws would be written in their hearts, and along with His laws He gave them the earnest of His Spirit and said, "As many as are led by the spirit of God they are the sons of God." (Romans 8:14). To be a part of this society or the holy nation under God one must experience the new birth. In sharing the scriptures with Nicodemus who was a leader among the Jews, Jesus stated that it was imperative that a person wanting a relationship with God be born of the Spirit of God, for without this experience no one can see or enter the kingdom of God.

In the New Testament economy, the leaders or the government of God rest on the shoulders of Jesus Christ, He is the head of the church, the government of the church is chosen by Him from among the people, and through them Christ as the head, emits His ideas, thoughts, will, plans, wisdom and long-term goals for the church. The leaders are to be subject to Jesus Christ as the people are to be subject to the government of the church.

As New Testament leaders the highest motive for serving God should be their desire to please Him. Everything written in the Old Testament about leaders is an admonition and warning for New Testament leaders. One of the greatest examples of a nation having a crisis in leadership is the life and tenure of service of King Saul, the first king of Israel.

As the dispensation of the judges came to an end, the Lord raised up a prophet by the name of Samuel. He was the last judge of the old order of judges and the first in a long line of prophets of the Old Testament order. He inaugurated the first two kings of Israel, King Saul and King David.

Saul was placed by God on the highest rung of leadership to provide government for God's people and to lead the army of Israel into battle against their enemies; he was the head of the armed forces of Israel. The government of that day comprised of the king, who was over national affairs, the high priest, who was over the worship and religious life of the nation, and the prophet who was God's voice to the king and the nation.

As the first king, the pioneer and the pacesetter, Saul should have set the God kind of watermark for the other kings of Israel to follow. But after he was anointed king, Saul's heart quickly turned away from God when the kingdom was established. He became rebellious, disobedient, selfish, arrogant, hardhearted, defiant, envious, and competitive; a man who loved the praise and attention of people more than the honor that came from obeying and submitting himself to God.

God took away His spirit and His anointing from Saul and an evil spirit was assigned to him. He spent his last days as a mad man pursing David the future king of Israel, the one God chose to replace him. He was jealous of David's anointing and wanted to kill him.

When God severed his relationship with Saul, Samuel was sent by God to anoint David to be king in his place. The last twenty years of Saul's life was marked by the absence of the presence of God. God did not speak to Saul by dreams, a personal word or through the prophet Samuel anymore. Jonathan, Saul's eldest son said it best, "My Father has troubled the land."

Like many of our present day leaders, King Saul's problems were rooted in pride and selfish ambition. He just did not want anyone to tell him what to do, and that included Samuel the Prophet, who was God's voice to the king. He refused to submit himself to the authority of God and became a law unto himself.

When a leader becomes a law unto himself, he sets himself in the place of God and will listen to no counsel, advice, wisdom or warning. When a person is in that state of defiance and rebellion only God can arrange his fall and destruction. Pride goes before destruction and a haughty spirit before a fall (1 Sam 2: 22-25).

Saul's legacy was marked by his disobedience, lack of character, ungodliness, lack of the fear of God and his disrespect for the office of Samuel, the prophet and spiritual leader of the nation. He left his footsteps in the sands of time as a leader that played the fool.

Saul was consumed with jealousy, a common problem among ministers today. The rivalry of Saul against David began when through the anointing on David's life he slayed a giant who was defying Israel. Every leader should have someone in his or her ranks with an anointing to slay giants, and solve problems that the ordinary man or woman cannot solve.

There are many would be giant slayers in local churches where the leadership suffers from insecurity like King Saul. Insecurity produces a spirit of control, intimidation, jealousy, selfishness, and rejection. These leaders use their authority to put member against member to provoke allegiance to the pastor only. They overlook those that have an anointing on their life for fear that the Lord would use them above and beyond the leadership's ability. When an insecure leader discerns that someone among their ranks is a "rising star" and I use that term loosely, they either retaliate like Saul did in the case of David, they use the person to do their dirty work, or they try to take the credit for that person's anointing and gift.

David knew Saul had his eyes on him, and was watching his every move; therefore, David behaved himself very wisely. Through his victory over the giant he became a captain in the army. King Saul promoted him as a captain over a division of soldiers. But as David continued to fight the wars of Israel and the Lord continued to give him success in every campaign, the women of Israel ascribed to David tens of thousands and to Saul thousands (1 Samuel 18: 5-9). This brought much wrath against David, insomuch that the king threw a javelin at him, but David got out of his way and fled for his life.

When there is a divine call on a person's life, their anointing, diligence, success, blessings, and promotion in the kingdom will automatically attract warfare. People love the significance of titles, labels and positions of authority, but seldom do leaders speak of their warfare. No one who has attained any measure of depth or height in God got there without experiencing affliction, adversity, sorrow, pain, frustration, tribulation and trials of their faith, even though they seldom speak about it. But all of the above produces the anointing on one's life. The greater the affliction the greater measure of grace and anointing is given.

It is the anointing that sets a leader apart for divine service, and there are several ways the anointing is produced in a person's life, such as:

1. One is anointed in one's calling.
2. One is anointed in tribulation and testing.
3. One is anointed in one's level of authority.
4. One is anointed over demonic princes.
5. One is anointed over the nations.
6. One is anointed over death.
7. One is anointed in royal gifts
   a. Word of wisdom
   b. Word of knowledge
   c. Discerning of spirits
8. One is anointed in power gifts
   a. Faith
   b. Working of miracles
   c. Gifts of healing
9. One is anointed in inspirational gifts
   a. Prophecy
   b. Tongues and interpretation
   c. Divers tongues
10. One is anointed in resurrection gifts and in specific areas of one's calling.
    a. Apostles
    b. Prophets
    c. Pastors
    d. Teachers
    e. Evangelists
11. One is anointed in other callings.
    a. Governmental gifts
    b. Elders
    c. Administration
    d. Helps
    e. Hospitality
    f. Intercessory prayer

Warfare produces an anointing and capability that every leader needs for their God-given assignment. This is called the trial of our faith. It produces grace and a weight of glory in and on the life of the leader which far exceeds the trials and the afflictions.

What King Saul failed to comprehend was the fact that God placed him in office. The choice of who was to be king was God's. Saul wanted to create a family dynasty so he could pass the throne on to his son Jonathan, who was his first born son. But as anointed as Jonathan was, he was not God's chosen to be the next king of Israel. As a prince in Israel, his anointing gave him the capability to be a battle strategist able to fight alongside his father in the wars of Israel.

However, when King Saul defied God's order to destroy the Amalekites, that action sealed his fate and the throne of Israel did not become a generational inheritance for Saul's son, Jonathan.

As a leader over God's people, Saul chose rather to listen to the people instead of the instructions of God given to him by the prophet Samuel. He willfully chose not to carry out the assignment against the nation of Amalek (1 Samuel 15: 22-23). This decision altered the course of his destiny, the destiny of his sons and the dynasty of the House of Saul.

One of the saddest stories in the saga of King Saul is the untimely death of his son Jonathan, who knew that God was no longer with his father, and that David, his best friend and brother-in-law, would be the next king of Israel. Yet Jonathan remained loyal to his father and refused to leave his father's side. In his final battle against the Philistines, Jonathan, two of his brothers and his father the king, lost their lives, and the nation mourned for its fallen leaders. The dream of having a family dynasty died with Saul and his sons on the hills of Gilboa.

But God never leaves himself without a witness or a plan and is never caught off guard or taken by surprise. God had a man in training to replace Saul while he continued in office for twenty years after the anointing and the presence of God departed from him. His fate was sealed and during those twenty years an evil spirit tormented him; all the while David was in God's dressing room of life, being prepared to become king at God's appointed time and season.

All leaders should know this, the one who will replace you is in the dressing room of life, getting prepared to take the baton from your hand to continue the race that you have started. Every leader has a tenure of service given to him or her by God. King Saul had a very good start, but he did not finish well, and his sons did not inherit a generational blessing. In the same way, leaders must realize that their disobedience will hinder the next generation and someone else of God's choosing will take their place, and that person may not be a natural son or daughter.

Evaluating Yourself: Examine, test and evaluate your own selves to see whether you are holding to your faith and showing the proper fruits of it. Test and prove yourselves [not Christ]. Do you not realize and know [thoroughly by an ever-increasing experience] that Jesus Christ is in you – unless you are [counterfeit] disapproved, on trial, and rejected? (Amplified)

Examine yourselves, whether you are in the faith; prove your own selves. Know ye not your own selves, how that Jesus Christ is in you, except ye be reprobates (failure)? But I trust that ye shall know that we are not reprobates (2 Cor. 13: 5, 6 KJV).

A Reprobate is a morally unprincipled person, one who is predestined for damnation, rejected by God and without hope of salvation.

I recently had a phone call from a pastor who called to tell the sad news of the death of a man of God, a pastor who was diagnosed with a rapidly moving cancer. The bereaved wife shared the story of what transpired. Her husband was hospitalized, he was in much pain and the doctors had him highly sedated to the point where he would feel nothing. They wanted him to be comfortable in his final days. However, while he slept soundly during the day, at night despite the fact that he was highly sedated, he screamed, shouted, fought, and kept rebuking an invisible entity that tormented him at night.

Unknowing to the congregation, this pastor had a secret life; he was a whoremonger who had fathered children by several women. The doctor explained to his wife that this nightly torment was not because of the physical pain, but it was something spiritual that he was experiencing. The wife took up a nightly prayer vigil at his hospital room to pray for him to rest before he passed away into eternity.

No one knows if he ever repented because he was so sedated, but after his death the wife felt the ramifications of his ungodly lifestyle when the mothers of these children started calling on her for money to support his children.

Leadership Is The Total Person Who Leads: Leadership for God's people involves spirituality, knowledge, skills, and an accumulation of experiences and a relationship with Jesus Christ. Leadership is needed to carry out Christ's program. People groups do not always know what to do or how to act; they need leaders. In the Body of Christ lessons must be taught, sermons must be preached, and Christians must be trained for the work of the kingdom. Someone must push the work forward, encourage the workers, pray for the sick, administrate every aspect of church life, as well as build according to the pattern. A leader must show the way by staying ahead of the crowd, the congregation, and the church.

Genuine Leadership: No one is ever truly elected to leadership. Public officials are elected to office, but not necessarily to leadership. An office in itself does not make one a leader, service is what makes one a leader. When an office is seeking a leader it will be a new day, for no one can be made a leader by election. Genuine leadership is the reward of honest, unselfish service that has won the respect and following of a group of people.

God's plan for the ages is based upon human leadership. When a deliverer was needed, God raised up Moses. When it was time for Moses to go off the scene, God raised up Joshua. Joshua was ready to take Moses' place. He was possessed with a spiritual understanding both of God's will and of his own responsibilities.

When God's people were in captivity in the kingdom of Persia, and they needed to be saved from possible destruction, a woman was needed. Mordecai said to Esther, "Who knows whether you have come to the kingdom for such a time as this" [Esther 4:14]. Queen Esther was God's leader at the right time.

Self-Sacrifice: Being a leader does cost, and the cost can be heavy. If you are looking at the price tag and it is too high, then put it down. There are many who started out on the pathway of leadership, but when they found out the cost, they rejected the high calling of God for a career. Sometimes the cost will mandate that the leader move his family to a foreign mission field to fulfill his destiny. Self-sacrifice may be a geographical move, a denominational move or a career move. If one is unwilling to pay this price, then one would reject the call and the opportunity.

The price of power is the price of giving up. Leaders who are successful are those who have planted their lives in the lives of others. To be a victorious leader one must be willing to give oneself up and over entirely, without compromise, to the will of the Father.

> Let your attitude toward one another be governed by your being in union with the Messiah Yeshua. Though He was in the form of God, He did regard equality with God something to be possessed by force.

> On the contrary, he emptied himself in that He took on the form of a slave by becoming like human beings are. And when He appeared as a human being, He humbled himself still more by becoming obedient even to death on a stake as a criminal! Therefore God raised Him to the highest place and gave Him the name above every name.
>
> -Philippians 2: 5-9. [CJB]

Finding and Accepting Responsibility: It is hard work when a true leader has found his or her calling. Men and women with strength of character, conscience, judgment, courage to act, and willingness to take the penalties of responsibility, are the stuff out of which leaders true are made. The journey is often strewed with heavy responsibilities because the leader is forever picking up what others have neglected.

A leader may labor unappreciated, unassisted, fighting almost single handedly, pushing the vision forward to make it easier for someone else who is coming to step into his or her shoes, but that is the price of leadership.

> I hated all my toil in which I toiled under the sun, seeing that I must leave it to the man who will come after me. And who knows whether he will be wise or a

fool? Yet he will be master of all for which I toiled and used my wisdom under the sun.

- Ecclesiastes 2:18, 19.

Abraham paid the price when he left his homeland to become the father of a great nation. Joseph paid the price in the pit and dungeon, yet he remained true to his ideal and later saved his family from starvation, when he had the opportunity to rule Egypt. David paid the price in humility to become "a man after God's own heart." Daniel purposed in his heart not to defile himself with the king's meat. Paul paid the price on the Damascus road, and all along his eventful life he paid heavy prices to be a powerful apostolic leader for Christ. Peter, James, and John left all and followed Christ.

When considered from a human standpoint, the price seems great. When seen through the eyes of faith and heart of love, a true leader has a sense of gratitude to do anything for Christ, who gave all for us; serving Him is a privilege, not a price.

Leaders are Defined by their Faith and Courage:

> Be strong and courageous, for you shall cause this people to inherit the land that I swore to their fathers to give them. Only be strong and very courageous, being careful to do according to all the law that Moses my servant commanded you. Do not turn from it to the right hand or to the left, that you may have good success where-ever you go.
>
> -Joshua 1: 7.

Courageous leaders are needed. Courage comes from a sense of the presence of God. Courageous leaders may have to break with convention to accommodate the vision and the leading of the

Holy Spirit. This may cause him or her to walk alone without companionship, fellowship or friendships.

Courageous leaders will often feel the weight of responsibilities when there is a lack of finances to fund the vision. When there is lack it is easy to feel discouraged. Times of depression will come to try the faith of the leader, but the courageous leader will seek to rise above fear and doubt.

Enthusiasm, optimism and courage will overcome many handicaps. Abraham believed God, and many a leader in this dispensation of grace can attest to the fact that God is faithful, and when the trial of their faith comes to prove them, their faith and courage will prevail.

Temptation: Temptation is common to all men. Jesus found himself confronted with the problem of lack of faith as he undertook the difficult task of training His disciples. He was amazed by their unbelief and remarked, "O ye of little faith." But Jesus had to experience His own personal temptation when He was driven by the spirit into the wilderness to meet His adversary, Satan.

He had to be proven that He had the strength and courage to resist the power of temptation. All leaders are faced with some form of temptation. Facing, overcoming, and enduring temptation is the foundation of the enduring success of a leader's ministry.

A leader's faith must be tested and tried, his or her ability to overcome must be proven in the face of the lusts of the eye, lusts of the flesh, and the pride of life. Every man is drawn away of his own lust and enticed; and when lust is conceived it produces sin, and when sin is finished it brings forth death. Lust is not confined to sexual sins, but humans lust for power, control, and

26

the adoration of mankind; idolatry and covetousness are also lust.

No temptation has overtaken you that is not common to man. God is faithful, and He will not let you be tempted beyond your ability, but with the temptation He will also provide the way of escape, that you may be able to endure it.

- 1 Corinthians 10: 13.

Dealing with Critics: The critics were alive and well in Jesus's day as they are today. They constituted one of His most aggravating problems. Wherever Jesus turned, He confronted the Scribes and Pharisees, who criticized Him at every opportunity and found fault with everything He did and said; they even tried to entrap Him with His own words. Herod knew that it was because of envy that they accused Him.

Leaders will always be criticized by their parishioners and peers. Jesus dealt with the Scribes and Pharisees by giving them the correct prophetic response. He knew that as religious as they were they had allowed Satan to give them a ministry of propaganda. They indulged in slander, gossip, spreading rumors, and lies because they were jealous and envious of His ministry.

There are six things that the Lord hates, seven that are an abomination to Him; haughty eyes, a lying tongue, hands that shed innocent blood, a heart that devises wicked plans, feet that make haste to run to evil, a false witness who breathes out lies, and one who sows discord among brothers.

-Proverbs 6: 16 -19.

Sometimes leaders have to deal with lies, ungodly slander, and critical reviews by addressing their accusers and their complaints. Some misunderstandings need an explanation especially when dealing with finances. If the leader's character is being questioned, this has to be dealt with before it spreads like wild fire throughout the congregation. Light has to be shone on rumors, slander, character assassination, accusations, and complaints before they become an infection that spreads throughout the church and affects members whose spirit are pure.

> Moreover, if your brother commits a sin you go and show him his fault – but privately, just between the two of you. If he doesn't listen, take one or two others with you so that every accusation can be supported by the testimony of two or three witnesses.

> If he refuses to hear them, tell the congregation, and if he refuses to listen even to the congregation, treat him as you would a pagan or a tax-collector.

> Yes! I tell you people that whatever you prohibit on earth will be prohibited in heaven; and whatsoever you permit on earth will be permitted in heaven.
>   -Matthew 18:15-17, CJB.

Ignorance: Jesus found the members of His group slow to learn. Even as He neared the close of His ministry, He was shocked to hear them asking about an earthly kingdom, and disputing with petty jealousy over who will be the greatest in the kingdom. Both James and John wanted to sit one on his right side and the other on his left side. Their selfish ambition blinded them to the reality of what they were asking for and the price that they will have to pay for such a place of honor.

Positions of honor in the kingdom can only be given by the Father and Jesus told His disciples so. Jesus himself had to pay the price of salvation by going to the cross; then He sat at the right hand of the Father in the position of High Priest and advocate general of the church.

In the Garden of Gethsemane Jesus was met with the baffling problem of sleepiness in His disciples, who calmly slept while He prayed and sweated blood, they were ignorant of the impending danger that awaited the church even though Jesus tried to warn them of the coming events.

Sometimes leaders are met with indifference, when they have put their life into some ambitious plan and they are trying to stir up interest among the members, only to discover to his or her dismay that they are asleep and unconcerned about the work of God. Jesus asked His disciples, "Can you not watch with me for one hour?"

The local church must have a fervent prayer life. The church's power is derived through intercessions and supplications. If the church is indifferent about prayer, Satan can assign spirits to destroy the church's influence, power and anointing due to the lack fervent of prayer.

Dealing with Members and the Spirit of Judas: All great leaders must learn how to deal with individual members of their congregation. Each member whether they are categorized as a ministry gift or a part of the congregation has a different personality. Each has a different level of education, spiritual understanding, wisdom and genuine interest in the success of the ministry. Many are more interested in a position in the church than in a relationship with Jesus Christ.

Judas was the treasurer of Jesus's ministry. He was a leader, one of the original twelve apostles chosen by Jesus Christ. He was given a position of honor and responsibility, but he had no interest in anything else other than what he could get out of the ministry for himself. As treasurer, his position gave him access to the ministry's finances, which he used at his discretion. Judas transacted business with the Pharisees and betrayed Jesus Christ for thirty pieces of silver. Greed, the lust for money was the dominant factor in Judas' life, certainly not a relationship with Jesus.

Jesus called His Father's house "A House of Prayer" but today many see the church as a place to transact business and more emphasis is placed on numbers; the amount of members acquired and the amount of money in the treasury, more than on developing leaders, discipleship training, leading people to Christ and teaching them about a lifestyle of commitment to God.

In dealing with Judas, Jesus knew that Judas would betray him; yet He never confronted him or accused him in front of the other apostles. He knew Judas was a traitor, a liar and a thief, but this caused Jesus to pray more earnestly for His other disciples. He said, "Have I not chosen twelve and one of you is a devil." Why did the all-knowing creator choose a devil? So that the word of God will be fulfilled (John 17:12). Like Lucifer, a covering angel that stood in the presence of God betrayed God; one of Jesus's own inner circle would betray Him also. This pattern of betrayal continues in ministry today.

Leaders must be discerning enough to know the spirit, the personality and the intent of the people around them, because the heart of man is desperately wicked and deceitful. Jesus gave Judas every opportunity for repentance, and leaders have to do the same, while allowing the person to make the final decision.

Peter, James, and John were handled differently from the other disciples. They had the strength of character, the aggression to deal with adversaries, and they were more advanced than the others in understanding and revelation. Jesus did not hold them back, but gave them special opportunities for service and development.

On several occasions we find Him leaving the rest of the group and taking these three with Him. They were with Him on the Mount of Transfiguration, they were permitted to see the raising of Jairus' daughter from the dead, and they went further with Him into the experience of Gethsemane.

Not every member can walk with a headship gift, there are those that are called into greater service and their gifts and abilities have to be developed, therefore, greater opportunities and exposure will be given to them to expand their capabilities. Consideration should be given to those who are capable but choose to work behind the scenes.

Apostle Andrew was an individual quite opposite from his brother Peter. He did not like the limelight. When they assigned him a part on the program, he was sure to be absent. Jesus did not drop his name from the roll. He adopted a wiser assignment which fit Andrew's personality. Andrew was an ambassadorial type of apostle, he made the connections and the introductions. He introduce Peter, who became the strongest apostle to Jesus.

A wise leader will recognize the fact that certain members have greater capacities and possibilities than others. All Leaders are not necessarily born leaders; they can be made. Unless one possesses some quality that would entirely disqualify him, then by persistent effort, faithful study, and prayerful persistence, one can learn.

In dealing with members, it is important for leaders to recognize and understand the many factors that have shaped and molded people's personality. Trauma impacts us emotionally, financially, socially, spiritually, and mentally. The issues of life have shaped our thinking, behavior and have affected the way we interact and relate to people. Who are we behind the anointing, spiritual gifts, college degrees, and positions of authority? That is the person God sees and knows.

Character Flaws in Leaders

Pride: When leaders are plagued with pride they have a tendency not to see their need for wise counsel, except when their weaknesses have been exposed and they become an embarrassment to their family and the church.

Prideful leaders justify their mistakes and their atrocious behavior by hiding behind their position, gifts, and anointing. If they are successful and there is no accountability, they act as though they are God, untouchable, undeterred, unchallenged, and every ungodly action is deliberate and justified. They surround themselves with "Yes" men who are spiritually shallow, and are more concerned about making money and impressing people with their accomplishments.

A prideful leader would rather lose a church member than take responsibility for his or her mistakes. If he is promiscuous, his wife is usually told by his enablers, [men with a vested interest in the finances of the church and their position], to turn a blind eye to his infidelities so she can hold the church together. This responsibility "to hold the church together" is based on the fact that his enablers feel that the wife may be the first lady but not the only lady in his life; therefore she should endure hardship, betrayal, abuse, disillusionment and the disrespect of his other women quietly, to prevent the members from leaving the church.

Prideful leaders, depending on their age, are usually unfaithful to their marriage covenant. Before these leaders are exposed, their sins are hidden from the church; and those who profit from the success of the ministry would provide a protective shield around them to protect them from being accused, persecuted or harassed by whoever brings their sins to light.

When someone is infested with the spirit of pride, the language that spirit uses is always, "I don't want anybody telling me what to do." "I will do it my way." "It's all about me." Why should I care about anyone; nobody cares about me." "I did this all by myself; nobody helped me." "Why should I give anybody anything, nobody ever gave me anything." Like King Nebuchadnezzar of ancient Babylon who declared, "Isn't this the great Babylon that I have made" (Daniel 4:30). Unfortunately, for the king, he forgot who raised him up to be a man of stature, successful, rich, and powerful. Eventually, Babylon the great city was destroyed forever.

In the dream, the stump of the tree was left in the ground, signifying that God will never remove the call from a person's life. He will provide opportunity for repentance, restoration and reinstatement, if the offender chooses to repent.

> I saw in the visions of my head upon my bed, and, behold, a watcher and a holy one came down from heaven. He cried aloud, and said thus, "Hew down the tree, and put off his branches, shake off his leaves, and scatter his fruit; let the beast get away from under it, and the fowls from his branches.
>
> Nevertheless leave the stump or his roots in the earth, even with a band of iron and brass, in the tender grass of the field; and let it be wet with the

dew of heaven, and let his portion be with the beasts in the grass of the earth."

And whereas they commanded to leave the stump of the tree roots; thy kingdom shall be sure unto thee, after that thou shalt have known that the heavens do rule.

-Daniel 4:13-15, 26. KJV

The Fruit of Pride:

a. Wherever pride is there will be contention.
b. Pride does not take heed to godly counsel.
c. Pride scorns wisdom.
d. Pride and stubbornness go hand in hand.
e. Pride and stubbornness precede a fall.
f. Pride brags about the things of the flesh.
g. Pride has an air of superiority.
h. Pride looks down in disgust at the less fortunate.
i. Pride hates to be corrected.
j. Pride does not give credit to anyone.
k. Pride wars against anyone pride considers as competition.
l. Pride will use any scheme or underhanded means to get the job done.
m. Pride does not fear the Lord.
n. Pride calls men "self-made" without acknowledging God.
o. Pride wants God's glory and power without God's input.
p. Pride hates to be challenged or questioned.
q. Pride always points the finger of blame at someone else.
r. Pride will never say, "I am sorry."
s. Pride is the nemesis of anyone who has more, does more, or has accomplished more.
t. Pride resists humility.
u. Pride is covetous.
v. Pride will not submit.
w. Pride is selfish and self-centered.

    x. Pride walks hand in hand with jealousy.

    y. Pride does not develop people, pride uses people.

Confessing one's faults and repentance is the key to healing and deliverance. This is a vital part of our daily spiritual growth, whether we are leaders or laity. No one is without sin but God. There is a sin that easily besets all of us, and examining our life in the light of God's word would make us realize that like Christ, we have to experience crucifixion of our flesh. We also have to be transformed by the renewing of our minds. Becoming Christ-like takes discipline, that is why we pray and study His word, but self-examination is a part of that discipline.

Being born into a sin infested and demon infested world is the cause of much testing, trials, tribulations and continued challenges for those who are in Christ. Whether we came from a broken home, or we were victims of abuse, infidelity, abandonment, incest, violent crimes, slander, reproach, blame, betrayal, or endured financial embarrassment, drug-addiction, hopelessness, incarceration, poverty, homelessness, etc., we all have experienced some sort of woe or we were the perpetrators of the pain that others have experienced. We must all purpose to abandon pride and throw ourselves on the mercies of God.

Unwise Counsel: A leader cannot take counsel from everyone. There is a key player in the story of the dispute between King David's two sons Ammon and Absalom that we need to pay attention to. The text says, (11 Samuel 13) Ammon had a friend, whose name was Jonadab, the son of Shimeah David's brother; and Jonadab was a very subtle man, [he was also his first cousin].

Ammon had a problem, he was in love with his sister, Tamar. She was a very beautiful woman and he lusted after her so much that he shared his feelings with his friend. Jonadab gave him unwise counsel, a plan that Ammon was foolish enough to follow. The ensuing action cost Ammon his life. He raped his sister Tamar, who was a virgin. This horrendous act enraged her brother Absalom, who set a plan in place to kill Ammon.

The murder of Ammon caused a rift in Absalom's relationship with his father, king David, and he lived in exile for quite some time. On his return to Israel the king refused to see his face and to reinstate him to public office, he was banished from the court. To get even with his father, the angry Absalom started a political campaign to overthrow his father and usurp the throne. Absalom stole the hearts of the men of Israel and caused civil unrest in the nation. The conspiracy was so strong that the people who followed Absalom increased more and more. David had to temporarily abdicate his throne and leave his house to find refuge outside Jerusalem from the impending civil war. The war resulted in Absalom's defeat and death (11 Samuel 18:9-1).

The only time Jonadab had anything to say about the problem he instigated, was to reassure David that only Ammon was dead when the news came that Absalom had killed all the kings sons. He knew that Absalom had determined at an appointed time to kill Ammon for raping his sister Tamar; yet he never gave counsel to his friend Ammon not to go the event where he lost his life (11 Samuel 13:30-33).

Many people try to give counsel that is self-serving. Self-serving counsel only benefits the one giving the counsel. All leaders do not have the gift of counsel, and being a leader does not automatically make someone a counselor or a problem solver. Counsel, godly wisdom, and experience, form a formidable team. However, we must all be careful because the fruit of the knowledge of good and evil in the wrong hands can be a dangerous weapon; because you will give your enemy license to use that knowledge against you.

God will at certain seasons in our life allow things to come our way so we will experience darkness. There will always be some trying situation that will test our resolve, our ability to cope, our character, our limits, our faith and patience, our strength to overcome. It is part of the maturing process. If you have never been in darkness you cannot appreciate light. If you have never experienced captivity you will not appreciate freedom. If you have never been sick how can you appreciate healing?

Wise counsel can only come from people that are mature in faith, courage, trust, experience, and have overcome adversity; people who know what demonic struggles are, and have been faced with challenges in life that only God can resolve. Jesus said, "In this world you will have tribulations, but be of good cheer I have overcome the world" (John16:33). A degree from a major university does not prepare you to overcome demonic struggles.

> Blessed is the man that does not walk in the counsel
> of the ungodly, nor stands in the way of sinners, nor
> sits in the seat of the scornful, but his delight is in
> the Law of the Lord and in His Law does he meditate
> day and night.
>
> ‑Psalm 1: 1‑2.

You may be called of God, but you cannot be a counselor if you are inexperienced, self‑centered, and unwise. Wisdom and experience is acquired during adversity and by a relationship with Jesus Christ. That means you learn and grow during the pressures and challenges of life. What causes a Christian to experience adversity?

a. When you have laid your life on the altar of sacrifice.
b. When you are serving to win the lost for Christ.
c. When your works enhance the lives of others and you represent God in all that you do.

d. When you are serving diligently in the kingdom of God.

e. When you are doing all to stand in holiness before God.

f. Disobedience also opens the door for adversity and the chastening of the Lord.

Adversity comes in different ways. When God begins to promote someone his or her first level of warfare will come from the church. Warfare will also be experienced in the market place, even from among family members who do not know the Lord.

Leaders must have the strength to bear their pain in the times of adversity, that strength can only come through sustained prayer, and the power of the word of God. Leaders cannot project their pain unto others, no matter how hurt they are. Being jealous of others is a waste of emotion, because you don't know what they have experienced to be successful. A powerful ministry is forged out of the fires of adversity. That is why we walk by faith and not by sight. Not only is there purpose to adversity, but there are benefits to adversity.

> Through Him we have also obtained access by faith into this grace in which we stand, and we rejoice in hope of the glory of God.
>
> Not only that, but we rejoice in our sufferings, knowing that sufferings produce endurance, and endurance produces character, and character produces hope. And hope does not put us to shame, because God's love has been poured into our hearts through the Holy Spirit who has been given to us.
>
> -Romans 5: 2-5 EVS.

Everyone will need wise counsel at some time in his or her walk with God. Our calling, ministry, and purpose must be prophetically aligned, defined, and declared. If not, some will arbitrarily take on assignments that were not given to them by God. Even Jesus experienced that in His ministry among members of His team.

> Then the mother of the sons of Zebedee came up to Him with her sons, and kneeling before Him she asked Him for something. And He said to her, "What do you want?" She said to Him, "Say that these two sons of mine are to sit, one at your right hand and one at your left, in your kingdom."

> Jesus answered, "You do not know what you are asking. "Are you able to drink the cup that I am to drink?" They said to him, "We are able." He said to them, "You will drink my cup, but to sit at my right hand and at my left is not mine to grant, but it is for those for whom it has been prepared by my Father."
>
> -Matthew 20: 20-23 EVS.

It is God the Father who has to determine your placement, position, level, and the scope of your call. And God puts in each leader a passion for what He has called them to do.

As a leader how would you define yourself? What are you most passionate about? Are you passionate about winning lost souls? That is your calling. Are you passionate about young people? That is your calling. Are you passionate about leading men to Christ and teaching men to be good fathers and faithful husbands? That is your calling. Are you passionate about worship and praise? That is your calling. Are you passionate about women's issues? That is your calling. Are you passionate about teaching and developing disciples? That is your calling.

It is the condition of your heart that determines who you are. It is through adversity that character is developed and manifested, and out of the heart flows the issues of life. We must maintain our identity with Christ, who is our life, no matter what crisis we are experiencing. All of God's children are developing, we are becoming Christlike. We go from stage to stage, grace to grace, strength to strength, glory to glory, victory to victory.

Spirit is greater than flesh, spirit is greater than our emotions, spirit has greater power than the soul. No one should completely trust everything that the mind configures because the mind is the battleground for control by the enemy. But when we walk according to the law of the Spirit, that law states that those that are led by the Spirit of God are the sons of God. When we live by the higher law of the spirit we are free from the law of sin and death; this enables us to take control over the issues of the flesh and the mind.

We should not let our emotions determine who we are, and matters of the heart should be handled in such a way that when we are afflicted, affliction will not crush us. When we are perplexed, in our perplexity we will not be driven to despair. When we are being persecuted we will not feel abandoned, forsaken and alone. And when we are physically stricken with infirmity, though our outward man may be experiencing adversity, the strength of the spirit man will sustained us because the spirit cannot be destroyed.

When adversity comes your way and you feel wounded and hurt, and you get depressed each time someone corrects you; if your emotions are easily damaged, if you suffer rejection when someone in authority says no to you; if you get offended when you are not recognized or when someone talks about you; then you are not ready for promotion. These are symptoms that you are too proud to receive wise counsel.

It is only when you can endure the hardness of adversity that you can become a good soldier in the army of the Lord. Anyone in military service has to undergo basic training, and if he or she would like to be considered for any unit of the Special Forces, he or she has to go through additional training for that higher level of service.

Every solider has to serve under whatever conditions he or she is called to; whether the mission is in a desert, mountainous terrain, swamp, jungle, city, snow, ocean, or the remotest regions of the world. The mission and the cause for which he or she is fighting takes precedence over personal feelings, emotions, philosophy, ethnicity, and the soldier's individual preference. He or she goes wherever he or she is sent. The same rule applies to the kingdom. God does the sending, God chooses the mission, and God does the equipping and the sending.

Warfare is adversity, and if you cannot walk with foot soldiers, you certainly cannot ride with horsemen. Horsemen are the people in high levels of leadership in the kingdom, men with governmental anointings. They rule from a heavenly position over cities, nations, and various regions of the world. They are principalities in the kingdom of God. They are men of war, generals in the army of the Lord and great grace is upon their lives.

If you cannot take the lead in a battle, then you have to be under leadership. Far too many people who strive for mastery fall apart in warfare and their feelings are too easily hurt. You may learn warfare from a text book, and that knowledge is good because it gives you the necessary information about battle strategies; but to be a soldier in God's army you learn warfare by experience. However, what is a challenge to one may not be a challenge to another, because we are so different by nature, experience, calling, perception, belief, and by our level of faith.

In warfare you have to know the cause. What are you fighting about? You have to understand the mission if it came from God, and you have to know the strategy that the Lord wants you to use. Sometimes the strategy is silence. God will give you a directive, "Have nothing to say about this matter, just talk to God." That is difficult for some people, because they love to tell their story, they tell it all to the wrong people. But what God is saying to you is, don't give the enemy any ammunition. Don't reveal your plans or your pain. Don't let the enemy know your need or your hurt. Just praise God. Praise is a vital spiritual weapon.

Joshua's Battle Strategy for Taking the City of Jericho.

Jericho had completely barricaded its gates against the people of Israel – no one left, and no one entered. The Lord said to Joshua, "I have handed Jericho over to you, including its king and his warriors. You are to encircle the city with all your soldiers and march around it once. Do this for six days.

Seven priests are to carry seven trumpets in front of the Ark. On the seventh day you are to march around the city seven times, and the priests will blow the trumpets.

Then they are to blow a long blast on the trumpet. On hearing the sound of the trumpet, all the people are to shout as loudly as they can, and the wall of the city will fall down flat. Then the people are to go up into the city, each one straight from where he stands."

-Joshua 6: 1-5.

A Word to Women in Ministry: There are many women in leadership in the Body of Christ. Some served in antagonistic environments where women with the call of God on their lives are not appreciated by male or females. Women who have accepted the call to kingdom ministry need to understand their warfare. They think it is just a "man" thing. It is men who are hindering women from becoming their best self. This does happen in society and also in the church. For example, if there is a female apostle in the midst and a male apostle, deference will be given to the male and not so much to the female, that is a fact. However, God spoke the women's warfare into existence when He told Satan in Genesis 2: 18;

a.   I will put enmity between you and the woman.
b.   Between your offspring and her offspring.
c.   He shall bruise your head, and you shall bruise His heel.

Women were born to fight. She has to especially if she is called of God, she cannot choose to be neutral and not engage the enemy. God will see to it that adversity will come her way to make her a prayer warrior. Whenever warfare arises against a woman in leadership that is doing the will of God, that my friend, is the enmity God was talking about.

A woman called into ministry must understand the importance of having a covering. The husband is the wife's first line of defense. If she does not have a husband with godly character, that is subject to Christ as his Lord; then she has to be in a church that recognizes her calling, the grace of God that is on her life, and is willing to accept her as a minister and provide the covering she needs. Her responsibility in all this is to pray that God will plant her in an environment where she can flourish as a tree that is the planting of the Lord.

God has a fixed order in the universe, Christ is the head of the church and the head of the man. The man is the head of the family of man, the head of the woman and the children because the man was created first. The woman brings structure into the family, and the man brings order into the family. A man does not rise to his best potential without having a family; and the woman is incomplete without her husband. A woman called to the ministry who is unmarried cannot be under a church covering that does not subscribe to women preaching the gospel.

> So they called them and charged them not to speak or teach at all in the name of Jesus. But Peter and John answered them, "Whether it is right in the sight of God to listen to you rather than to God, you must judge. For we cannot but speak of what we have seen and heard."
>
> -Acts 4: 18-20.

The Need for Quality Leadership: The greatest honor that can come to any person is to be set aside by the Holy Spirit to serve Jesus Christ. To lay down one's life, is to die to self and to take up the cross daily to follow Christ. It is to give the reins of one's life over to God in complete surrender. It is to enlist without reservation in the work of reconciliation, restoration and deliverance of souls.

When a person has made a complete commitment to the work of Jesus Christ, it is only then he or she can say, "My life is hid with Christ in God and I am not my own; nevertheless not my will but the thy will be done," which is total, complete and unconditional surrender. Many have been called to that level of commitment, but few have made the quality of commitment God demands, which is total surrender; hence the reason why the Bible says, "Many are called but few are chosen."

For some the cost of surrender is based on what they will lose compared to what is to be gained. Some want to know ahead of the commitment what are the benefits. They want a guarantee of success before they set off on the journey toward spiritual destiny. Some do not want a cross, trials, persecutions, or afflictions. I heard one Pastor say, "I told my relatives, come and help me build a church I am going to be rich." Some do not want to make the necessary sacrifices to start a ministry. Some said, "Yes" but their motives were wrong because they saw ministry as a vehicle for fame, money and power.

God did not give everybody the capacity and grace to manage a city type church with thousands of members. Many may desire that type of ministry but they may not have the grace, character, strength, ability, courage, dignity or management style to function on a governmental level in that leadership position.

The saddest thing that can happen to a person, who believes in his or her heart, that he or she has labored in the vineyard of God, is to come to the end of life's journey, and on that day of reckoning, come before the throne of Christ to receive his or her reward and hear Christ say to him or her, "I never knew you," or "I don't know who you are," because their name and service to God was never recorded. Their so-called ministry was never initiated by the Holy Spirit, and was never sustained by the power and grace of God. Like Simon the sorcerer they just bewitched people into believing that they were men or women of God when in truth they were imposters.

It is possible that a person can serve in leadership based on his or her intellect and professional ability and not based on his or her calling and relationship with God. We need professional people in the church, along with business people and people with skills that would assist in implementing the vision. But the key to successful leadership is a genuine relationship with God, courage, wisdom, guidance, and direction of the Holy Spirit.

The church of this generation has forgotten one vitally important element in leadership. Every leader should have the spirit of Christ. Poor quality leadership stems from the fact that the person in leadership does not have the Spirit of Christ, is not grounded in the word of God and does not have a prayer life even though they are ordained ministers.

> For who knows the inner workings of a person except the person's own spirit inside him? So too no one knows the inner workings of God except God's spirit.

> Now we have not received the spirit of the world but the Spirit of God, so that we might understand the things God has so freely given us.
> -1 Corinthians 2: 11, 12.

When I was growing up in Church, the leadership in those days would never appoint a person in leadership who did not experience the baptism of the Holy Spirit. We had praying churches back then; churches who derived their power and anointing by the intensity of their prayer life. It was mandatory that every leader attend prayer meetings.

Intercessory prayer ignited the fire of God on the altar each time the church was in session. The Holy Spirit had His way from start to finish, no one controlled the program, the Holy Spirit was in charge. Sometimes there was no preaching, but people were at the altar crying out and surrendering to God. Holy fire was present in the House. But it ceased every time a leader tried to control the move of God.

For those who live according to the flesh set their minds on the things of the flesh, but those who live according to the Spirit set their minds on the things of the Spirit.

For to set the mind on the flesh is death, but to set the mind on the Sprit is life and peace. For the mind that is set on the flesh is hostile to God. It does not submit to God's law; indeed, it cannot. Those who are in the flesh cannot please God.

You, however, are not in the flesh but in the Spirit, if in fact the Spirit of God dwells in you. Anyone who does not have the Spirit of Christ does not belong to Him.

But if Christ is in you, although the body is dead because of sin, the Spirit is life because of righteousness. If the Spirit of Him who raised Jesus from the dead dwells in you, He who raised Christ Jesus from the dead will also give life to your mortal bodies through His Spirit who dwells in you.

-Romans 8:5-11.

Because the call of God is a high calling, it is the highest vocation that an earth dweller can attain. To serve as an ambassador of the kingdom of Heaven, to lead souls to Christ Jesus, to unfold the mysteries of the word of life to mortal man, and to see the life changing effects of the word in a person, is far greater than anything that can be attained by man. It is outstanding, powerful, and miraculous, it is supernatural. Nothing can gratify or satisfy the soul of a leader more than to see the tangible effects of lives transformed by the power of God.

The core of a leader's heart is the place from which ministry flows. Along with the word of God, leaders can use their life experiences or testimonies of deliverance to minister unto people.

Some hide their pain behind a mask of pride and allow bitterness, un-forgiveness, jealousy, resentment, hate and all the rancor of spiritual diseases that the heart of man can accommodate, ruin their relationship with Christ and others.

Due to disappointment and hurt, a leader can become spiritually deficient by harboring in his or her spirit the darkness of unforgiveness. Unforgiveness leads to other spiritual deficiencies, such as hate, anger, resentment, retaliation, sabotage, subtlety, craftiness, cunning, manipulation and strife. An unhealed leader produces a poor quality of leadership due to the darkness caused by these faults. If you are easily hurt your strength for leadership is too weak.

If then you have been raised with Christ, seek the things that are above, where Christ is, seated at the right hand of God. Set your minds on things that are above, not on things that are on earth. For you have died, and your life is hidden with Christ in God. When Christ who is your life appears, then you also will appear with Him in glory.

Put to death therefore what is earthly in you. Sexual immorality, impurity, passion, evil desire, and covetousness, which is idolatry. On account of these the wrath of God is coming.

In these you too once walked, when you were living in them. But now you must put them all away: anger, wrath, malice, slander, and obscene talk from your mouth. Do not lie to one another, seeing that you have put off the old self with its practices. And have put on the new self, which is being renewed in knowledge after the image of its Creator.

-Colossians 3: 1-10 ESV.

The gift in the leader determines the quality of his or her leadership. These gifts are fivefold ministry gifts, creative gifts, gifts of administration, communication, hospitality, technology, music, arts and crafts, etc. All these gifts are needed in the house. The church is an old institution that has to align itself with every succeeding generation.

The church of the 21st century has at its disposal the kinds of media and communication that is necessary and available for the church to be relevant in this generation. Along with new technology, God is giving the church new revelation and great grace. It is the age of supernatural, kingdom manifestation, and power. God is raising the water level of the church through quality ministry gifts, through which He has empowered His church.

- Quality has to do with characteristics or attributes.
- The natural or essential character of someone.

Quality leaders produce quality ministries. A quality leader gives a quality presentation. Apostles have the ability to check the water level and the quality of a church or ministry gift. Quality leaders should not only have spiritual gifts, but they should also possess qualities such as good morals, which is virtue, godliness, wisdom, holiness, knowledge, righteousness, truth, faith, love, goodness, patience, kindness, courage, and divine strength. A quality leader should live and function within the boundaries of the Word of God and the leading of the Spirit of God.

A quality prophet gives a quality prophecy; a quality prophecy has to be inspired by the Holy Spirit, because a quality prophecy has to be truth. It is not the word or thoughts of the prophet that comes to pass; it is the word of God that comes to pass, [Not maybe or perhaps, or I think God is saying this or that]. Quality leaders operate on a kingdom level. The kingdom is way above our carnal mindset. Kingdom law is the highest law, and quality leaders must have the spirit of the kingdom and the attributes of the King, Christ Jesus.

When we live on a lower level, that lower level affects every area of our life. To produce a quality ministry we have to go into a realm or an environment where kingdom keys are provided. David had the keys to the kingdom, therefore David aligned his kingdom with the kingdom of heaven, by building the Tabernacle of David, and placing prophetic singers and a choir all around the ark to worship the Lord continuously.

The kingdom of God is for quality leaders who are disciplined, creative and whose mind is in sync with the mind of God. It's not about starting a ministry but it is about the quality of our service. When leaders copy, imitate, and emulate it is because there is no vision or inspiration, they are trying to operate on a level that was not given to them, and often they are trying to operate outside the boundaries of their calling.

Every house has to be tested, every ministry has to be tested, every gift has to be tested, every leader has to be tested, and we all will be tested with the spiritual elements of wind, fire, flood, and rain. Your maturity will be tested, your obedience will be tested, and your wisdom will be tested. If you are one of those leaders building a ministry around yourself, and you call the ministry by your name, you will be tested with fire and when you die your ministry will die with you. Ministry must be generational, and a line of succession must be in place.

A quality leader does not commission spiritually, immature people without supervision, no matter how gifted he or she is. Spiritually immature people with gifts are children with no understanding of the ways of God. When we elevate a novice whose Christlike characteristics and understanding have not yet been developed, there must be accountability to a headship gift.

A novice will not bring honor to his or her office if he or she does not know order, proper protocol, the fear of God and the word of God. Every leader must learn how to walk in the dignity and decorum of his or her office. His or her spirit must be regal. You cannot be an officer in the house of God and behave like a gangster or someone dragged in from the street.

Familiarity: We all want friends and connections in the ministry, Jesus called his disciples friends. But sometimes leaders get too familiar with the wrong people. Some acquaintances cannot respect the office of a leader if they become too intimate with them as a personal friend. Boundaries has to be in place because familiarity can become a dangerous weapon if a leader is surrounded by people with a different set of moral values.

Apostles, prophets, teachers, pastors and evangelists are gifts given by God for the perfection of the saints, for the work of the ministry, for the edifying of the Body of Christ (Ephesians 4:11, 12). Sometimes people attach themselves to an anointed ministry gift for selfish reasons. These leaders should prayerfully choose who he or she wants to be their Armor Bearer, Assistant, or Administrator merely because too much familiarity will cause disrespect and friction in the relationship. The enemy within is more dangerous than the enemy on the outside. It is the ones closest to the minister that has the opportunity to make an accusation, lay blame, and assassinate the character of a leader.

Even though we are to love the people of God, all the people in the house of God are not God's people. The wheat and the tares are growing together until the time of harvest. That is one of the strategies of the enemy, to plant people in the house of God who are not the people of God. People gossip about leaders all the time and wise leaders must learn to keep their personal life very private because closeness to a leader is a position of trust.

The Dignity and Grace of The Leader: A leader is a gatekeeper and a watchman. In Pentecostal type assemblies, when there is an out-pouring of the Spirit, the head leader should not be on the floor acting out of control as the people. Somebody has to be watching, somebody has to be discerning what is manifesting in the house. Every spirit that manifests in the house is not the Spirit of God.

Daniel was a prophet who served in government under Babylonian and Persian kings. He was a man of God and an Executive President in the highest level of government under the king. Daniel had an excellent spirit because he walked in the dignity of his office as a government official and a man of God.

The behavior and decorum of every leader is judged by the people to whom they minister. People do not want their leader to be like them, they want their leader to be honorable, dignified, gracious, wise, upright, with integrity, intelligence and discretion.

Paul's charge to Timothy:
> Remind them of these things, and charge them before God not to quarrel about words, which does no good, but only ruins the hearers. Do your best to present yourself to God as one approved, a worker who has no need to be ashamed, rightly handling the word of truth. But avoid irreverent babble, for it will lead people into more and more ungodliness.

> Now in a great house there are not only vessels of gold and silver but also of wood and clay, some for honorable use, some for dishonorable. Therefore, if anyone cleanses

himself from what is dishonorable, he will be a vessel for honorable use, set apart as holy, useful to the master of the house, ready for every good work.

-2 Timothy 2: 14-16; 20-26 ESV.

The Gangster Mentality among Leaders: Have you ever wondered why it is so easy to join some churches, but it is so hard to leave? Because the dominant spirit and culture of the church is intimidation and harassment. Some leaders act like gangsters, they will gladly receive you when you want to be a member, but once you are in they begin to treat you as their property.

What prompts this type of behavior among leaders? This behavior is rooted in selfishness, control, fear and rejection. The fact that some leaders try to take the place of the Holy Spirit in the lives of people stems from control.

Why does leaving some churches have to be so difficult?: The rationale is if the member leaves, especially one that is a tither and gives huge sums of money to the church, then their leaving will affect the church's bottom line.

When leaders get so hurt about a member moving on that they cannot be civil, it is evidence or proof of the condition of the leader's heart. There are instances where departed members have been confronted, harassed repeatedly, and verbally abused. This type of behavior only demonstrates the immaturity and selfishness of the leaders or their subordinates.

If the Holy Spirit leads a person to join a church, it is expected that when his or her season is over at that church, then it is up to the Holy Spirit to lead him or her to another well, to drink the water over there.

Depending on the level of one's call, the current local church may not have the capacity, strength, level of anointing to upgrade a called person to the next level in ministry. Some pastoral and evangelist churches do not have the ability to nurture one that has a governmental anointing. The water level of the church may be too low, there may not be a functioning governmental gift in the house, or there may be a pecking order in the church to which one has to subject oneself.

In the initial stages of my call to the ministry, I became a member of a large church where there was a move of God taking place. During prayer the Holy Spirit revealed to me that He wanted me to leave that church. He said, "If you remain here you will miss God's timing for your ministry, there are too many people ahead of you." There was a pecking order in the house that I was not aware of.

Later on, I came to realize that there were people waiting in line for a long time to be set forth in the ministry at that church, but it was never going to happen because of the way the ministry was structured around the Pastor and his family.

Too many people with calls of God on their life miss the timing and purpose of God by aligning themselves with a church structure based on nepotism, which cannot accommodate the call of God on the life of anyone that is not a family member or a very close friend of the Pastor. The church or the ministry where God assigns a person, should be the place of discipleship training and ministry development, until the time God calls him or her into higher service.

One major crisis we have in ministry is that there are too many wounded, soulish, un-delivered, hurting leaders, who are emotionally unavailable. Yet they are trying to lead people to wholeness or completeness in Christ; a status which they themselves have not yet attained. They act as bosses or lords over God's people because they do not have a shepherd's heart.

A shepherd's heart is a gift from God. When a person is designated as a ministerial assistant or junior pastor in a house that has a chief shepherd or a chief apostle, and he or she does not have the gift or heart of a shepherd, it is most likely that his or her focus will be on the title and position instead of their responsibilities to the people. Leaders who have not been processed by the spirit of God usually have an attitude and tone that is defiant, bossy, disrespectful, outrageous and ridiculous; totally without love and compassion. They make outrageous demands because they can and they want to be honored by the people of God without showing them the equivalent in respect.

Rejection is the major reason for this gangster-like behavior of so many in leadership. Control is a by-product of rejection. What is driving many unhealed leaders is the prestige of ministry, the honor of men, the position of power, and the need for significance. They want to be praised like God, and honored by their parishioners, yet they are jealous of the accomplishments of others, this has given rise to the spirit of competitive jealousy in the church.

One aspect of true leadership is the ability to be firm, courageous and strong, yet not superimposing his or her will on their constituents, but a true leader leads by faith and love; faith works by love (Galatians 5:6b). A leader who is insecure and afraid of rejection, draws strength from his or her position as leader, and compensates for his or her insecurity by dominating, controlling and bullying the people of God.

God is bringing apostolic grace and unity to the House of God by raising up able leaders, full of the Holy Spirit and wisdom, that will bring unity and balance to the house by preserving the spirit of unity in the bond of peace.

Domineering and Controlling Leaders: In the book of Revelation, the Lord rebuked the Church at Pergamum and Ephesus for tolerating leaders who taught the doctrine of the Nicolaitans. At Thyatira there were also some Nicolaitans since it also had the same teaching of immorality and idolatry (Revelation 2: 20-25). Here, the name Jezebel was mentioned. The name "Jezebel" is synonymous with the wicked Phoenician queen who was the wife of King Ahab. Jezebel, the false prophetess caused sexual promiscuity and idolatry to flourish in the church at Thyatira, and like the Nicolaitans was responsible for raising up domineering leaders in the church.

> But I have a few things against you, because you have there some there who hold the teaching of Balaam who taught Balak to put a stumbling block before the sons of Israel, to eat food sacrificed to idols, and practice sexual immorality. So also you have some who hold he teaching of the Nicolaitans.
> – Revelation 2: 14,15 ESV.

A second example of domineering leadership in the New Testament church is that of Diotrephes. One who pridefully desired to be exalted above the brethren. We have much of that in the church today. Leaders, who want to be exalted, honored and celebrated by their parishioners. Like Diotrephes these leaders don't have an ear to hear the truth about themselves and are easily offended when admonished, ignored, or corrected.

> "I wrote something to the Church, but Diotrephes, who loves to be first among them, does not accept what we say. For this reason, if I come, I will call attention to his deeds which he does, unjustly

accusing us with wicked words; and not satisfied with this, neither does he himself receive the brethren, and he forbids those who desire to do so, and puts them out of the church. Beloved, do not imitate what is evil, but what is good."

-3 John 9-11a.

The spirit of Diotrephes presents the ever present problem of leaders with prideful, domineering characteristics who want to have the pre-eminence among the brethren. They love to take the lead, they have a take-over spirit, they love to exercise their authority, they love to push themselves forward no matter who is in charge, they love to tell the pastor how to manage the church, they are eager to be a leader. They try to expel people from the congregation who refuse to comply with their demands. They love self-exaltation, they love to admonish people, while they cannot receive correction. They are presumptuous, self-willed, and hate to be rejected or ignored. They are unteachable, love attention, and make unjust and open accusations against other leaders and people who do not comply with their demands, or pay them the attention they crave for.

The apostle Peter gave an admonition to domineering leaders:

So I exhort the elders among you, as a fellow elder, and a witness of the sufferings of Christ, as well as a partaker in the glory that is going to be revealed: Shepherd the flock of God that is among you, exercising oversight, not under compulsion, but willingly, as God would have you; not for shameful gain, but eagerly; not domineering over those in your charge, but being examples to the flock. And when the Chief Shepherd appears, you will receive the unfading crown of glory.

-1 Peter 5: 1-4 ESV.

Those who dictate and impose their position and their will upon others, usually find it very difficult to submit except it is advantageous to them. The prophet Ezekiel gave a most appropriate word to the shepherds (leaders) of Israel.

And the word of the Lord came unto me, saying, Son of man, prophesy against the shepherds of Israel, prophesy, and say unto them, Thus said the Lord God, "Woe unto the shepherds of Israel that do feed themselves! Should not the shepherds feed the flocks?

Ye eat the fat, and ye clothe you with the wool, ye kill them that are fed, but ye feed not the flock. The diseased have ye not strengthened, neither have ye healed that which was sick, neither have ye bound up that which was broken, neither have ye brought again that which was driven away, neither have ye sought that which was lost; but with force and with cruelty have ye ruled them.

And they were scattered, because there is no shepherd; and they became meat to all the beasts of the field, when they scattered. My sheep wandered through all the mountains, and upon every high hill; yea, my flock was scattered upon all the face of the earth, and none did search or seek after them.

Therefore, ye shepherds, hear the word of the Lord. As I live, saith the Lord God, surely because my flock became meat to every beast of the field because there was no shepherd, neither did my shepherds search for my flock, but the shepherds fed themselves, and fed not my flock; Therefore, O ye shepherds, hear the word of the Lord.

"Thus said the Lord God, behold, I am against the shepherds; I will require my flock at their hand, and cause them to cease from feeding the flock. Neither shall the shepherds feed themselves anymore; for I will deliver my flock from their mouth, that they may not be meat for them.

For thus saith the Lord God; Behold, I, even I, will both search for my sheep, and seek them out. As a shepherd seeketh out his flock in the day that he is among his sheep that are scattered, so will I seek out my sheep, and will deliver them out of all places where they have been scattered in the cloudy and dark day.

And I will bring them out from the people, and gather them from the countries, and will bring them to their own land, and feed them upon the mountains of Israel by the rivers, and in all the inhabited places of the country.

I will feed them in a good pasture, and upon the high mountains of Israel shall their fold be; there shall they lie in a good fold, and in a fat pasture shall they feed upon the mountains of Israel.

I will feed my flock, and I will cause them to lie down, saith the Lord God. I will seek that which was lost, and bring again that which was driven away, and will bind up that which was broken, and will strengthen that which was sick; but I will destroy the fat and the strong; I will feed them with judgment."

-Ezekiel 34: 1-16 KJV.

Leaders Who Need Counsel: I have had the privilege of listening to single female ministers over the years who were very angry with men of God that had disrespected them and caused them much hurt (a continuing problem in the church). Single women who are called into the ministry are especially vulnerable to predatorily, immoral, and domineering men that are in positions of leadership.

One single female pastor in particular, was so full of resentment and bitterness for all the wrong that was done to her in a particular organization, that not only did she leave the organization, but carried that hurt with her to another house and kept telling everyone about her experience.

Over a period of time the hurt had taken root in her heart, and became a root of bitterness. When anyone tried to give her a word of exhortation and comfort, she would retaliate with prideful rage. She did not believe she had unforgiveness in her heart. She was just sharing how she was wounded in the house. She was the victim, she was disrespected, she was violated, but the man of God refused to apologize. She would not be comforted, because she was waiting on God to vindicate her. But years later, God who is long suffering and abundant in mercy spoke to her about her unforgiveness and she humbled herself and repented.

The moral of the story is this; the possibility of being wounded in the house of God is real. But the mistake our sister made is this; she allowed that wound to fester in her heart for so long that it affected her judgment, her personality, her behavior, her ministry to other women, and how she treated others. Without realizing it, she had become just like the person who inflicted the hurt on her, because now she was the one hurting others.

I listened one day as I waited for another woman of God, who was counselling a sister about her turbulent marriage with an unsaved husband. When she concluded her counsel, I could tell she was disgusted. She walked away with a scowl on her face. I stepped up and asked her, "Is that counsel working for you with your unsaved husband? She said, "No."

She had all the theories, all the Biblical facts, and definitions, but no experience, meaning that she was not an overcomer and more than a conqueror in that area of her life. Her unsaved husband was more outrageous and dangerous than the husband of the woman she was counseling. Her husband was always threatening to kill her and commit suicide, yet she would not separate herself from that volatile situation. He eventually carried out his threats, but God was gracious, he shot himself first and died, allowing her to escape.

How can a leader take a person to a place in God where they have never been? How can they take a person into a place of healing and deliverance when they have not experienced healing and deliverance? A leader cannot impart what he or she does not have. This is a truth not only in the natural but also in the spiritual. A person cannot give what they don't have.

You cannot impart instructions to live by, when you are not living by those same instructions. You cannot tell people what to do when you are not doing it yourself. You cannot imply that people must trust God for what they need, when you are not trusting God for what you need.

Leaders must realize and understand that it is not just the position or the title that makes them a leader, but there is a lifestyle of good works attached to the position. Righteousness and peace work together. Faith works by love, so faith and love goes hand in hand. God told Joshua, "Be strong and courageous" (Joshua 1:7).

A position of leadership needs courage, faith, truth, integrity, knowledge and Godly wisdom to function effectively. But an immoral lifestyle disqualifies a person from being an effective leader.

Many potential leaders are like seed sown on stony ground. They have the potential and they start out with high hopes, but soon they wither under the pressure of difficulties because they have no foundation upon which to build. Reliability is a foundation stone of Christian leadership. It is required that a servant of God be found faithful. Therefore, a Christian leader must have certain characteristics which qualify him or her to serve.

Spiritual and Moral Characteristics:

Consecration: This is a prime requisite of a Christian leader. Consecration is making one's life count for Jesus. It involves whole hearted devotion to God, whole-hearted surrender to Christ as Lord, whole hearted love for God, whole-hearted dependence on the Holy Spirit as a guide. A consecrated leader is one that is sensitive to God's guidance, one who abides in Christ, one who seeks God, one who is completely surrendered to God, living daily in His presence.

Humility: As God sought for great leaders, a man among men, you would think that those He chose were anxious for notoriety or to occupy conspicuous places. But to the contrary, When Moses was offered the chance to be a leader of the Israelites; he shrank from the responsibility, feeling his unworthiness. Through many hard battles fought with Pharaoh and having to endure the murmurings of the people – he remained humble and constantly leaned upon God.

Now the man Moses was very meek, more than all
people who were on the face of the earth.

- Numbers 12: 3.

Faith: Faith accepts and believes where it cannot prove; faith
trusts to the limit and then commits everything to God. Faith is
the currency of Heaven.

"Without faith it is impossible to please God"
—Hebrews 11: 6.

Selfishness: Of all the places where a selfish spirit is not to be
desired, is the place of leadership. It is a requirement that a
leader has the spirit of Christ, which is an unselfish spirit. A
leader must prefer others more than self, and care not for the
glory or the honor that might come in rendering service to
mankind.

"Do nothing from selfish ambition or conceit, but in
humility count others more significant than
yourselves. Let each of you look not only to his own
interest, but also to the interests of others. Have this
mind among yourselves, which is yours in Christ
Jesus."

-Philippians 2: 3-5 ESV.

Integrity: Honesty, sincerity and truth should be a part of a
leader's character. Many leaders fail in the area of integrity
when they compromise their faith, their word, their
righteousness, and their principles of morality and decency.

Let integrity and uprightness preserve me.
- Psalm 25: 21.

O Lord who shall sojourn in your tent? Who shall dwell on your holy hill? He who walks blamelessly and does what is right and speaks truth in his heart. Who does not slander with his tongue and does no evil to his neighbor, nor takes up a reproach against his friend.

In whose eyes a vile person is despised, but who honors those who fear the Lord. Who swears to his own hurt and does not change. Who does not put out his money at interest and does not take a bribe against the innocent. He who does these things shall never be moved.

-Psalm 15:

Executive Skills, Education and Ability: In qualifying as a Christian leader, one's mental alertness should be considered. A leader should be a little above the mental level of his group. He should be so equipped by the Holy Spirit that while his subordinate leaders think on a carnal level, the chief executive should be quicker in thinking and more alert in acting. There are many successful leaders who do not hold college degrees. They keep mentally alert by constant study. Education is not limited to Schools of Thought or Bible Seminary.

Just as professionals have to keep pace with the changing trends in science and technology to be relevant; The spiritual leader has to keep abreast with the changing seasons in the kingdom, to know what is present truth. He or she should attend workshops and conferences which will help the leader keep abreast with the movements of Christ's Spirit in the Body of Christ, and to receive impartation, revelation and words of knowledge from ministry gifts that are in tune with the frequency of heaven.

Knowledge of organizational methods, and planning are keys to success. Leaders have to constantly sharpen their skills and abilities to be on the cutting edge in leadership. There is an art and skill to leadership. An anointed charismatic leader has great influence and is capable of winning the hearts of the people because of his or her charisma. Charisma is a special quality of leadership that captures the popular imagination and inspires allegiance and devotion.

When a leader has no charisma, no leadership skills, just a title, and he or she cannot empathize with people, and has no love for the people, that leader often rules arbitrarily. Often these types of leaders are more interested with programs, rules, regulations, and the bottom line. Such a leader disrespects him or herself by being hostile and irreverent, and are often puzzled when they are shunned and disliked by the people; because in his or her mind they are doing the will of God. But what leaders with bad attitudes fail to realize is this; a leader has to serve God and the people with the right spirit and attitude. The sons of Zebedee wanted to call fire down from heaven to consume the people, when the people did not receive them; Jesus told the sons of Zebedee, "You do not know of what sort of spirit you are" (Luke 9: 53-55 Amplified).

All leaders must realize that without people they would not have an organization, a business, a ministry or a church. If they understood that fact, leaders would be much more appreciative of the people that serve. No human can by themselves do everything that needs to be done. Have you ever heard of any leader having a members appreciation day, of course not.

The present day attitude of many church leaders especially independent, non-denominational churches is this; "My church is my family's business." Their church or their family business is so structured that family members are put in positions of leadership whether they are capable, saved or not. If it is a large ministry or church the entire family could be on the payroll, while most of the work still has to be done by volunteers.

Leaders must be careful with allowing family members who are unsaved and not delivered, to take up positions of leadership in the church. A spiritual leader must know how to develop leaders who are loyal and are not family members. Some family run churches go into free fall and into court to settle disputes when the founder dies. They fight each other for control and money, especially if the spouse is incapable of taking over the reins of leadership.

Pastoring is just a job for many leaders void of the mind of Christ and the heart of God, they are only working for a paycheck. Some leaders focus only on preaching, because they do not have the capability of managing a large enterprise like a mega church. Success in ministry is more than members and the offering. What are the long range goals of the ministry? What is the vision and mission of the church? What is the divine mandate? Where do we go from here if we are busting at the seams? Is the church equipped to transition into an army?.

The man with a real experience is the man to fear because he is the man who knows. Plans have to be workable not theoretical or imagined. Each leader who is appointed by the Senior Pastor must bring skills to the table, so he or she can build on the foundation experience that he or she possesses.

A leader must be resourceful, determined, reliable, persistent, and hard working. Jesus worked as a Carpenter, Paul worked as a Tent-maker, Peter, James and John were Fishermen, and Luke was a Physician. Elisha was plowing with twelve yoke of oxen when he was called. David was a Shepherd, living with his sheep out there on the hills of Judah. All great leaders know the value of work. The only thing that follow us into eternity is our works.

To be considered as a great leader one must have a determination to work, to build something in people or to build something tangible for God despite the obstacles. Every leader must have the will-power to forge ahead, make decisions, and have the ability to stay on the job. Many churches have closed their doors when will power weakens, when the warfare becomes too intense, when the financial needs are insurmountable, and a support structure is not in place. When a leader lacks the appropriate mentality, correct judgment, and fails to plan so a crisis can be averted, then leadership for that person is just a job and not a calling.

Understanding the Mandate of Ministry: If the mandate on the church is not defined, and there is no kingdom application, impartation or enhancement of one's calling, why would anyone want to invest time, money and energy in any enterprise that lacks vision and purpose?

This is the reason why some churches become religious institutions of manmade rules and regulations filled with customs and traditions that make the Word of God void, and put unnecessary burdens on people. When there is no prophetic insight, no move of the spirit and the anointing on the church needs to be upgraded, the church becomes stuck, and the people become weary, then the leadership has to rely on programs to entertain and keep the interest of the people to prevent them from straying.

If the church does not reproduce itself with a younger generation, a kingdom seed, eventually that church will become unproductive and die. No church should strive to be just a family church. The reason why the tribe of Judah prevailed over the tribe of Ephraim was because there were more sons in Judah than any other tribe. There is no way any family can produce that many children to be called a family church. Every church needs people outside of their blood line. Jesus began a new generation of sons of God, not born after the will of the flesh but after the will of God; giving access to both Jews and Gentiles to be a part of the family of God.

An unwise leader is someone who fails to seek God for godly wisdom, understanding and direction; one who fails to be equipped mentally, spiritually, and otherwise for the divine calling of shepherding people.

A wise leader is one who relies on the Spirit of God for revelation, clarification, insight and direction. Mentally, he may possess the qualities of a genius, but most of the people God has called were ordinary people with ordinary ability that God had to equip so He could get the glory out of elevated them from the back to the front, from the bottom to the top.

> For consider your calling, brothers; not many of you were wise according to worldly standards, not many were powerful, not many were of noble birth. But God chose what is foolish in the world to shame the wise. God chose what is weak in the world to shame the strong. God chose what is low and despised in the world, even things that are not, to bring to nothing things that are. So that no human being might boast in the presence of God.
>
> -1 Corinthians 1: 26 -29.

The Spirit of the Scribes and Pharisees: Jesus said to the crowds and to his disciples.

"The teachers of the law and the Pharisees sit in Moses seat. So you must obey them and do everything they tell you. But do not do what they do, for they do not practice what they preach. They tie up heavy leads and put on men's shoulders, but they themselves are not willing to lift a finger to move them.

Everything they do is done for men to see; they make their phylacteries wide and the tassels on their garments long; they love the place of honor at banquets and the most important seats in the synagogues; they love to be greeted in the marketplaces and to have men call them 'Rabbi'. But you are not to be called 'Rabbi', for you have only one Master and you are all brothers.

-Matthew 23:1-8.

The spirit of the Scribes and Pharisees is very prevalent in the church today. How can we identify this spirit among us? Some of the identification marks are criticism, condemnation, envy, slander, pride, jealousy, hate, destruction, self-exaltation, selfishness, covetousness and exaggeration of one's importance. That spirit will move heaven and earth to destroy a person's ministry.

When Jesus would not preach the doctrine of the Scribes and Pharisees they made plans to destroy Him. The Roman Governor, Pilate knew that it was because of envy they had Jesus arrested. Pilate could find no fault in Jesus, therefore to convince Pilate that they had a case; they found witnesses who brought false charges against him, because they needed a plausible reason to put Him to death.

Many who are called to ministry will be wronged by leaders whose opinion they value, who they trust and respect highly. Some never get over the hurt, but young ministers need to learn early in their walk with God, not to place so much confidence in a leader that they fail to see their humanity. The arm of flesh is weak, and leaders make mistakes, some are too prideful to admit when they are wrong and would rather lose a valuable member and a relationship rather than say, "I am sorry."

Most problems between people in leadership are of a spiritual nature. When a leader has the spirit of a Pharisee and encounter a subordinate who functions with a stronger anointing, the spirit of envy will cause him or her to covet that person's anointing and gift. Leaders with the wrong spirit are prone to envy. Some will go so far as to sabotage a person's ministry or would rather believe every lie or accusation made against the person they consider a rival. Jesus could not work with the Scribes and Pharisees, their envy and religious mindset was a stronghold that produced demented behavior.

Discerning the Spirit of a Pharisee: A Pharisee pretends to be very spiritual, but his or her heart is deceitful. A Pharisee will use their office to make unconscionable demands on people who lack discernment. A Pharisee demands that people not only respect them but fear them. A Pharisee's primary motive in ministry is to use people. A Pharisee lacks the love of God, compassion, consideration for others, and have an overt sense of self. A Pharisee loves the spot light, and hates when people are promoted and honored. A Pharisee willingly opposes anyone that God is using above and beyond them. The Pharisees attended all of Jesus's meetings to find fault and to gather evidence so that they could accuse Him. Pharisees bring false accusations and promote slander to destroy another minister's reputation.

Leaders and their Assistants: When Elijah was threatened by Jezebel he ran for his life, his attendant or servant had to run with him, but when he arrived at Beersheba he left his attendant there (1 Kings 19:1-3). The warfare that was released against Elijah after his victory at Mt Carmel was so intense that the man of God became discouraged and physically exhausted.

He had to separate himself from his armor bearer, and continue the journey alone into the desert, where he fell into a deep sleep. On two occasions the angel of the Lord woke him up to eat, because of the physical demands of the journey ahead, which was a forty days and nights journey walking to Mt Horeb the mountain of God.

In contrast, during Moses administration whenever *Moses* went up into the mountain of God, Joshua his minister always accompanied him. Joshua was in training to be Moses' successor, but this no name servant of Elijah could not meet the spiritual or physical demands of the position.

Many strive to be the minister of someone anointed and high profiled mainly because they seek notoriety, not understanding the spiritual demands and warfare of an anointed and high profiled leader. The carnal mind thinks that proximity to an anointed leader will bring them certain benefits and it does. But when one seeks the position without consulting God, one's motives are questionable. But when a word and a directive to fill that position comes from God, then it is the will of heaven that the chosen person filling the position is being positioned by God to prepare him or her for ministry.

The anointing on a ministry gift is transferable, as in the case of Moses and Joshua, and Elijah and Elisha. But what happens when the minister is unqualified to receive that transference of the anointing as in the case of Gehazi, the servant of Elisha?

Then the ministry gift has to separate him or herself from the person and a more appropriate candidate has to be selected.

Being a minister's assistant is more than carrying a person's bag, driving him or her to scheduled appointments or bringing him or her water to drink. A minister's assistant must have certain physical, mental, and spiritual capabilities and qualifications. The ministry gift becomes a mentor, a coach or an instructor to the assistant. But when anyone becomes a minister's assistant without hearing from heaven, the intensity of the warfare will cause him or her to be discouraged.

If the ministry assistant is someone who is trying to establish his or her own ministry by being connected, when a better opportunity presents itself, he or she would depart, not taking into consideration that God has a due season for everything under the heavens.

Too many armor bearers or ministry assistants have betrayed the trust of those they serve, and have disqualified themselves for transference of the anointing. An untrained, spiritually immature ministry assistant does not know how to intercept an attack, how to defend, protect, guard and most of all how to intercede for a ministry gift. The most important role of a ministry assistant is that of a spiritual watchman and an intercessor.

Why does a ministry gift need an assistant? From my own personal experience when there is a heavy anointing on me after ministering, it takes me a period of time to transition from the spirit. People talk to me and I don't remember what I said to them. I always forget my personal items; they are left behind, lost, or misplaced. An assistant is also needed to assist me as I minister at the altar.

The chosen person must become the eyes and ears of the ministry gift, taking notes, reminding the ministry gift of the time, the next item on the agenda, when the next appointment will be, making sure the items on the minister's table are accounted for. The assistant also follows up on phone calls, responding to invitations, making sure the ministry gift is comfortable and not placed in a negative or compromising situation by other people.

The assistant must be intelligent, must have good character, know how to take the initiative, must represent the ministry well, must know how to serve the ministry gift with dignity, dress well, guard the minister's personal business, protect him or her from predators and abusers, and must have a fervent prayer life.

Stay In Your Lane: People are always looking for attention or significance, not understanding there is warfare on every level of ministry. This is never a consideration for people that are driven by the desire to be seen, the need for notoriety fuelled by jealousy. Even if they are spiritually immature, lack wisdom and understanding they still want a title and a position of honor.

At the end of the day most people cannot even define their calling, for they are trying to emulate everybody and they do not understand that a gift has to be developed before it begins to be fruitful. Leaders have to function in their calling to be elevated in their calling. The anointing God gave you is suitable for your assignment. When God adds more responsibilities to you, He will increase your level of anointing to accommodate the assignment and the new level. You cannot copy what everybody does. There are footprints and there are imprints. Abraham left footprints in the earth and Jesus leaves imprints in our spirits.

When Satan took the glory and honor of man away from Adam; not only did Adam loose his covering, but emotionally he fell into a state of rejection because of his separation from God, his life source. It was his intimate relationship with God that gave Adam his significance and identification. A man or woman who has issues with rejection or soulish issues will always try to find what is missing in his or her life through intimate sexual relationships, grabbing the spotlight for attention, or attempts to compete and compare what they are doing and what material possessions they have, with what others have and are doing.

The emptiness or the hollowness in the soul is the cause for the constant need to be loved, accepted, honored, celebrated, wanted, and the need for notoriety. When the soul is fragmented the person has personality and emotional issues. The solution is inner healing to bring him or her to the state of wholeness. Outside stimulus covers up an internal issue.

All leaders should find the time for self-examination. Some leaders may think of themselves very highly, having an exaggerate opinion of their own importance, but how do the community of believers feel about them? If a person justifies his or her bad behavior instead of being remorseful, that person is not ready to be ordained as a minister. When church authorities look at the gift in a person and not at their bad character, and give them ministry credentials God will hold the church authorities responsible for the damage this person does to the people of God (Ezekiel 3:17-21).

After God rejected Saul, Samuel cried all night, because his spirit was grieved. He felt responsible for Saul because he ordained him as King, even though the directive came from God. The bible warns us as leaders "To lay hands suddenly on no man". Some would-be leaders are not ready to be elevated by ordination, even though there is a call of God on their life; their character is soiled, and they have proven to be unreliable, unrepentant, unethical and wanting.

There is a due season for every purpose under the heaven. First, Christ has to be formed in the hidden man of the heart, and in the process of time the characteristics of Christ has to be evident. We call this fruit, otherwise the attitude and personality of the believer will be a deterrent to others who are seeking after God.

A leader should always pray the prayer of repentance and continually ask for God's goodness and mercy to be a constant in his or her life. Being a leader does not mean that one will not make mistakes, but mistakes have to be handled with discretion so that the people of God will not be traumatized by the mistakes of unethical leaders.

Much prayer should precede the act of elevating someone in ministry. The reason for this is to ensure that the person has been disconnected from the kingdom of darkness, bad habits, and a lifestyle that is inconsistent with godliness. In the spirit realm many people are still wearing their old garments of unrighteousness. Transformation has not taken place in the spirit.

The gifts and calling of men are before repentance. The ex-prostitute though saved may be still wearing the garments of a street woman in the spirit. The celebrated man of God may still be wearing filthy garments depicting his attachment to his sins of adultery. No one can call a person into the ministry, that call or summons is reserved for God, the Father only. There are some things that His sons do not have the authority to do.

God has to change our image in the spirit and give us a change of garments, the garment of praise and the garments of righteousness, so we can walk in the new image of Christ. This is the reason why there must be a period of preparation for people called into the ministry, a period of development, transformation, and equipping to enable the called ones to walk in what they were predestined to become. This period of preparation takes place prior to commissioning.

Some leaders are not ready to be what God has called them to be, but the call is there. If leaders are commissioned before they are ready, in whatever state they are in when they are commissioned they will remain. The liar would continue to lie, the fornicator would continue to fornicate, the thief will continue to steal, the person who is conniving, subtle, lacking integrity, and manipulative would continue as they were before ordination. The act of ordination does not change a person's character. Christ ordained twelve apostles and he confessed that one of them was a devil.

When leaders exercise authority with the wrong spirit, nothing in the spirit realm will move, nothing will change, but when authority is exercised with the word given by the Spirit of God, that word comes to pass. So it is not the word of a man, it is the word given to a man by the Spirit of God. That word is truth. It is wrong to speak on behalf of God when God has said nothing. God is not a liar.

The Spirit of Emulation: Emulation is one of the works of the flesh listed in Galatians 5: 20. [KJV] To emulate is the desire or ambition to equal or surpass, because of jealousy or envy; the desire to imitate or copy, trying to equal or excel, to rival successfully.

I was ministering at a church when the Lord said to me, "There is a spirit of emulation in this house." To emulate Christ is acceptable, we are becoming like Him; but to emulate someone else because you covet their gift, you covet what that person does or has, is wrong. Emulation is an antecedent for jealousy.

When we are dealing with spiritual things, there is a level of understanding and consciousness we must have before we embark on doing things that were not given to us by God. We must know they are different operations of the Spirit and levels of authority even if the gift is the same.

When I was first called as an apostle, I went to fivefold ministry seminars and apostolic conferences to listen and learn. I did not know how to be an apostle; the calling did not come with instructions, only with an assignment. For the gift to be developed, I had to acquire the wisdom and revelation necessary to function as an apostle in my sphere of authority. What my function, sphere of influence and authority was I had no idea.

I could not emulate other apostles because each apostle has a different assignment and level. I had to gain knowledge not just in the word of God or by revelation, but I had to sit at the feet of someone who was operating on that level of ministry, and had a depth of knowledge that could only be released by revelation. Someone who had tasted the powers of the world to come and could activate the gift of Christ in me. They had to know what they were talking about.

The gifts and anointing God gave to each leader allows him or her to function in his or her respective calling as the Holy Spirit leads. Leaders ought to have an anointing of creativity, this anointing comes from God. Leaders are graced with the inspiration for creativity, if they don't have it, they should ask God for it, or allow someone with the gift to impart it to them. If a leader constantly copies everything others do, that leader will also copy their mistakes.

Original ideas come from the mind of God. God is a Creator, a Great Designer and an Architect. The heavens declare His glory; the beauty of creation unfolds to us the manifold wisdom of God. Creation testifies of his attributes and abilities.

His sons are endowed with His wisdom and creativity, and we can design, create and implement things that are excellent, and consistent with His character and attributes. Man turns to religious tradition and custom that is not relevant or inconsistent with the word of God, because he or she does not know God. The Scribes and Pharisees made the word of God void by their tradition. Oftentimes culture, customs and tradition are hindrances to the release of the gift of Christ and the kingdom of God.

> And he said unto them, "You have a fine way of rejecting the commandment of God in order to establish your tradition."
>
> -Mark 7: 9.

Knowing the Gift of Christ: There is another area of crisis in the Body of Christ which we must address. There are ministers who do not know the gift of Christ, their level, their capacity, their ministerial assignment, or their measure of rule; they are all over the place imitating other men of God and trying to be something in God that God did not call them to be. Some ministers have many gifts, one gift may be more dominant than the others, and may be used more frequently, and perhaps they are identified by that dominant gift.

I once belonged to an organization that appointed any and everybody to be a Pastor as long as he or she could exhort the scriptures. The Presiding Bishop wanted to enlarge his jurisdiction by planting many churches. It was all about the numbers. His method of operation was to uproot a family and plant them in a city or town and charge them to start a church. Then every month the hierarchy officials would pull the finances out of every local church via the overseers office. Many of these churches were too small to survive or operate without funds and eventually had to close down.

These men were appointed as pastors not because of the call of God, but they were selected randomly and expected to fill the church with family members, but many of these churches never amounted to anything; primarily, because the leader did not have the gift or the grace of a pastor, did not have a pastor's heart even though he or she had the position of a pastor.

Many of these Pastors lacked the anointing, the ability and divine capacity, and had no vision of church building. But instead of acknowledging they were not pastors, they accepted a position which elevated them to a place of prominence in the organization because their egos were being stroked. It must be understood that the calling of an apostle, prophet, teacher, pastor and evangelist are gifts given to men by God, to edify the church and to bring the church into maturity.

Many of them with young families suffered financial hardship, due to the demand for funds made by the upper echelon leaders of the organization. A small church with mostly family members did not have the capacity to meet all the demands for money. The pastor had to meet the demands from his personal income, or place those demands on the church. These churches were constantly having fund raising events, while the spiritual life of the church suffered, causing many of them to go out of existence.

Most of these pastors did not understand that pastoring was not their gift. Some were intercessors, some were deacons, some were administrators, some were of such poor quality wayside soil, and so carnal in their deliberations, with no revelatory word to feed the sheep. They could not impart or activate any spiritual gifts and the people remained stagnant, and deficient while the pastor collected his monthly tithe allotment.

All ministers should know their calling and their dominant gift. God gave to the church apostles, prophets, teachers, pastors, evangelists. There are governmental gifts and there are other gifts. [1 Corinthians 13:27] I heard someone say "God called me to be an evangelist but God did not call me to preach." My question to that person was, "What does an evangelist do?"

Ministers on every level must be aware that Satan has given demonic principalities rule and authority to manage and control every city, region, nation, and territory for the dark kingdom. Demonic principalities are the rulers of the darkness of this world. And they can emulate every gift given by God to mankind.

God gives every minister a measure of rule according to rank, qualifications, equipment, and commissioning. How do ministers of the gospel deal with the demonic princes in an International Jurisdiction that they were not assigned to? There must be a collaboration of ministry gifts. Working within the framework of partnerships, networks, and covenants provide protection and give access.

Many ministry gifts that do not have influence in the International Arena can go there through partnerships, they are able to work with and support other ministries in that geographical location. However, where there are no partnerships, covenants or networks, spiritual rank is the determining factor.

Though called as an apostle to the Gentiles Paul was forbidden by the spirit to go into Asia when he wanted to. God knew that as zealous as Paul was, he needed to be upgraded before he could confront the demonic strongmen over Asia. The Apostle Paul had to learn an important lesson in his ministry about levels in the spirit and divine timing.

> "When they had gone throughout Phrygia and the region of Galatia, they were forbidden of the Holy Ghost to preach the word in Asia. After they were come to Mysia, they assayed to go into Bithynia; but the spirit suffered them not to."
>
> - Acts 16:6, 7.

Some ministers however, override the leading of the Holy Spirit and engage themselves in activities for which they are not ready. Finally, Paul was permitted to go into Asia. The region was infested with demonic activity and he needed a higher level of anointing to do battle with the principalities assigned to Asia. God gave Paul a special gift. God wrought special miracles by the hands of Paul. So that from his body were brought unto the sick handkerchiefs or aprons, and the diseases departed from them, and the evil spirits went out of them. (Acts 19: 8-12).

That gift was not given to him when he first became an apostle, it was given to him when God determined the time had come for Paul to go into Asia, he needed a new level of anointing and certain weapons to counter the demonic principalities in that geographical region.

Evil Spirits Carry Diseases: Asia was so infested with demonic activity because of idolatry, that the people were stricken with demonic diseases. God gave Paul a special gift of healing and sent him on an assignment into Asia. Apostles are sent ones, they are sent on assignment by God. When an apostle is sent he or she has to be equipped. God did not allow Paul to go into the region of Asia until he was equipped to deal with the demons in that region.

Unclean spirits carry every debilitating disease that ever existed. When an unclean spirit is cast out the victim, the disease usually goes away and the victim is cured, but the devastating effects of the demonic disease may have taken a toll on the physical body of the victim, and a work of restoration has to be done by the Spirit of Grace. Therefore God wrought special miracles by the hand of Paul, a healing and restorative ministry, but Paul's testimony of his experiences in Asia even after God equipped him for the mission, was about the hardship he and his team experienced.

> "We do not want you to be uninformed, brothers, about the hardships we suffered in the province of Asia. We were under great pressure, far beyond our ability to endure, so that we despaired even of life. Indeed, in our hearts we felt the sentence of death. But this happened that we might not rely on ourselves but on God, who raises the dead. He has delivered us from such a deadly peril, and He will deliver us."
>
> 11 Corinthians 1: 8, 9.

If Paul had not taken heed to the spirit and went into Asia prematurely, outside of divine timing and the will of God he would have died. His ego made him feel he was ready for ministry in Asia, but the spirit told him not so. The spirit knew the power of the territorial princes in Asia, but Paul didn't.

Many leaders with anointings on their life do not understand if they operate outside of their calling there will be disastrous results. Unbelieving ministers have taught that if a person is saved he or she cannot have a demon, which is wrong. Presumptuousness has caused many people to operate outside of their covering and calling, without consultation from God because they are prompted by their gift and not the giver of the gift.

Know Your Measure: Paul understood that God has given to every called minister a measure of faith, grace, a measure of rule, and a measure of anointing. Paul realized that even though he was an apostle, he needed a divine upgrade to go into Asia.

Just as you need a government issued license to drive a car on the streets of any city and country, in the spirit you need a Kingdom of Heaven issued license to have access to secret knowledge, intelligence, wisdom of the operations of the dark kingdom, and the works of the people who belong to the dark kingdom. The kingdom of darkness is a secret society that also operates on the earth. Only God can give you access, increase your discernment, wisdom, knowledge, anointing and the power you need to operate on that level of access.

In Revelation we read Jesus sending a word to the seven churches in Asia; these churches were established when Paul was sent into Asia. Paul and his team preached all over Asia and the Bible says, "All of the Jews living in Asia heard the word." (Acts 19:10)

God gave the apostle Paul a pioneering breakthrough anointing and sent him into a region held in the grip of darkness by demonic princes. Paul and his team had to break through the forces of darkness to preach the gospel in Asia. They came under such demonic oppression and backlash that he reported that they were in such despair, they felt that life was not worth living. Demonic oppression can make a person feel like committing suicide.

> For we do not want you to be unaware, brothers of the affliction we experienced in Asia. For we were so utterly burdened beyond our strength that we despaired of life itself.

Indeed, we felt that we had received the sentence of death. But that was to make us rely not on ourselves but on God who raises the dead. He delivered us from such a deadly peril, and he will deliver us.

On him we have set our hope that he will deliver us again. You also must help us by prayer, so that many will give thanks on our behalf for the blessing granted us through the prayers of many.

-2 Corinthians 1:8-11.

Too many ministers want to go into geographical areas of the world just to put the trip on their résumé. What they don't seem to realize is that unlike the days of the early church, the gospel has been preached in many areas of the world, but apostles are being sent throughout the world in this season to release the spirit of the kingdom of God. But many parts of the world are still held in the grip of idolatry, and worship of false religion initiated by the rulers of the darkness of this world.

If a ministry or minister is not kingdom minded, what does he or she have to offer people besides religion and programs? The reason for networks and partnerships is to give ministers the opportunity to have the prayer covering they need to venture out into the world to preach the gospel of the kingdom. The power of God is very evident and more potent in some third world countries and the reason for that phenomena is that the people resort to prayer at all occasions and every opportunity, and are eager to hear the word of God; while in established so-called first world countries, if the church service goes beyond ninety minutes there are those in the congregation that are upset.

Every leader should know the scope of his or her calling. This is where their authority lies. Some ministries are local, some are global, some are assigned to a certain geographic area, or to a people. The apostle Paul's assignment was to the Gentiles, Peter's assignment was to the Jews. It is only when God enlarges your territory and increases your anointing that you have the grace to go beyond your stated purpose or calling.

If you are a leader in the house of God named "Bless the Lord Ministries," your authority lies within the boundaries of that house of God. You are not a leader in "Upon this rock I will build my church ministries" you do not have any authority in that house because you are a pastor, prophet or apostle. Each house has leaders with divine authority and their own set of rules and protocol. This is very important for prophets to understand; your gift functions where there is relationships and fellowships.

A leader in one house does not have any authority in another house except he or she is a presiding governmental apostle, prophet or bishop. Simply speaking, a man who has a family has authority in his own house, but he has no authority over another man's wife and children. In the same scenario, when a leader goes to another church he is a guest of the man or woman of God that gave the invitation. The invited minister has to conduct him or herself by adhering to the protocol of the house.

A pastor may allow his leaders certain liberties, but those liberties do not extend to another house with whom they fellowship. Where there is order the spirit of chaos has no liberty. What is normal in a house that has no order will be abnormal for a house that has order and structure.

When ministers are being trained, their training should include house protocol and procedures for ministry outside of their local church. There are people that should never be allowed to go outside of the local church to minister without the consent of the Pastor, because they will embarrass their pastor, the church and themselves.

Disorder Is a Constant Problem: The word iniquity implies a generational disorder. The reason why we are destroyed for the lack of knowledge is because of our generational disorder. Order can be defined as:

a. The sequence or arrangement of things or events.
b. An established method or system, as of conduct or action in meetings, worship, court proceedings, etc.
c. A command, direction, or instruction, usually backed by authority.

In dealing with order, we have to look at creation. God created the heavens and the earth. The earth was without form and void. God began to create a system in the universe called cosmos. From this word we get cosmological which is another word for order. When we are dealing with the cosmos or God's order we are dealing with things that God has specifically placed in order for the universe to function. Everything in the universe functions in a fixed order of sequence. The variations of seasons work with the sun and moon as the earth orbits around the sun and climatic conditions are changed. The sun gives light to the moon, the stars and the earth, for without light all vegetation will die, and eventually all life forms will perish.

In the military, when an army defeats another country in war it can establish dominion and a new order for that country. When Satan defeated Adam he became the prince and power of the air and he acquired dominion and established a satanic order. Satan is not the god of the earth; he is the god of this world. The words 'this world' means an order that was established. So long as he is the god of the world he established, everyone that's under his auspices must then function the way he functions.

The Bible says, "The earth is the Lord's," therefore for Satan to access God's earth he has to use human beings who have been given rights to the earth. He uses his order that he imposed on them so he could draw from the earth's greatest resource which is mankind.

Order is also a characteristic or a trait. For example, Karen is a young lady who has been raised in church, and has been very involved in the ministry; she has the call of God on her life, has no tattoos or piercings and is a straight "A" student. At eighteen she gets involved with a young man who has no salvation, and does not go to church. He sets his eyes on this gift and decides he is going to have her.

Even though she is raised right, if she allows this undisciplined guy to sweep her off her feet and she marries him, then after the marriage she realizes he has four kids with four different women, he does not want to work, and he is used to women taking care of him, no matter how she tries to keep the house tidy, he is so messy that they are constantly fighting about the clutter around the house. When order marries disorder it produces disorder.

If a great church family moves to another state because God has blessed them with an opportunity for promotion on the job, and they find themselves in a church where the music is good, the praise and worship is great, the people are well dressed, but the pastor has issues with infidelity and finances; he does not pay his bills, his character is out of order and the church is experiencing crisis after crisis because the pastor has opened a door in the spirit for certain demonic entities to infiltrate the house. Moving to that place of disorder will have a profound effect on the life of this family, this place of disorder will impart something in their life that they never had before.

They came from a place of order, they had order in their lives before they came to this church and God blessed the man of God with a promotion. When order comes under the authority of disorder, it will eventually produce disorder. If they do not leave that church, that spirit on the pastor will affect, the husband and father of that family.

Lot, Abraham's nephew was a man that was totally out of order. His herdsmen were fighting Abraham's herdsmen; therefore Abraham had to ask him to move out. Abraham said to him, "You choose where you want to go." But because Lot was out of order, he did not say to the man who raised him, "You choose first" but he chose first. He gravitated towards Sodom and Gomorrah, a place of absolute disorder.

When God determined to destroy the place, Abraham had to intercede for the city because Lot lived there. Angels had to pull Lot out of Sodom before God destroyed it, but Abraham never invited Lot back to his house, the reason is, when you get rid of disorder, you don't invite it back.

The lack of order is due mainly to ignorance, lack of home training or parental discipline. Some people did not grow up in homes where there was structure, order, any form of discipline or consequences for bad behavior. Disorder, unruly behavior, and in some cases criminal activity was their way of life. When they accepted Christ and their call to the ministry, the biggest hindrance to their spiritual growth and development in the ministry is receiving correction and accepting spiritual discipline. The bible says about such people, "The way of the transgressor is hard." (Proverbs 13:15)

But there are designated places of order ordained by God for His people to learn order, discipline, and self-control. These might be significant places where order is demanded and expected. The military, a training school, a particular field of endeavor, or profession where the trainee has to accept the rules and regulations in order to graduate, or they may have to report to a disciplined oriented, orderly, organized, unsaved, professional person.

Time Management: Time is of the essence, that is a remark that I have heard for many years. What is time and how important is time to the plan of God? God has set times and seasons for everything He has on His agenda.

Time is something that is not tangible, it exists and occurs in a continuum in which events occur in irreversible succession from the past, through the present, and into the future; as in moments, minutes, hours, days, months and years; sunrise to sunset. In Genesis 1: "God called the light day and the darkness night and the evening and the morning was one day."

Within this continuum, there are things that need to be accomplished, so a monthly calendar is important for leaders, setting time limits are important. One meeting with a client should not last all day. You should not allow people to just show up and take all of your time without checking with you to see if you have anything on your agenda for that day. The devil loves to waste a minister's time with things that are non-productive.

When time is important to you, you will not let anybody waste your time, and you will not waste other people's time. There is a time to start and a time to finish. We should practice or get in the habit of starting on time and ending on time; but always leave room for unforeseen circumstances because we are not in control of everything. God is in control. I am not talking about failing to plan, but not planning will lead to failure. This is why we need to follow the supreme leader, the Holy Spirit; He keeps us in the will of the Father. If we override the Spirit's leading we will make mistakes.

God may detain us in His presence because He wants to do something among His people. God can do that, He is God. When you enter into another environment as a guest speaker, make sure you know what time the service starts and what time the service concludes. Some preachers may believe this is an opportunity to display their gifts to the annoyance of the Pastor that gave him or her a set time to conclude ministering.

Some years ago we had a visiting minister at our church. During the week we usually dismissed the service at 9.00 pm. The pastor had to leave early on an emergency and this minister used this opportunity to continue the service well past midnight. Even though the majority of the people left, a few remained until the end. This made the deacons who were responsible for closing the church very angry. Was there a move of God taking place? No. This minister just wanted to prophesy to everybody. That was his last opportunity to minister at our church because he lacked wisdom.

Leaders should have a daily, weekly and monthly schedule. This will enable the leader to manage his or her time wisely. Sometimes leaders have to redeem the time. Too much time over here today may result in the leader having to take back time tomorrow. Pastors have to make the time to study and spend time in God's presence, but members usually expect the pastor to attend every emergency and all their picnics and social events, which is wrong.

God included rest in His schedule, and told man six days you shall labor but on the seventh day you must rest. God called His day of rest 'Sabbath' and leaders should acknowledge the fact that God has given man a day of rest.

A day can be a period of time to separate from everything and go on a "Sabbatical" because our spirits cannot be engaged in warfare all the time. Pastors cannot take care of people's problems all the time; he or she will grow weary because of the lack of rest. There should be rest days when leaders should not receive any phone calls except there is an emergency. A rest day is also a day that the leader has set aside to be alone with God.

Jethro, Moses' father-in-law gave him a plan to incorporate the tribal leaders of Israel in the governmental structure of the nation. His plan was to divide the nation into groups of ten, fifty, hundreds, and thousands, and place leaders over them, lest Moses wear himself out and weary the people.

Fellowship is great, but people will always place a demand on your time. Wise time management should include spending quality time with the Lord, your spouse, and immediate family.

Interpersonal Skills: God invested Himself in people, God's business involves people. People are souls, the soul is eternal. The soul will spend eternity either with God or away from God in eternal darkness. If there were no souls to save, Christ would not have died, and there would be no need for the Church or Church leaders. People make leaders relevant. Without people there would be no need for pastors, apostles, prophets, evangelists and teachers. Without people there would be no nations, governments, laws, wars, industries, farmers, ships, trade, buildings, streets, cars, etc. Satan's warfare with God is all about people.

Leaders must learn the art and skill of managing people. Discernment will help the leader perceive the various personalities that are present in the house. But wisdom will give the leader the courage and the technique to develop other leaders. How does a leader deal with wounded people, undisciplined people, those that lack courage, those that are presumptuous and unwise, the selfish, the emotional, the weak, the unfaithful, the strong-willed, the jealous, the angry, the cunning, the liars, the proud, the wicked, the stubborn, the unteachable, the thief, the unlearned, the backslider, the discouraged, the mentally challenged and the helpless; the whole montage of people Christ came to save?

When God raises up a leader, He gives that leader responsibilities that have to do with people. His salvation plan includes reconciliation, deliverance, and restoration of people into the image and likeness of God. People are the earth's greatest resource, for a church to grow and fulfill its commission, it must have people. For a business to be successful it must have customers. For any enterprise to be successful it must have people.

When David became a captain in Saul's army, the way he carried himself among the men under his command, caused them to respect him as a leader. David went in and out among the people and behaved himself wisely. When David left Saul's employ and was on the run from Saul, the men who were dissatisfied with Saul's leadership defected from Saul's army and joined David's band of mercenaries.

Every leader must ask God for wisdom and the spirit of counsel to deal with people. Psychology enables us to understand people's disposition. It makes us aware that behind all that clamor and bad attitude is an unloved, unwanted, rejected person that is looking for nurturing and love. They may never have told anyone their story, but everyone has a story.

Ungodly Pastors' Wives: A pastor can be a male or female, but because the majority of pastors are men, we will use them as our point of reference. In some cultures a pastor's wife is referred to as the first lady of the church. This title is given to her for deference and to distinguish her from the other wives of ministers in the church. If she is a minister she is supposed to carry the Biblical description of her calling: elder, pastor, evangelist, apostle, etc.

Pastor's wives warrant some attention in this book. In the church of today, many of them are in a place of honor and leadership in the house of God. It came to my attention during my teenage years in church that some pastors' wives were not saved. My first encounter was with a family who lived next door to the church; only a driveway separated the church from their home.

The wife would sit at her kitchen window and listen intently to everything that went on in the church each time there was a service, but she and the children never attended any of the services and never went to another church. She avoided the advances of the visiting missionaries and always had an excuse when anyone particularly the women, invited her out to one of the services. Her children followed her pattern of behavior and they never became a part of their father's ministry.

My second experience was with a young pastor whose wife came to church to keep her eyes on her husband. She did not want him becoming too friendly with the ladies in the church. She was not a part of the church. This man of God was actually afraid of his wife. She would grab at him in the presence of any female he spent too much time speaking to.

Her bad attitude caused so many problems in the church that the members rarely spoke to her. One day a family member suggested that she go to the organization's national ladies retreat, and she did. It was during the small group counseling session, that she was ministered to and accepted Jesus Christ into her life.

Another experience I had was with a woman who was having an affair with the pastor while he was engaged to be married to someone else. The mistress got pregnant and reported the affair to the church authorities; but he refused to acknowledge that the baby was his.

After the scandal died down he continued cheating on his fiancé with this woman and she became pregnant with his second child. This time the leaders of the organization removed him from his position as pastor and his fiancé broke off the engagement.

In his distress he was persuaded by a group of men to marry the mother of his children and start a church, which he did. This unsaved, angry woman became the first lady. That unrepentant, obnoxious spirit with all the rancor of Jezebel fought with every member of the church, and harassed the ministers until she drove them out. God warned the pastor in a dream not to remove the people who were the pillars of the church. This kept her quiet for a little while after the dream was told to the congregation. But before long she continued her rampage and her quest to exercise her power and the authority of the first lady. It took sometime, but finally everyone left and the church was disbanded.

The church must accept the fact that there is a difference between a man's wife and the ministry gift of a pastor.

- A wife is a woman chosen by a man to be his life companion; the marriage ceremony seals the covenant between the two of them.

- A pastor is a ministry gift and a divine calling. God gives a person a pastoral gift, a prophetic gift, an evangelistic gift, a teaching gift, an apostolic gift, as well as other gifts and talents.

- Every pastor's wife is not called into the ministry. A man or woman cannot make his or her spouse a minister if he or she does not have the gift of God or the call of God on his or her life.

Pastors' wives fall into various categories because men are given to appetite. If a man and his wife were married before they were saved, his choice of a wife was determined by what an unsaved man wanted in a woman. Some unsaved men who grew up with a God-fearing mother at home usually know the difference between a woman of the streets and a woman that he can make his wife. He will often choose someone like his mother or someone his mother will be pleased with or because of his rebellion he will go to the other extreme and marry a Delilah or a Jezebel.

Pastor's wives should complement the office of their husbands and bring balance to his ministry. She does not have to be a minister to be effective if she is a praying woman. If she has the spirit of counsel, if she is wise, learned, devoted, humble and sincere, then these qualities will be admired and appreciated in a pastor's wife.

Choosing a wife after the call has its advantages because the man can now choose someone going in the same prophetic direction. When a ministry gift of a pastor and his or her companion complement each other they become yoke fellows, a good ministry team, a good match because of their harmony and the power of agreement.

When choosing a local church for membership, one must not only follow the leading of the Lord, but one must also take into account the relationship between the pastor and his wife, for what is on the head trickles down to the body. When a pastor has no respect for his wife and disrespects her in front the church, and talks about her to the other women in the house, not only is he destroying his marriage but as the gatekeeper he is opening the door for the Spirit of Harlotry to infest the church.

When the marriage took place before the call into the ministry, we have to take into consideration that the spouse may not want to be a part of the community of people that worship and serve Jesus Christ. One would think that if a husband has accepted the Lord that his wife would be elated, but that is not always the case. Many marriages have ended in divorce because one spouse gave his or her life to the Lord Jesus Christ and accepted the call into the ministry. In other marriages the couple remained married but the unsaved partner blatantly refused the lifestyle of a Christian and a consecrated minister.

In recent years male Pastors have given their wives the title of co-pastor. Is co-pastor a calling or a title? A pastor is a fivefold ministry gift that was given by God for the work of the ministry, the perfection and edification of the church. Only God can give a person the gift of a pastor, prophet, evangelist, apostle, teacher or any other spiritual gift. Men can give titles, men can appoint people for service in the church, but God gives the gift and the anointing for the call.

There is a measure of grace and faith that accompanies the gift of Christ. God never does anything without a witness; someone has to bear witness to the call of God on a person's life. If there are no witnesses, then we should pray for God to use someone to bear witness to the call of God, so we don't walk in presumption and error. Why is that necessary? Witnesses who hear directly from God legitimize or sanction what heaven is saying or releasing in the earth.

When a man of God has chosen a wife based on his fleshly appetite, and not the leading of the Lord, he usually chooses a certain type of woman. Delilah, Jezebel, Vashti, Penninah, Herodias or the strange woman. None of these women have the character to be a first lady. There is nothing lady-like about them and they do not qualify to be first ladies or carry the title of co-pastor. Under the heading of the strange women we will include the repeated drug offender, the alcoholic, and the covenant breaker who is always cheating on her husband.

Delilah: Delilah was a treacherous seductress. Samson was a judge [pastor] in Israel that fell into the clutches of crafty Delilah. She was paid large sums of money by her people to find out the source of Samson's strength. Women like Delilah are often used by the kingdom of darkness to seduce men of God, who have an uncontrollable appetite for the flesh.

Delilah is skillful; she knows the art of seduction quite well and the weaknesses of men. She only seduces men with money, influence, power, position and prestige. She is a weapon in the arsenal of Satan. The source of her power is her beauty and her weapons are flirtation, flattery, seduction and her promiscuity. With these weapons she initiates men unknowingly as proselytes into the kingdom of darkness. She has broken many homes, divided many churches, seduced and captured many men of God.

When the godly wife runs from Delilah and divorces her husband or the husband divorces the wife and marries Delilah, that spirit not only becomes the first lady, but it is given a seat of honor in the house of God. Even though the women in the house of God will warfare against that spirit, and hold Delilah in contempt, the pastor will use his authority to defend and protect his mistake. Churches that have been impacted by Delilah usually split or members show their dissatisfaction by leaving the house.

Penninah: is the type of woman that is only suited for the bedroom not the boardroom and certainly not the pulpit. Her female anatomy is what makes her relevant. She is contentious and carnal minded. Her bossy, meddlesome behavior, coupled with her spirit of harassment, confusion, jealousy, and manipulation keep warfare and strife activated among the women in the house. She is always in people's business and lives vicariously through her children, or family members. She is not a lover of people, but she needs them to make her relevant. Godliness is not one of her traits, and without her husband's position she would have no identity of her own, and will not be celebrated as a leader among the people of God.

Jezebel: Much has been written and preached about Jezebel, the wife of Ahab, king of Israel. Jezebel was a witch, a high priestess who brought her evil religion with its demonic worship practices into the nation of Israel. Jezebel is like so many controlling women who are married to men of God, they do not want to stay at his side as a wife, mother, lover and friend, his eyes and ears, his prayer partner and the manager of the home. They want to rule alongside their husbands, because they are jealous of the attention people give to their husbands. Jezebel was controlling and manipulative. Much of the crimes against God that her husband committed were initiated by Jezebel.

To avoid having a contentious home environment, many male pastors who are married to a woman with the spirit of Jezebel, would rather give in to the demands of the wife for attention and a place of rule in the house of God, because he knows that by being uncooperative she can make life difficult for him at home and at church.

These husbands compromise because of the demands placed on them by their wives, to put her in charge or to make her the co-pastor, when he knows that she does not have the grace, anointing, ability or call of God to carry the weight of responsibility if something unforeseen should happen to him. Not only do these men compromise, but they support and condone their wife's disorderly, rebellious, manipulative and controlling ways.

Ahab married a woman whose spirit was disorderly. He himself was out of the will of God. When disorder marries disorder the result is disorder. Ahab used his authority to give license, privilege, and his blessing to his wife to commit all kinds of debauchery and wickedness in Israel. She used his authority to cut off the prophetic ministry in Israel by killing the prophets of the Lord. She in turn became his co-ruler in the kingdom, usurping his authority, and using the king's signet as her badge of authenticity.

Ahab made it mandatory for the people to worship Baal, his wife's false god, by rearing up an altar for Baal in the house of Baal, which he had built in Samaria. He also made a grove and did more to provoke the Lord God of Israel to anger than all the kings of Israel that were before him. And there was none like Ahab, which did sell himself to work wickedness in the sight of the Lord, whom Jezebel his wife stirred up.

Why would a servant of God marry a witch? Women prey on men with the same tenacity men do that prey on women. It is always the assumption that the woman is the victim, but that is not always the case. When a servant of God is bewitched by an evil woman and marries her, it's because he was blinded by witchcraft and his own lust.

> But every man is tempted when he is drawn away of
> his own lust and enticed.
> -James 1:14.

Men of God lose credibility in the kingdom of heaven when they allow a false gift to operate in the Lord's house. As naive as some

Christians are, they would believe Jezebel is a prophet of the Lord, because they do not know the difference between prophecy and a spirit of divination, manipulation and control.

Everything Jezebel does is done under the pretense of God [Jehovah]. People who are not filled with the Spirit of God, nor have the gift of discernment and who do not know the Word of God will also be bewitched by her. One of her traits is to overrule the pastor in every decision. She calls herself a prophet, she usurps authority and seduces God's servants to live immoral lives. She is diabolic and dangerous. She establishes false worship, and allows lawlessness to fester among the people. She practices her craft in the house of God, and initiates many unsuspecting followers in the kingdom of darkness.

Vashti: is known as the beautiful Persian queen who was dethroned and was replaced by Esther, a Jewish girl, during the reign of Xerxes, King Ahasuerus of Persia. Vashti was not just beautiful, but was a wealthy young woman who lived a lifestyle of privilege and excess. Vashti was the typical wife that a great man like the king would choose to adorn his palace. She was not only beautiful, but spoiled, selfish, high-minded, scornful, stubborn, and ungrateful. She lacked the discipline, maturity, poise, wisdom, and grace needed to complement her husband's high position as a world ruler, and to fulfill the demands of her exalted position as queen without being an embarrassment to her husband.

In the story of her short reign as queen (Esther 1) The outspoken Vashti embarrassed her husband, the new king, during his inauguration. She did so before the chief executives of the nation, visiting dignitaries, governors, military officials, all of whom were present at Susa, the capital, along with all the leading ladies in his vast empire that were attending the inaugural celebration.

Vashti's beauty was her only asset but it was only skin deep. Her bad attitude was well documented as the reason for disfavor in the kingdom. She rose to prominence because of her beauty, which was the primary reason she was chosen to be queen. As queen in the society of that day, she had no authority in governmental affairs, her responsibilities were to be social, a hostess at parties when the king entertained heads of state, special envoys, visiting dignitaries from other nations, and to respond when the king asked her to accompany him at an event. It was a marriage of convenience, typical of the marriages that were common in those days; however, the king admired her beauty.

A Pastor's wife with the demeanor of Vashti cannot relate to her husband's position as a pastor. As far as she is concerned, being a pastor is his job. His family life is separate and demands more of his time and attention. Pastor's wives with the demeanor of Vashti purposely separate themselves emotionally from their husband's role as a pastor and from the people to whom he ministers. But she will tolerate those who are making a financial commitment to the first family's welfare. But she has no love or compassion for people apart from enjoying the things that the people can do for her or give to her. She remains aloof, snobbish, critical and apart from the people who cater to her needs and pamper her, she has no friends, and only wants to enjoy the company of her family members.

One pastor's wife with a Vashti temperament came to one of our meetings. We had extended an invitation to her husband to be a guest speaker at one of our week-long events. She showed up the last day of the event and stood before the people when given an opportunity to speak and told them, in typical Vashti style, "I am not here to meet any of you; I am here to be with my husband." She came to collect the money that the church gave her husband on the last day of the meeting, so she could go shopping. She embarrassed her husband to the extent that he just hung his head and became very quiet, as she went on with her tirade before the audience.

This pastor said to some of his colleagues that he had considered divorcing his wife on many of those occasions when she had embarrassed him; but he took into consideration the impact it would have on the church and the fact that his father, who was also a pastor, divorced his mother and how it had devastated the family, and ripped the church apart. He did not want to impose that pain on his children or on the church. His solution was to make her the pastor, leaving her in charge of the church while he spent most of his time on the road and out of the country ministering.

Herodias: Herod had ordered the arrest of John the Baptist, and bound him with chains and cast him into prison, because of Herodias, his Brother Philip's wife, whom he had married. John said to Herod, "It is not right for you to have your brother's wife." Therefore Herodias had a grudge against the man of God. But Herod feared John and protected him, knowing him to be a righteous, holy man who he liked listening to.

Finally, an opportunity presented itself on the king's birthday. Herod gave a great banquet for his high officials and military commanders and the leading men of Galilee. Herodias' daughter danced before them and her dancing delighted the crowd and Herod was pleased.

However, to impress his officials he made a request to the young dancer. "Ask me for anything you want, and I'll give it to you, up to half of my kingdom." Without hesitation the girl went to her mother, Herodias for instructions; her mother seeing an opportunity to get rid of her nemesis John the Baptist said, "Ask him for the head of John the Baptist." Even though the request disturbed the king, he had to follow through because of his oath which was made before his dinner guests.

The spirit of Herodias is that spirit that influences husbands who are men in authority. Herodias uses the authority of her husband and influences him to terminate, or destroy the ministry of people she considers too anointed, and too independent; someone she is jealous of, someone she cannot control, anyone considered by her to be a rival, who will take the spotlight away from her, or who is doing something from which she cannot benefit.

When the spirit of Herodias is in the house of God, her husband is just a figure-head, the man in the fore-front, but she is the one behind the scenes that uses him like a puppet. Herodias is really the one who is in charge, the one dictating the pace and order of the house.

The Herodias spirit retaliates against ministers that speak truth, that bring order and correction to the house. She hates true governmental prophets that speak "Thus said the Lord." Anyone in ministry that is attached to that house where her husband presides, that speak against anything she condones, they will experience the wrath of Herodias. It's a spirit that causes the death of prophetic ministries. It stifles the ministry of the prophet, and causes the demise of that ministry gift in the house. Herodias is cunning, deliberately crafty, wicked and will tolerate no one getting in her way. She retaliates when opposed and uses her influence over her husband to get him to carry out her diabolical, vicious, vindictive schemes.

The Story of Abigail: 1 Samuel 25; tells us a story of a man named Nabal and his beautiful wife named Abigail. Nabal was a wealthy man. The bible does not say how Nabal acquired his wealth, whether he was an astute business man or if he inherited his wealth, but he is described as a great man because he had great possessions and lived in prosperity. Nabal had a reputation for being brutish, disrespectful, unwise, churlish, disgusting, unreasonable and prideful; a man so harsh with his insults to others that he was called a man of Belial, no one could speak to him. (Belial was a term used to describe a person that was evil). His wife on the other hand was described as a woman of good understanding, and of a beautiful countenance.

David had an issue with Nabal. David and his men had provided protection for Nabal's shepherds while they were in the wilderness, and on a day when Nabal was shearing his sheep, he had a great feast, one that was fitting for a king; on hearing about the feast David sent some of his young men to ask Nabal for some food in return for what David and his men had done for him. But Nabal insulted the men and sent them back to David empty handed. On hearing Nabal's insulting remarks, David became so angry that David told four hundred of his men to strap on their swords, He was determined that he was going to kill every man in Nabal's camp that night.

The news of the impending destruction reached Abigail, Nabal's wife, she was told the story of what transpired when David's men came to greet Nabal and to ask for food. Abigail went into action to avert the impending evil, she took an abundance of the food that Nabal refused to give David and his men, and without telling her husband anything Abigail intercepted David and made her peace offering to him, using her wisdom and humility to appease David.

David came to the realization that God had sent this woman to meet him, he said to her "Blessed be thy advice, and blessed are you for keeping me this day from coming to shed blood, and from avenging myself with mine own hand." When the evil was averted, Abigail went home and found Nabal so drunk that she did not say anything to him until the morning. On hearing about the crisis that she averted, Nabal suffered a heart attack and after ten days the Lord struck him down and he died. God avenged David, and this wise woman became David's wife.

Every great man needs a wife with the wisdom, discretion and inner beauty of Abigail. She was a woman of peace, a woman who could arbitrate and bring solutions to situations that could be devastating to the husband's calling, his family and ministry. All men of God need to realize that the enemy of their souls would use any scheme possible to destroy them, and to have an Abigail as a wife is an asset that they must recognize, encourage and be devoted to.

If we look at Abigail's demeanor we do not see a woman that was insecure, jealous, seeking attention or trying to compete with her husband. Her husband was a great man because he had material possessions, she was a great woman because of her wisdom; she knew how to influence, negotiate and persuade a great man in such a way that he would realize his mistake and change his mind.

The words Abigail used to appease David made him see the error of his ways, vengeance belonged to God not to David; she made him think about the regret that he would have when he became king, and the effect it would have on his reputation. He was angry because he was insulted by an evil man and was about to commit a crime in Israel. And out of that anger blood would be on his hands. David was going to give an account to God for all the innocent lives that would be lost that day because of his issue with one man.

When God avenged David by the death of Nabal; David knew that Abigail would be an asset to him; he admired her wisdom, her skill in arbitrating the problem and bringing it to a peaceable conclusion, and for what she had done, she became his wife and what Nabal refused to give away, was given to David by the Lord.

> And when David heard that Nabal was dead, he said, "Blessed be the Lord who had avenged the insult that I received at the hand of Nabal, and has kept back his servant from wrongdoing. The Lord has returned the evil of Nabal on his own head." Then David sent and spoke to Abigail, to take her as his wife.
>
> 1 Samuel 25: 39.

False Ministers: False Christ, false prophets, false apostles, false teachers, false pastors is a problem dealt with throughout Scripture. The false ministers of Pharaoh battled with God's true servants Moses and Aaron, and they were able to duplicate many of their miracles and demonstrations of spiritual power. The name Balaam is synonymous with ministry that is tainted and motivated by money. The Old Testament prophets decried the false priests and shepherds of their day. Paul is particularly strident in his attacks against false ministers in the New Testament.

It is essential that we acknowledge the source of all false ministers as Satan himself. Paul said; "And no wonder! For Satan himself transforms himself into an angel of light" (2 Corinthians 11:14). In this statement, Paul links the work of false apostles with something beyond mere error. He links it with hell itself. This fact must guide the Church in its response to false ministers today.

God has graciously provided the Church with gift ministries in the form of true apostles, prophets, evangelists, pastors and teachers (Eph.4:11-13). The stated purpose is that going forward we will not be children in understanding, tossed to and fro and carried about with every wind of doctrine, by the careless indifference of discourteous men, with their cunning craftiness and disrespect for the truth, whereby they lie in wait to deceive. (v. 14)

Imposters and predators will always surround the fivefold ministry. Satan tries to duplicate everything that God has established. He has the ability to transform himself into an angel of light. Paul speaks of true ministers, and immediately refers to their opposition by false ministers. We are being equipped by God so we will not fall prey to the false ministers that are always prowling around the Body of Christ seeking for opportunity to influence the church with the spirit of error.

For every ministry gift God has ever created, Satan has presented a counterfeit. The ministry gifts of Ephesians 4:11 are no exception, and in this context we must understand false ministers because Christ has given the Church the apostle, prophet, evangelist, pastor and teacher. Satan (as a false Christ, 2 Cor. 11:4) has created five crude and dangerous imitations to impersonate them:

1. **Predators**: Jesus warned us of false prophets that would appear in sheep's clothing, but inwardly were ravenous wolves (Matthew 7:15).
2. **Hirelings**: Jesus spoke of false shepherds (or false pastors) who would come to kill, steal, and destroy as hirelings. They would fail to protect the sheep, and instead would scatter and abandon them (John 10:10-13).
3. **Heretics**: The apostles Paul and Peter both warned of the existence of false teachers who would peddle fables and heresies to bring swift destruction to God's people (see Tim. 4: 3,4; 2 Pet 2: 1).
4. **Deceivers**: It is clear that false evangelists can be identified as those who spread a false gospel (Gal. 1:9).

5. **Imposters**: Jesus spoke to the angel of the church at Ephesus of false apostles, men who were liars, claiming apostleship though they were not sent by God (Rev. 2:2).

The counterfeit nature of these men may flow from one of two corrupt foundations. Some false ministers are false because they are apostates, that is, they have fallen away from a once legitimate faith (2 Thess. 2:3). Like Judas, they begin by having a valid experience with God, but because of internal weaknesses and lack of character, they turn away from Christ to a life marked by error.

We may assume that some false ministers are total imposters who have never had an experience with Christ. In either case, they are regarded as deceived and dangerous people encouraged by the devil to bring harm to God's people.

All false ministries have common roots. How did Judas become a betrayer? For any man to come to this kind of deception, some dark dynamics must be at work deep within him, but only two major motives are mentioned in Scripture. The bible does not excuse deviant behavior on some childhood trauma or environmental deficiency. False ministers practice their evil behavior either out of the love of money or the sin of pride.

That money should be the root of this evil is not surprising. It appears that Judas was affected by this power himself. Great profit can come from the resources of naïve people who are told they are giving to God.

Why Leaders Fall: Human beings often think of consequences after they have given in to temptation and the reality of how much their mistake is about to cost them hits home. Every man is drawn away by his own lust when he is enticed, when lust is conceived it results in sin.

Humans make bad decisions when they follow the dictates of the flesh. The flesh is always contrary to the will of God. Some mistakes are deliberate sin; some are made because of ignorance, others through temptation because they are weak in certain areas. However, every servant of God is responsible for his or her own destiny. God has given man principles of life in the word of God to direct us. When these principles are ignored, man becomes his own lord, and his pride is the prelude to his destruction.

Temptation is common to man but God is faithful; He will not suffer us to be tempted above and beyond our capacity to endure, but will make a way out, so we can be delivered out of the snare of temptation.

Every leader should know his or her area of weakness, if not, he or she should seek God about the things which He has unknowingly delivered him or her from and is still delivering. Serpentine spirits go after flesh and attach themselves to those unsanctified areas where the flesh has a stronghold. What was the chief sin in your life that prevented you from living an overcoming life? What habits had you so bound that it controlled you, or possessed you? These are the weaknesses one has to guard oneself against.

Many accept the call of God and received their ministry credentials, but never repented of their secret sins and addictions because they were never expose. Secret sins like pornography, drug addition, harlotry, etc. will take you further than you want to go. When these hidden sins become unresolved issues and they continue to be ignored, the addiction goes deeper and further and the person becomes a victim of his or her secret sins.

Some ministers involved in secret sexual sins can so compartmentalize their life that they can stand behind the pulpit and preach a great message without feeling any remorse or conviction, all the while their secret sins involve molesting young women or boys in the house of God, having numerous adulterous affairs, keeping a mistress on the payroll of the church, using church money to take their lovers on vacation, raiding the church's bank account and a host of other discrepancies.

This is the danger of belonging to a church where the leadership has no one to be accountable to for his or her actions and all his or her discrepancies are swept under the rug. Usually, other church leaders become enablers and sins against God are covered up by those men who supposedly "have the leader's back."

When women fall into sin, they are dealt with harshly by their counterparts. They are judged indiscriminately by men and women. Insults and derogatory names of all kinds are hurled at the women, and they are thrust out. But men on the other hand cover up the indiscretions of other men and allow them to continue serving in their capacity especially if it is a paid position.

The admonition in the word says:
"For if we sin willfully after that we have received the knowledge of the truth, there remains no more sacrifice for sins, but a certain fearful looking for of judgment and fiery indignation, which shall devour the adversaries.

He that despised Moses' law died without mercy under two or three witnesses. Of how much sorer punishment, suppose ye, shall he be thought worthy, who hath trodden underfoot the Son of God, and hath counted the blood of the covenant, wherewith he was sanctified, an unholy thing, and hath done despite unto the Spirit of Grace?

For we know him that hath said, Vengeance belongs unto me, I will recompense, saith the Lord. And again, the Lord shall judge his people. It is a fearful thing to fall into the hands of the living God."

-Hebrews 10: 26 -31.

Many, many, many leaders do not know the fear of the Lord. That is why it is so easy for them to be liars, to speak for God when God has not spoken; to give the church their opinion whether right or wrong and pretend as if it is a Rhema word from God.

Many today entered the ministry with pure hearts, until the devil shows them the great opportunity they have to manipulate and control God's people; and they do it under the pretense that they are doing God's work, but manipulation and control are the seeds and sins of witchcraft.

The House of Eli: Nepotism is favoritism shown or patronage granted by persons in high office to relatives or close friends. And such was the case with the high priest Eli during his tenure as priest in Shiloh.

Eli's sons were very wicked men. They had no regard for the Lord. Now it was the practice of the priests with the people that whenever anyone offered a sacrifice and while the meat was being boiled, the servant of the priest would come with a three-pronged fork in his hand. He would plunge it into the pan or kettle or caldron or pot, and the priest would take for himself whatever the fork brought up.

This is how they treated all the Israelites who came to Shiloh. But even before the fat was burned, the servant of the priest would come and say to the man who was sacrificing. Give the priest some meat to roast; he won't accept boiled meat from you, but only raw.

If the man said to him, Let the fat be burned up first, and then take whatever you want, "The servant would then answer, No, hand it over now, if you don't I'll take it by force."

This sin of the young men was very great in the Lord's sight, for they were treating the Lord's offering with contempt.

Now Eli, who was very old, heard about everything his sons were doing to all Israel and how they slept with the woman who served at the entrance to the Tent of Meeting.

He said to them, "Why do you do such things? I hear from all people about these wicked deeds of yours, No my sons, it is not a good report that I hear spreading among the Lord's people.

If a man sins against another man, God may mediate for him; but if a man sins against the Lord, who will intercede for him? His sons, however, did not listen to their father's rebuke, for it was the Lord's will to put them to death.

-1 Samuel 2: 12-17, 22.

In this scenario we see Eli, in his position as Senior Pastor, and his sons as ministers serving in the House of God. Under the Levitical priesthood, those of the lineage of Aaron inherited the priesthood. The Levitical priesthood was a generational inheritance of the sons of Aaron, who were of the tribe of Levi. The sons of Levi were not able to continue forever because of death. However, since Christ's death, burial, and resurrection, the Levitical order of priesthood has been discontinued and was replaced by the order of Melchisedec, a new order of priesthood that was based on the power of an endless or the eternal life of the High Priest.

Using Eli's house as a back drop for our discussion we surmise that whenever there is a family dynasty in a house of God, correction and discipline are very rarely given to family members. They walk under the covering and protection of a parent who is the senior minister, and they are never or seldom chastised by the church for their indiscretions, sins, failures, or short comings.

Another scenario of nepotism is that favoritism is shown to those who give great sums of money to the church. Often, depending on the spirit of the Pastor, these acts of kindness tie the pastor's hands, so that no reprimand or correction is ever given to any of his financial supporters, even when they step out of their place of subordination and begin to take over the house by telling the pastor what he or she should or shouldn't do. They usurp the authority of the pastor by chastening the members while the pastor keeps silent.

A spirit of compromise is the reason why many leaders show favor to their benefactors and family members who are out of order. Even when God puts a check in the spirit of His chosen leader and informs the pastor about the person's motives, they over-ride the Holy Spirit's alert and look the other way, in so much that they make excuses for their disorder. But that same leader will render harsh criticisms, correction, and even discipline to other members, especially single women, for the least error they make, which is a double standard of justice.

Eli was ready and willing to call out Hannah and rebuke her because he thought she was drunk, when in reality she was praying within herself to God, due to her burdened soul and grieving spirit, caused by the torment she was experiencing from her rival Penninah, and the fact that God had closed up her womb. Eli could not discern her heart.

So Hannah rose up after they had eaten in Shiloh, and after they had drunk. Now Eli the priest sat upon a seat by a post of the temple of the Lord.

And she was in bitterness of soul, and prayed unto the Lord, and wept sore. And she vowed a vow, and said, O Lord of Hosts, if thou wilt indeed look on the affliction of thine handmaid, and remember me, and not forget thine handmaid, but wilt give unto thine handmaid a man child, then I will give him unto the Lord all the days of his life, and there shall no razor come upon his head.

And it came to pass, as she continued praying before the Lord, that Eli marked her mouth. Now Hannah, she spoke in her heart; only her lips moved, but her voice was not heard; therefore Eli thought she had been drunk. And Eli said unto her, "How long will you be drunk? Put away your wine."

And Hannah answered and said, "No, my lord, I am a woman of a sorrowful spirit; I have drunk neither wine nor strong drink, but have poured out my soul before the Lord. Count not thine handmaid for a daughter of Belial (lawless or worthless person): for out of the abundance of my complaint and grief have I spoken hitherto.

-1 Samuel 1: 9-16.

But the Bible states that Eli's sons were wicked men, who slept with the women at the entrance of the tabernacle, they also stole the offerings of God and caused the people to abhor the Lord's offerings. Yet Eli did not address his sons' behavior until he heard the complaints of the people. And still he did not use his authority as High Priest to set them down, or dismiss them from service in the holy place, but left it up to God to do the judgment because he did not want to offend his sons.

The problem with a family dynasty is that apart from the founding father or mother who birthed the ministry, the family is denied the opportunity of ever birthing anything spiritual. They take their inheritance for granted. They have a sense of entitlement because they are the king's son or daughter, and everything is handed to them. They never had to count the cost or pay for anything. They know nothing about laying a foundation, they have no experience with struggling to build a ministry, and the sacrifices that it takes to bring a ministry to maturity.

There are many men that roam around the Body of Christ as predators not building or birthing anything, but looking for an opportunity to take over someone else's ministry by camouflaging themselves as a spiritual cover. Many women have fallen prey to these rogue ministers, who see the church as an opportunity for a paycheck, and the woman as someone they can deceive and bring under subjection to their cunning wiles and schemes.

As creator, God put laws in place to govern the universe. The earth He gave to man to govern. Man operating on a governmental level has put laws in place to govern society, to keep law abiding citizens safe by prosecuting law breakers. Man has a judicial system for judgment and justice to keep order in society. God also has a system of judgment and justice, and His laws for governing the universe and the kingdom of man was given to man in the volume of the book we know as the word of God.

Under heaven's judiciary, there are sins against God and sins against man that are arbitrated by God. Jesus Christ is our advocate or defense attorney who pleads our case before God's throne. Satan is the prosecuting attorney, who makes accusation in his capacity as the accuser of the brethren. Eli so rightly said, "If a man sins against a man, he can get justice in the courts of man; but when a man sins against God, who will entreat God for him in the court of heaven, who will be the defense attorney to plead his case?"

Due to presumption, pride, stubbornness, wickedness, and self-deception, when a leader's spirit is out of order, he or she takes on a rebellious attitude; believing in his or her heart that being used of God makes him or her untouchable and uncorrectable, and he or she can do whatever is right and pleasing in his or her own eyes and the people must submit to the leader no matter what he or she does or says. Leaders with this disposition and warped, prideful mentality hate governmental apostles and prophets that bring order to the Body of Christ.

Because the priests were set in office by God, the people could not do anything about Eli's two contrary sons, only Eli could. In his position as High Priest, he represented the government of God. There was no king in those days, no governmental prophet to speak to the nation on behalf of God. God was the judge and jury; He alone could deal with the corruption in the House of God perpetrated by the priests of God.

If ministry in a family is a generational inheritance, it means God has chosen the family down through the generations to minister to Him in the House of God because of their faithfulness and God's predetermined will. These families carry a generational anointing and are like glory carriers.

When leaders like King Saul become unfaithful, rebellious and disobedient to God, sometimes the throne or the inheritance does not pass on to the next generation. In contrast, King David was faithful to God and God gave him a generational blood line to sit on his throne. Jesus was of the same tribe as David, and He is a natural heir to David's throne.

In most instances, a generational, spiritual inheritance ceases when sins against God in a family are not dealt with. This also happens when a family turns aside after other gods, and a Godly generational heir does not materialize.

In the case of Eli's house, God not only destroyed the House of Eli, but He cursed Eli's bloodline, and raised up Samuel as a prophet to the nation and priest to replace Eli's sons. The mantle of government was passed on to someone who was not of the bloodline of Eli.

> And the Lord said to Samuel, "Behold I will do a thing in Israel, at which both the ears of every one that hears it shall tingle. In that day I will perform against Eli all things which I have spoken concerning his house. When I begin, I will also make an end.
>
> For I have told him that I will judge his house forever for the iniquity which he knows; because his sons made themselves vile, and he restrained them not.

And therefore I have sworn unto the house of Eli, that the iniquity of Eli's house shall not be purged with sacrifice nor offering forever.

-1 Samuel 3: 11-14.

If a leader wants to discipline others, he or she must also discipline those that are closest to him. If discipline is left up to God, always remember that it is a fearful thing to fall in the hands of the living God. Eli learned that the hard way. The called ones in the family who are expected to serve in leadership must be an example to the congregation. When leaders lose their fear of God and honor their children or family members instead of God, there will be divine consequences.

God asked Eli a question through the man of God. "Why do you scorn my sacrifice and offering that I prescribed for my dwelling? Why do you honor your sons more than me by fattening yourselves on the choice parts of every offering made by my people Israel? Are we doing the same thing in the church today?

A Servant's Heart: In order to serve others you must have a servant's heart. Many want to be in ministry today without serving. Some want to get up front and personal with ministry gifts for the transference of their anointing, but care nothing about the person. Their only interest is for a door to be opened for them or the notoriety that comes with the relationship.

People who pursue fame instead of pursuing God fail to understand this principle. Jesus told his disciples, "And whosoever will be chief among you, let him be your servant." (Mathew 20: 27) Servant-hood must precede commissioning. If the individual is only serving to gain an opportunity to impress people and display his or her gifts, he or she must realize that gifts were given before conversion or repentance. Your gift or your talent is not you. Your character defines who you are. God knows you from the inside out; at the core of your heart. You cannot pretend with God.

If you ask a person for his or her résumé, he or she will tell you in writing about their education, accomplishments, job history, and market place experience that qualifies him or her for the job. These are the proof that the world uses to evaluate a person. But how is a person evaluated in the spirit realm? God said about Jesus, "This is my beloved son in whom I am well pleased" (Matthew 3:17).

In what way did Jesus please the Father? He pleased God by His obedience. He pleased God by becoming a servant. As a servant He humbled himself and became obedient unto death. It was the Father's will that He should taste death for every man. Even though His crucifixion was horrendous, in His obedience He looked beyond to see the joy of many souls being delivered from the powers of darkness and entering into relationship and sonship with Him and His father.

Servants are workers together with God. They serve their master Jesus Christ. Whatever their assignment may be, they do it in the name of Jesus. A servant thinks about pleasing his or her master and doing his or her job efficiently. The servant knows that he must maintain a good relationship with his master, so he tries to please the master by being obedient and contrite.

When a leader does not have a servant's heart he or she sees him or herself as a lord over God's heritage. He or she treats people as property to be used at will, and service is measured by what people can do for "me".

When God gives the church a pastoral gift He also gives that person a pastor's heart. There is a built-in programming in the heart of shepherds that causes them to nurture and care for their flock. Sheep instinctively know the voice of their shepherd; they also know the voice of a wolf in sheep's clothing; because the sound that a shepherd emits is quite different from the sound that a wolf emits. Jesus is the chief shepherd and His sheep know His voice. Shepherds serve the sheep. Hirelings have the heart of a wolf, they do not serve the sheep, they ravish the sheep.

The Spirit of Jealousy: One of the greatest causes of division and sabotage in the Body of Christ is the Spirit of jealousy. When there is a lack of cohesiveness, much back-biting, criticism, unforgiveness, competition and emulation in the house, one does not have to do much investigation. These are the fruit and proof that a spirit of jealousy has infested the church.

Covetous people are consumed by this spirit. Jealous people want what you have. What they fail to realize is that most low to moderate income people pretend to be well off by using credit cards, and living with a lot of debt, trying to impress people that they are blessed.

This sin is rampant among ministers. They are jealous of another minister's anointing, spiritual gift, and ministry. They align themselves with people whose anointing they covet, but as soon as another ministry gift comes along they switch their allegiance. They are motivated by who can get them to where they want to go, and give them what they want.

Jealous people are not loyal and cannot be trusted. They are only around because there is nothing else available, but they do not love anyone else but themselves. They use people; they do not reproduce themselves so that another person can carry their anointing. They have the spirit of Judas.

Some years ago, a female pastor was a guest speaker at our women's conference. I was a young minister at that time and there was much I did not understand. This woman ministered about the spirit of jealousy. I was appalled! What in the world do Christians have to be jealous about? We are all facing the same enemy. Our warfare may be different but we are all in the struggle. What is she talking about? I could not see it at that time.

On another occasion I went to a ministers' conference. All the senior ministers and pastors were seated up front and the junior ministers were seated behind them. Even though I was a junior minister at that time, the Spirit of God began to point out to me the different pastors who were not getting along with each other. I was amazed! I did not expect that behavior from senior people in the ministry, I was really naïve.

When I became a Pastor, we taught our congregation to pray and a strong anointing was present. I did not think that a congregation of our size would be a problem for another pastor with a larger congregation. To my amazement, our congregation was on the hit list of one particular pastor who strongly believed that we should not be in existence, we should be a part of his church.

He lodged complaint after complaint to the regional overseer claiming we were in his territory and should be a part of his congregation. He ignorantly continued his rampage trying to convince everybody that he was right, even though we were situated in two different towns separated by a large river. He also believed that no other church in that region should experience a move of God that he was not a part of; he wanted to own whatever God was doing and claim it as something he was responsible for.

I cried out to God, "Lord what is going on?" God said to me, "Pay attention to the spirit of jealousy." In the course of my years in ministry there were leaders I held in high regard, but I soon realized that wherever there is selfishness, covetousness, and insecurity, the spirit of jealousy will be present.

The anointing does not make a person exempt from jealousy. When there is a spot or blemish of darkness in a person's spirit, jealousy will manifest itself. All you have to do is listen to their remarks and comments. Watch their attitude, the way they receive or don't receive you and you will discern if you are dealing with the spirit of jealousy. There is one thing a jealous person cannot do; that is, pay you a compliment. It is easier for them to say something negative because that is what jealousy is a dark negative deposit in someone's spirit.

I was invited to hold a series of meetings at a church, it lasted for five weeks. The Pastor gave me the option of remaining for as long as I wanted to, not only was he able to rest, he also enjoyed my teaching. By the end of the third week I had a very terrible experience.

I was sitting in my office when something came into the room and began wrapping itself around me and began to squeeze the life out of me; I jumped to my feet and cried out "My God what is going on?" At the same time I reached for the phone to call my prayer partner. She answered immediately, and we began to pray.

It was a serpentine spirit that attacked me, but when we began to do warfare it let go of me and slithered away. We stayed on the phone discussing the incident and she began to share with me what she was experiencing at her local church. The Holy Spirit said to me, "It is a spirit of jealousy."

There are other dominant spirits that infest people who are part of the visible congregation we call "The Church." Wherever people are, there will be evil spirits. Human beings are a magnet for spiritual encounters and infestation because man is a spirit, he has a soul and lives in a body. Evil spirits can carry out their destructive agendas against mankind when they inhabit or influence humans, and they are often used by humans to carry out their evil agendas against people that they want to destroy.

Other Dominant Spirits In The Church Are:

a. Harlotry - Sexual promiscuity, adultery, and fornication.
b. The Spirit of Error - Doctrines of devils, False doctrines.
c. Racism - Racial and cultural bias, hate and segregation.
d. Gender bias - Crimes against women. Disrespect and sabotage against women in positions of authority.
e. The Spirit of Mammon - The ungodly pursuit of money as an object of worship.
f. Religious Spirits – Strict adherence to a religion, or a religious community or a religious sect.
g. Pride - Haughty behavior and exaggerated self-esteem, resulting in an overly high opinion of oneself.
h. Idolatry - Excessive devotion or worship of a person, a thing, or oneself. The practice of sorcery, witchcraft, and divination.

In the church there is a form of idolatry perpetrated by those who advocate that God only uses men to preach the gospel. They form a sect of believers who believe the male alone is set apart by God for ministerial service and men are the only messengers of God in the earth. This is a part of the women's warfare against the serpent. This form of idolatry condones crimes against women in the house of God, disrespect for women in ministry, and the alienation of women from leadership positions.

The Lore of Full Time Ministry: Full time ministry may look glamorous to some people, especially those inexperienced with the nuances of ministry. Newly ordained ministers are seldom, if ever taught about managing finances, and the need to separate personal finance from the finance of the ministry or church. In building a ministry there is always the ever present need for money; kingdom building requires or demands finances, and God expects His people to finance His work in the earth. But before venturing into full time ministry, one should begin setting aside money for the needs of the ministry in a separate account, and begin the process of getting out of debt. Far too many ministers are irresponsible with their personal finance, and they expect the church to pay for their extravagance and indiscretions with personal finances.

Most leaders practice the art of gouging (exacting exorbitantly, extorting or scooping) their people for money each time there is a an assembly, instead of putting a plan of action in place for the church to finance itself. Discussions about money should take place in a private business meeting with church members only, instead of discussing financial incidentals before visitors and non-members.

Before any minister decides to become a sacrificial lamb and step into full time ministry without any means of financial support, he or she should count the cost. Newly organized churches with inexperienced pastors that are in full time ministry with a young family, must understand that the lack of financial support will have devastating effects on the family, and will put them in a position of always being needy and having to endure the pain of rejection when a tithing member leaves the ministry.

People in full time ministry must have some means of financial support; many who do not have a pastoral calling have presumptuously started churches primarily to have a means of support. Some ministers perceive pastoral work in the same way they perceive a secular job, but the difference with a secular job, and a person called of God into ministry is this; the one called of God is accountable to God, and the one employed on a secular job can be fired or can quit; but no one can quit God and God does not fire anyone. Any worker who puts his hand to God's plow and quits is not fit for the kingdom of heaven. But when one does not know the will of God and is operating on his own instincts without the collaboration of heaven, if one's objective is money, that love of money will open the door to other temptations.

In the American economy a meager church cannot take care of a family. If someone wants to go into full time ministry without counting the cost, personal financial pressure will turn their ministry into a side show, because of the needs of the first family and the pressures it place on the constituents. People have left churches because of that pressure, especially if they are going through a season of hardship themselves.

Counting the cost includes, how much the first family is willing to deny themselves. It takes years to build a strong tithe paying membership. In the meantime the spouse should be willing to support the family financially by holding down a job. Members come and go all the time; you cannot depend on the financial support of the membership when pastoring a small church. If you are called by God your dependency has to be on God first, then on whatever financial arrangements you have made, such as having a job or a business that will take care of the family's personal and financial needs.

In full time ministry your level of living will depend on your level of income. Too many ministers with small churches try to live above and beyond their means especially with the availability of credit cards; trying to proof that God is blessing them with material things while depending on the small church to pay their bills and to feed them. Many who have stepped out prematurely to live by faith, found out the hard way that they were not ready for a life of sacrifice, and have ended up in dire poverty. Some lost their home to foreclosure, and others lost their family to divorce.

The lack of finances have made many ministers leave the ministry to go into business or to go back into secular work, making full time ministry a bad experience. Those that have endured without financial support, run from church to church, fellowship meetings and events to get opportunities to preach so they could get an offering. Yet they will not stop incurring debt. After a while their body will suffer from the stress of ministry; trying to meet the demands of people, and the stress of always having to look for ways and means to get a dollar.

As the church grows the finances grow, patience means that the pastor has to wait until that growth takes place. Fruitfulness comes after growth. Growth and fruitfulness must come before the pastor could afford to buy that expensive car or a new house in an upscale neighborhood. The pressure of money has caused a lot of ministers to get into relationships outside the will of God, or under a ministry covering that cannot take them into their prophetic destiny.

When I use the term 'young ministers' I am not referring to age, but to the time and season of their calling. I was called into ministry in my earlier twenties; I started pastoring at age thirty two, then God changed my direction and called me into another phase of ministry before I became an itinerant ambassadorial apostle. There are people who are beginning to pastor in their fifties and sixties. I often say when people with calls of God on their life spend too much time in the Devil's service; when they finally accept the call of God on their life, God has to do an accelerated program with them to get them to the place of spiritual maturity that they should be at their current age.

When a person starts running for God in their fifties and sixties there is no room for error, they have a course to complete and a vision to accomplish like every other minister. Their vision cannot be based on what they see others in ministry do. They have to seek God for wisdom, and realize they cannot run at the rate at which a younger man can run. They cannot make the mistakes that a younger man can make, because he has time on his side to recover and start afresh. The one thing an older person should have is wisdom and some of the fruits of wisdom are discretion, prudence, integrity, discernment, understanding, courage and good character.

Sometimes with the call of God on one's life, comes the call of other people who will try to call you into their service. People who want you to do for them what they do not want to do or cannot do for themselves. People will, if you let them, put burdens on you that God did not give you the capacity or strength for. Then then will try to make you feel guilty for not doing what they want you to do.

Every young minister has to examine him or herself to see if they know what is the good, acceptable and perfect will of God for their life. There is a wonderful word in the dictionary that ministers need to use when their spirit is sending out a warning signal, or there is an alert in their spirit, and that word is "no". If the minister is not in a habit of asking God to order his or her footsteps, and he or she has low self-esteem issues, insecurity issues, rejection issues, the need for prestige, privilege, and the need for attention, then what looks and sounds good maybe fulfilling an emotional need, but is it the will of God?

Covetousness, need, thievery and greed can take you to place where you don't want to go. These sins can make you associate with people that you should not associate with; and have relationships with people that will put a stain on your character, cast doubt on your integrity, and make you do things for money that is not consistent with the character of God.

Full time ministry may sound like you are going full speed to do the will of God. But is it God's will or your will? There is a time to every purpose under the heavens. Far too many ministers in full time ministry, who lack financial support, have allowed the stress of ministry and lack of finances to make them sick. Stress is a killer, it leads to high blood pressure and other ailments.

Determining Your Affiliation: Independent apostolic, prophetic churches are currently in the present move of God, and are releasing the Spirit of the Kingdom. Most of them are a prototype of the Antioch church in the book of Acts. The church of Antioch was a sending church. They sent apostles, prophets, and ministerial teams all over the world with the message of the kingdom. Sending churches teach, train, and equip the called ones. They are capable of determining by the Spirit of God the placement of each son of God in the body of Christ and they can activate their spiritual gifts.

The difference between an apostolic, prophetic church and a pastoral church is that pastoral churches gather but do not send, and for the most part do not like to release people into their destiny. With no prophetic voice in the house, people with calls of God on their life have to hear directly from God. God never leaves himself without a witness. Not only must a person hear God's call and know that the spirit is summoning them, but someone else must bear witness to the call of God on their life.

The organizational structure or denominational structure also determines whether the pastor should go into full time ministry. Pastors who are employed by an organization or a denomination have their salaries and benefits decided on by the organization; and the organization considers their position as pastor their life's vocation or a job.

In some denominational structures, pastors are rotated from location to location periodically. This is decided by the governing council of the church, or a council of Bishops. They are appointed and given the charge to build under the auspices of that organization which is their covering. However, in some of these organizations the pastors' salary is determined by the tithes collected by the local church, or it is determined on an administrative level by the governing council of elders or deacons in the local church. These pastors usually have special functions and appreciations to boost their income.

Then there are pastors who venture out to build on their own, we term these pastors and ministries as 'Independent, Non-denominational Churches' who either function on their own or are in a network, headed by a chief apostle or bishop. Their vision does not fit the denominational wineskin.

Independent churches can also be family oriented. The line of succession is based on the next eligible person in the family. The leadership comprises of a husband and wife team. The pillars of the church are other family members, or faithful believers who are appointed as elders and deacons, and other professional people who can assist the church with its vision and strategy.

Before going into full time ministry one should consider a few things:
    a. Health Insurance.

b. Other sources of income if the church is too small to support a pastor.

c. Paying into social security, so that the Pastor will have another source of income when he retires, but also the Pastor will be able to get health insurance from Medicare. [USA pastors only], other countries may have their benevolent fund for seniors.

d. A Pastor should include in his or her contract with the local church a retirement benefit clause that will enable him to receive a retirement income from the church he has built.

e. Depending on the size of the church an appropriate plan should be put in place when the pastor retires, if the pastor's only income was the local church.

When the church begins to stretch out and to enlarge, a pastor must accept the fact that he or she cannot continue to micro manage the church; he has to delegate responsibilities to other proven leaders in the church. The wisdom of Jethro, Moses father-in-law, enabled Moses to put a leadership team in place that is still relevant today.

He was advised to provide for the people; leaders over thousands, hundreds, fifties and tens. [Exodus 18:17-26] In today's church economy we will call these leaders pastors. Large churches need pastors [New Testament word] or elders in the house to assist the senior pastor or apostle with the care of the people. In this way the senior pastor or the apostle can keep his or her focus on the overall vision, ministry of the word, prayer and delegation of the business aspects of the church to qualified people.

Some people are more suited to a smaller church. They complain about not being able to relate to their pastor, not being connected to the body, and not feeling that they are in the 'loop'. They feel like an outsider even after being in the church for an extended period of time. This feeling of not being connected makes people leave a church to look for a more relatable church experience.

A pastor encountered a situation one day when he was out shopping. Two ladies approached him and addressed him as pastor, and began to have a conversation with him. His response was "Do I know you? how do you know me?" They said, "We are members of your church." The pastor was so embarrassed that he apologized. Back at the church he asked his elders to put in place a method and a plan where once a month he could visibly meet and greet the new members of the church.

Too many pastors still believe that because they have eight hundred members on role, that those same eight hundred members are still there, over an extended period of time. They count numbers and money. If the church has an eight hundred seat auditorium and it is filled with eight hundred bodies every Sunday, it does not mean that they are all members. Visitors, children and the indigent church hopper attend church on a regular basis. They are a part of the crowd of people who visit a different church every month looking for a "home church" with all the amenities that they want, but they are not financial supporters of any ministry.

Some pastors will say we have one thousand members on role, when hundreds of those members are no longer a part of that congregation and have not attended that particular church for several years. They just walked away and their names are on the role of several churches across the state or the city, and six hundred new people have filled the pews. Some have been gone so long that no leader in the present church knows who they are. Also the leadership cannot just count the membership by those who pay tithes and offerings because young people and the aged seldom, if ever, have money to do so.

Except a member is a part of the administration and ministry team, Pastors with large churches have no other way of knowing who comes and goes except if they pay offerings with a check, or credit/debit card. The modern church must have computer applications in place to keep up with personal information. Members have to be taught to take into consideration that their home church expects them to call the office and let someone know when they have re-located, when there is a crisis, when someone is deceased, and if they need a visit from an elder.

Any pastor whose management style is micro managing every department of the church, would eventually find him or herself having a hard time dealing with growth and expansion due to his or her desire to control everything and his or her refusal to delegate authority.

Called to the Mission Field: Some are called to the house and some have answered the call to missions. Many ministers want to go to the mission field in another country when they have never done missionary work in their own country. Why go to the slums in Africa when there are slums in America? Why take care of the poor in another country and neglect the poor in your own country? Why go to another country knocking on doors to tell people about Jesus, and not do it in your own community.

I do believe that some ministers want to go to the mission field just to put something on their résumé. When a church or ministry gift takes it upon his or herself to visit another country without the leading of the Lord, they are being unwise. Usually they bring back a negative report because they were not received by any church or ministry covering in that nation. There were no crowds flocking to see them, there were no honorariums, there were no special services designated to hear them minister. Some of them even ended up in the wrong hands, for there are false ministers and predators everywhere.

You cannot go to the mission field with the mindset of a tourist. Tourists stay in five star hotels, resorts, or vacation destinations. Before you decide to travel to the mission field, check your heart; why do you want to go to the mission field? Is it to preach? There are many, many preachers that travel the world preaching the gospel. It is safe to have a church receive you and cover you wherever you are going, for there is danger everywhere.

I have come to the conclusion that people with those aspirations who are not called to the war on a global scale, have no knowledge of strategic level spiritual warfare. You cannot go to the battlefield looking for prestige. First, you must know something about the religious climate of the country you plan to visit. Where ever religious principalities abound, there will be warfare waged against you, the warfare may be subtle or outwardly aggressive depending on the length of your stay.

If you are going to the mission field you must know in what capacity you are going. First and foremost, can you speak the language? If you are going with an internationally known ministry whose work is well documented, it will be an added benefit to you, because that ministry will serve as your covering, especially if the ministry has a contact person or a church in a position of influence in that nation, or a contact in government. These contacts will always be an added benefit if the need arises.

A person can travel as a part of a support group, as part of the intercessory team, or as a person filling one of the necessary functions that is needed for a large ministry to operate on foreign soil. One has to learn the rudiments of international travel; every country has its own national security laws for admission into the country.

There is a difference in traveling on your own to another country because you are a missionary, and in being invited by a church as a guest speaker. If you are invited then the covering church in that nation is responsible for you until your departure. If you are a person going from place to place with no contacts, you will have to find your own way by faith. Don't be surprised if in this age of national security that you may be detained and eventually deported.

If you are going with someone who may not be well known, but he or she has experience with international travel, and is informed about the protocol of international ministry, cultural diversity, cuisine, custom and tradition, monetary exchange, immigration, customs, excise law, religious preferences and practices. This may be to your benefit, that person can help you with the information you need to make your trip a pleasant experience. You may find that it is necessary to educate yourself about these things before entering another nation as a missionary, with the mindset of a tourist. Ministers must know their boundaries in a foreign land to avoid being embarrassed.

High minded, prideful ministers seldom exercise wisdom when they leave their jurisdiction and enter another man's field of endeavor. Let me inform you, "You are not in charge everywhere." As one Pastor said to me, "I give you access to my people and my pulpit but don't bring another preacher in my pulpit." I said to him, "I will never do such a thing." Yet presumptuous preachers do it all the time without stating their intentions to the head of the house.

Finally, there are Pastors who will never allow another ministry gift in their pulpit. Primarily, because they do not want "their" money leaving the house. Yet they will maneuver and position themselves, to get other unsuspecting pastors to open a door of opportunity for them to speak at their house, and minister to their people without any intention of reciprocating the favor.

The pastoral gift by itself cannot perfect the church. Many pastors need another level of anointing, another level of revelation, to bring the church into a kingdom dimension. Governmental apostles and prophets are equipped to release the Spirit of the kingdom in areas of the globe where God is manifesting His glory and souls are being saved, delivered and set free.

2. THE ESSENCE OF LEADERSHIP

Essence is defined as: the inward nature of anything; the true substance; the fundamental nature or the most important quality; the indispensable characteristics and relations of anything.

APPOINTMENT, POSITIONING AND PURPOSE

Leadership key #1:
-   **You are Positioned According to Your Purpose.**

God has arranged a place for every member of the Body of Christ, and has placed him or her in position as He pleases. Every member is positioned according to his or her divine purpose in the body.

> I myself have selected your fellow Levites from among the Israelites as a gift to you, dedicated to the Lord to do the work at the Tent of Meeting.

> But only you and your sons may serve as priests in connection with everything at the altar and inside the curtain. I am giving you the service of the priesthood as a gift. Anyone else who comes near the sanctuary must be put to death.
>
> - Numbers 18: 6-7.

In this passage of scripture the Lord is speaking to Aaron and Moses, and He said that the tribe of Levi, (better known as the Levites), was a gift given by God to do the service of the Tabernacle.

Their appointment, position and purpose were as follows: God said to Moses,

> "Appoint the Levites to be in charge of the Tabernacle of the Testimony – over all its furnishings and everything belonging to it. They are to carry the Tabernacle and all its furnishings; they are to take care of it and encamp around it.
>
> Whenever the Tabernacle is to move, the Levites are to take it down, and whenever the Tabernacle is to be set up, the Levites shall do it. Anyone else who goes near it shall be put to death.
>
> The Israelites are to set up their tents by divisions, each man in his own camp under his own standard. The Levites, however, are to set up their tents around the Tabernacle of the Testimony so that wrath will not fall on the Israelite community. The Levites are to be responsible for the care of the Tabernacle of the Testimony."
>
> -Numbers 1:50-53.

Aaron and his sons were given charge of the hallowed things of the Tabernacle by reason of the anointing. The priest was a service gift and the priesthood was a service ministry.

Leaders are given as gifts by God to His people. They are obligated to the service of God, which is to serve God's people.

In Old Testament times, whenever the Jewish people were in trouble, God would put His spirit upon someone He chose from among the people. God would give that leader his authority, a specific assignment, and commission him to lead God's people to victory.

1. Moses was commissioned to deliver the children of Israel out of Egypt.
2. Joshua's assignment was to bring the children of Israel into their inheritance.
3. Judges were sent to help God's people overcome repeated oppression.
4. Kings were anointed with wisdom and power to rule the nation and to fight wars.
5. Prophets were sent by God to warn, rebuke and redirect the people to the true worship of Jehovah.

Leadership key #2:
- **Leaders were God's Answer to the Needs of His People.**

Under the New Testament or New Covenant, leaders have the responsibility to:

- Preach the message of the kingdom.
- Deliver the people from the grip of the power of darkness.
- They are mandated to teach God's people to observe and keep God's commandments, statues, and laws.
- They are anointed to develop disciples into sons, and develop sons into soldiers.

Apostles, prophets, teachers, pastors, and evangelists are given to the Body of Christ to equip her and bring her into sonship (Ephesians 4; 11-13). Fivefold ministry leaders are gifts. Just as the Levites were given to the priests (Aaron and his sons) as gifts to serve in the Tabernacle, fivefold ministry leaders are given by

Jesus Christ our High Priest as service gifts to the Body of Christ.

These New Testament ministry gifts were given by God as an expression of His love. It is with this understanding that we must see God's leaders as God's gifts to men. They are not to be idolized but respected, encouraged, and supported. It is by God's design and will, that able men and women, full of the Holy Spirit, men of truth, and wisdom, hating covetousness, accept the call of God and step to the forefront to lead the way for God's people.

These callings were ordained before the foundation of the world. God foreknew us, and predestined those He has chosen as leaders, to be His voice to the people, the nation, and to the world.

Just as a person must have a profession or a vocation in the secular world, in the kingdom of God, leaders anointed by God have a vocation or a profession. They are ambassadors for Christ, sent into the world with a message of reconciliation.

Therefore, if anyone is in Christ, he is a new creation. The old has passed away; behold, the new has come.

All this is from God, who through Christ reconciled us to himself and gave us the ministry of reconciliation; that is, in Christ, God was reconciling the world to himself, not counting their trespasses against them, and entrusting to us the message of reconciliation.

Therefore, we are ambassadors for Christ, God making His appeal through us. We implore you on behalf of Christ, be reconciled to God.

-2 Corinthians 5: 17 - 20.

At the appointed time God summons those people He pre-ordained, called, and chose before the foundations of the world.

ABRAHAM'S SUMMONS:

The Lord had said to Abram, "Leave your country, your people and your father's household and go to the land I will show you. I will make you into a great nation and I will bless you. I will make your name great and you will be a blessing. I will bless those who bless you, and whoever curses you I will curse, and all the people on earth will be blessed through you.

- Genesis 12: 1- 3.

MOSES' SUMMONS:

Now Moses was tending the flock of Jethro his father-in-law, the priest of Midian, and he led the flock to the far side of the desert and came to Horeb, the mountain of God.

There an angel of the Lord appeared to him in flames of fire from within a bush. Moses saw that though the bush was on fire it did not burn up. So Moses thought, "I will go over and see this strange sight – why the bush does not burn up."

When the Lord saw that he had gone over to look, God called to him from within the bush, "Moses! Moses!" and Moses said, "Here I am." "Do not come any closer," God said, "Take off your sandals, for the place where you are standing is holy ground."

Then He said, "I am the God of your father, the God of Abraham, the God of Isaac and the God of Jacob." At this, Moses hid his face, because he was afraid to look at God.

The Lord said, "I have indeed seen the misery of my people in Egypt. I have heard them crying out because of their slave drivers, and I am concerned about their suffering, so I have come down to rescue them from the hand of the Egyptians and to bring them up out of that land into a good and spacious land, a land flowing with milk and honey – the home of the Canaanites, Hittites, Amorites, Perizzites, Hivites and Jebusites.

And now the cry of the Israelites has reached me, and I have seen the way the Egyptians are oppressing them. So now, go to Pharaoh and bring the Israelites out of Egypt.

-Exodus 3: 1-11

Leadership Key # 3
·Leaders Are Chosen From Among The People:

Moreover thou shalt provide out of all the people able men, such as fear God, men of truth, hating covetousness; and place such over them, to be rulers of thousands, and rulers of hundreds, rulers of fifties, and rulers of tens.

-Exodus 18: 21.

Then the Lord said to Moses, "Gather for me seventy men of the elders of Israel, whom you know to be the elders of the people and officers over them, and bring them to the tent of meeting, and let them take their stand there with you.

And I will come down and talk with you there, and I will take some of the spirit that is on you and put it on them, and they shall bear the burden of the people with you, so that you may not bear it yourself alone."

-Numbers 11: 16, 17.

So Moses went out and told the people the words of the Lord. And he gathered seventy men of the elders of the people and placed them around the tent.

Then the Lord came down in the cloud and spoke to him, and took some of the Spirit that was on him and put it on the seventy elders. And as soon as the Spirit rested on them, they prophesied. But they did not continue doing so.

-Numbers 11: 24, 25.

As soon as Moses' spirit rested on them they prophesied, because Moses was a prophet. However, the seventy elders did not continue to prophesy because they were not Prophets. Being able to prophesy does not make one a Prophet.

God told Moses to gather these seventy men who were tribal leaders; they were chosen to assist Moses with governing the people, and to assist in judging small matters among the people. The hard cases were left to Moses.

God took some of the spirit and the anointing that was on Moses and imparted it to the seventy elders. Delegating some of Moses' authority to lead and govern to the seventy elders.

The responsibility of governing the people of God must come from God. The seventy tribal leaders had delegated authority, meaning they were subject to Moses, who was subject to the authority of God. Moses was the chief shepherd. You can discern the heart of a shepherd by his intercessory prayers for the people. Moses intervened with intercession, he pleaded with God not to pass judgment on Israel.

Furthermore, the Lord said to me, I have seen this people, and behold, it is a stubborn people. Let me alone, that I may destroy them and blot out their name from under heaven. And I will make of you a nation mightier and greater than they.

So I turned and came down from the mountain, and the mountain was burning with fire. And the two tablets of the covenant were in my two hands. And I looked and behold, you had sinned against the Lord your God. You had made yourselves a golden calf. You had turned aside quickly from the way that the Lord had commanded you.

So I took hold of the two tablets and threw them out of my two hands and broke them before your eyes. Then I lay prostrate before the Lord as before, forty days and forty nights I neither ate bread nor drank water, because of all the sin that you had committed, in doing what was evil in the sight of the Lord to provoke him to anger.

For I was afraid of the anger and hot displeasure that the Lord bore against you, so that he was ready to destroy you. But the Lord listened to me that time also.

And the Lord was so angry with Aaron that he was ready to destroy him. And I prayed for Aaron also at the same time.

-Deuteronomy 9: 13-20.

Moses took an intercessory position before the Lord by laying out prostrate on the ground forming an intercessory barrier between God and the people.

On Mount Carmel Elijah took an intercessory position by putting his head between his legs and praying for rain. (1 Kings 18: 41-46).

Rizpah, Saul's concubine, took an intercessory prayer position by taking sackcloth and spreading it for herself on a rock, from the beginning of harvest until rain fell from the heavens. When King David heard what she had done, he took the bones of Saul and his son Jonathan, and the bones of Rizpah's sons that Saul fathered, and the sons of Michal, Saul's daughter and buried them in the land of Benjamin their tribal inheritance.

David had hung the sons of Saul to appease the curse on the land brought on by the blood-guilt of Saul on his house because he put the Gibeonites to death, after they had covenanted with Israel in the days of Joshua. When David buried them in the land of Benjamin. God responded to the plea for the land. (2 Samuel 21:10-14)

When leaders are chosen from among the people, it is important that the leaders have the spirit of the chief shepherd. One of the roles of the chief shepherd is to be a mediator before God for the people. God holds the chief shepherd accountable for the flock. The chief shepherd must be an intercessor.

Joshua's Commissioning, Appointment, Ordination, and Elevation took place before the people.

Moses said to the Lord, "May the Lord, the God of the spirits of all mankind, appoint a man over this community to go out and come in before them. One who will lead them out and bring them in, so the

Lord's people will not be like sheep without a shepherd."

So the Lord said to Moses, "Take Joshua son of Nun, a man in whom is the spirit, and lay your hand on him. Have him stand before Eleazar the priest and the entire assembly and commission him in their presence.

Give him some of your authority so the whole Israelite community will obey him. He is to stand before Eleazar the priest, who will obtain decisions for him by inquiring of the Urim before the Lord.

At his command he and the entire community of the Israelites will go out, and at his command they will come in." Moses did as the Lord commanded him. He took Joshua and had him stand before Eleazar the priest and the whole assembly. Then he laid his hands on him and commissioned him, as the Lord instructed through Moses.

- Numbers 27: 15-23.

The command to ordain and elevate Joshua came directly from God. The above text clearly calls Joshua, "The man in whom is the spirit." It is important for us to know the spirit of the leader, before he or she is elevated to high office.

Joshua had to stand before the proper governmental authorities in the nation of Israel, the ones who had the authority to legally elevate him, not only in the presence of the people, but in the presence of a great cloud of witnesses in the spirit realm.

The spirit realm must know who we are, what is the level of our authority, and the stated purpose of our commission so that the universe can cooperate with us. When Joshua spoke to the sun and told it to stand still, the sun obeyed Joshua because all of creation recognizes a manifested son of God. Elijah had the authority to close and open the heavens because the universe knew who he was, a governmental prophet who was an ambassador of the kingdom of Heaven.

When the seventy elders were appointed, Moses did not lay his hand on them. God took some of the anointing off of Moses and imparted it to the seventy elders. They needed a portion of the spirit of Moses to serve in leadership.

But in this instance of Joshua's elevation and ordination, the Lord did not take a portion of the spirit of Moses and impart it to Joshua. Joshua already had the spirit, which was imparted to him by his service to Moses, and his appointment as Captain of the army of Israel.

Having the spirit, God instituted the next phrase of elevation. Joshua had to stand before Moses and Eleazar and they laid their hands on him and ordained him. He was ordained and commissioned to walk in his calling. This had to be done by the proper authorities for it to be legal and binding in the spirit. Moses and Eleazar the High priest were the proper governmental authorities of that time.

Under the New Testament order before a person is ordained, commissioned, or released to walk in his or her calling, there are certain things that have to be taken into consideration.

1. Their works: What that person is doing to prepare him or herself to walk in their calling.
2. Are they serving around the house of God?
3. Are they supporting the work of the ministry?

4. They must be proven. The governing authorities must judge the quality of their work, their sacrifice, their worship, their obedience, their faithfulness, and how they relate to the governmental officials of the church. Are they respected by the people?

5. If they are doing nothing before they are ordained, they will do nothing after they are ordained, commissioned, and released. They will have the label as a minister without doing the work of the ministry.

6. Their lifestyle is important.

7. Their reputation in and outside of the community is important.

8. Their character is important.

9. Their family life is important.

10. Their level of maturity is important.

Then their availability, stability, reliability, and dependability must be proven. The call may be there, but is the person ready? Is the person spiritually mature enough to handle the responsibilities of leadership in the house of God? Does the person have the interpersonal skill and wisdom to manage people?

A true leader is known by his or her spirit. The church has to take a closer look beyond the gifts and talents which are given before repentance, in order to see the heart, the inner core of the individual. This is because a position alone does not make one a leader. One must also have the heart, mind, and the thought processes of a leader.

Leaders must be equipped mentally, spiritually, emotionally, and be physically able to take up their responsibilities. If a person is lazy, if they have a spirit of slothfulness, they should not be a leader of anything. If they say, "I am in charge" or they act as though they are in charge, then they should be able to tell exactly what they are in charge of. The first thing a leader should be in charge of is his or her own spirit.

> A man without self-control is like a city broken into and left without walls.
>
> -Proverbs 25:28.

Many leaders acquire the position of dominance over people without ever examining their own spirit. The Bible asks the question, "Know you not yourself?" Too many leaders are guilty of unforgiveness, harboring bitterness, resentment, jealousy, lust, rebellion, covetousness, pride, envy, and are servants to corruption while they are using the word of God to minister truth to others.

Leadership Principle #4
-   **Leaders Carry the People in their Heart.**

This principle is seen in the Old and New Testaments.

> You shall take two onyx stones, and engrave on them the names of the sons of Israel; six of their names on the one stone, in the order of their birth.
>
> As a jeweler engraves signets, so shall you engrave the two stones with the names of the sons of Israel. You shall enclose them in settings of gold filigree.
>
> And you shall set the two stones on the shoulder pieces of the ephod, as stones of remembrance for the sons of Israel. And Aaron shall bear their names before the Lord on his two shoulders for remembrance.
>
> So Aaron shall bear the names of the sons of Israel in the breast piece of judgment on his heart when he goes

into the Holy Place, to bring them to regular remembrance before the Lord.

And in the breast piece of Judgment you shall put the Urim and the Thummim, and shall be on Aaron's heart, when he goes in before the Lord. Thus Aaron shall bear the judgment of the people of Israel on his heart before the Lord regularly.

-Exodus 28:9-12; 29-30.

For I am confident of this very thing, that He who began a good work in you will perfect it until the day of Christ Jesus. For it is only right for me to feel this way about you all, because I have you in my heart.

-Philippians 1:6-7.

One stone was for remembrance, one stone was for judgment. In Acts 10:1-23 a Roman centurion named Cornelius, who was not a Jew, built a memorial or a remembrance before God in the spirit, because of his prayers and alms giving. In Acts 5, Ananias and his wife lied to the Holy Ghost before Peter and they experienced the judgment of God.

Far too many strive for a label or a position of leadership without understanding that there is a relationship that exists in the spirit dimension between a God chosen leader and those who follow.

A leader chosen by God, has the authority to appoint other leaders among the people to assist in the work because no leader can do the work without help. Moses did not realize this until his wiser father-in-law made him aware that not only was he going to wear himself out but he will also wear the people out.

If God indeed has given that authority to a person, then that authority also includes the ability to release blessings upon others. The leader who understands this truth can be used powerfully to accomplish the will of God in the earth.

The Apostle Paul said to the Philippian church, "Because I have you in my heart...." Therefore Paul was obligated to intercede for the church, as Moses was compelled to intercede for the people because he also carried the people in his heart.

> For I long to see you, that I may impart to you some spiritual gift to strengthen you. That is, that we may be mutually encouraged by each other's faith, both yours and mine.
> -Romans 1: 11-12.

Just as Aaron carried the names of the children of Israel on his breast piece each time he went into the Holy of Holiest, leaders are supposed to carry the people in their heart each time the leader goes before God.

Under the New Covenant, because of the shed blood of Jesus Christ, the Holy of Holies is a sanctuary within the spirit of a born again leader; it is Christ in you the hope of glory. And the names of the people should be written on the leader's heart, so as the leader goes before God in prayer, God can reveal to the leader who is struggling, who is under attack, who is giving up, who needs encouragement and so on.

The connection between shepherd and sheep is supposed to be so strong, that when there is a disconnect in the spirit realm, a corresponding alert should be felt in the leader's spirit letting him or her know that the connection is broken; or they should hear the Spirit of God call the name of the person, or urge the leader to pray for that person.

When God brings a weakened member to the leader's attention, and the leader's spirit is troubled, or there is a groaning in the leader's spirit for that person, God is putting the leader on high alert, that the member is not doing well.

> Jesus told Peter, "The devil demanded to have you that he might sift you as wheat, but I have prayed for you that your faith may not fail. And when you turned again, strengthen your brothers."
>
> -Luke 22:31.

The Shepherd is the first level of protection for the church. He is the first line of defense for the members. He is the gatekeeper, he is the watchman. When the leader is not conscious of a member, it is because the connection is broken, that member's spirit will feel the impact, he or she will feel disconnected. He or she will feel alone, like a distant stranger in the local church and they will eventually leave the church to go somewhere else to make that connection or simply drop out of church completely.

Some churches become revolving doors when the spiritual connection has been broken and members no longer feel connected to the anointing and the spirit of the house. Some leave because of offense, some leave because of free will. Some leave because they feel ignored. Some leave because they never felt connected or at home.

In very large churches the pastoral staff usually has no idea who the members are or if they are still attending the church. A large church is not for everyone because it does not provide the intimacy and atmosphere some people need.

As leaders intercede, their intercessions must include the prayer Jesus prayed for his disciples.

While I was with them, I kept them in your name, which you have given me, I have guarded them, and not one of them have been lost except the son of destruction, that the Scriptures might be fulfilled.

-John 17:12.

Jesus "guarded" over those who were given to Him. He kept them. It is in this fashion that the leaders of God's people must hold those given to them within their heart.

In understanding this spiritual principle, leaders must also understand that every person has authority over his or her own life. Jesus lost Judas, who chose to go his own way. People have the power of choice. As Joshua addressed the nation of Israel, he said to them "Choose you this day whom you will serve."

Leadership principle # 5
- **Leaders are not to be Mentally, Morally or Spiritually incapable.**

Leadership for God's people demands integrity, uprightness, righteousness, holiness and truth. A leader must not be immoral. The true church is a nation of people. The true church is a place where the spirits of just men become mature. Leaders called and chosen by the Spirit of God must be capable mentally, morally, and spiritually. If you are disabled in character you do not meet the qualifications for leadership.

A morally disabled leader will hurt the church. A spiritually disabled leader cannot function effectively in his or her calling. If a person is mentally disabled he or she should not be in leadership. A leader needs a sound mind to function effectively in his or her calling. The mind takes the brunt of warfare from the enemy, because the mind harbors the thoughts and ideas that come from the mind of Christ, and what comes from the enemy.

As ministers of reconciliation, we must all bear witness of the saving grace of our Lord Jesus Christ. Ministry is a life-calling, and the assignments for ministry are designated by God. Far too many are copying, emulating, competing, and positioning themselves outside of the pre-ordained will of God. Many have started ministries out of a spirit of competitive jealousy and the need for attention, and some of the called ones have started ministry out of God's designated season.

That same spirit was among the disciples as they discussed among themselves, "Who will be the greatest?"

> Within minutes they were bickering over which of them would end up the greatest, but Jesus intervened. "Kings like to throw their weight around and people in authority like to give themselves fancy titles."

> It is not going to be that way with you. Let the senior among you become like the junior; let the teacher act the part of the servant.
>
> > -Luke 22:24-26.

Leadership key #6
-    **The Essence of Leadership is Love.**

God is love. Love is divine, holy, and pure. Jesus is the embodiment and expression of the Father's love. Love was not willing that any should perish, so Love gave His only begotten son as a sacrifice for sin.

All leaders must have this attribute of God. The Holy Spirit spreads the love of God in our hearts. If you don't know God, then you don't know love. Demonstrating love, compassion, mercy, and kindness is reflective of the spiritual strength of a mature believer that is rooted in the essence of Christ Jesus.

Life is all about choices. If you are hurt by someone, it is easy for your flesh to retaliate, to get even, and to stay angry or you can choose to walk in unforgiveness. But if you allow your flesh to dictate how you relate to the problem, and to the person, no matter how well you function in your gift or how anointed you are, you will be as one described in 1 Corinthians 13.

"Though I speak with the tongues of men and of angels, and have not charity, I am become as sounding brass, or a tinkling cymbal. And though I have the gift of prophecy, and understand all mysteries, and all knowledge; and though I have all faith, so that I could remove mountains, and have not charity, I am nothing."

"Charity never fails, but whether there be prophecies, they shall fail; whether there be tongues, they shall cease; whether there be knowledge, it shall vanish away. For we know in part, and we prophesy in part."

And now abides faith, hope, charity, these three, but the greatest of these is charity."

Leaders must include in their prayers – "Lord teach me the depth, height, length, and breadth of your love.

That Christ may dwell in your hearts by faith; that ye being rooted and grounded in love, may be able to comprehend with all saints what is the breadth, and length and depth, and height; And to know the love of Christ, which passes knowledge, that ye might be filled with all the fullness of God.

-Ephesians 3: 17-19.

Operating in love is not a sign of weakness. Love is a divine characteristic of the sons of God. Love makes a leader approachable, but the lack of love makes a leader a scorner, a scoffer, cynical, and sarcastic.

Love does not mean that as a leader you don't use corrective discipline. Love does not mean that as parents we don't discipline our children. We discipline them certainly, but we do so because we carry our children in our heart. We discipline because we love. Leaders must discipline like God disciplines, with the end in mind; with the eternal destiny of the soul in mind that this person must not perish, or be lost.

> My son, do not regard lightly the discipline of the Lord, nor be weary when reproved by Him. For who the Lord disciplines He loves, and chastises every son whom He receives.
>
> - Hebrews 12: 6.

In America, state government has enacted laws that forbid parents from administering corrective discipline to children. There are government agencies in place that would remove children from homes where they are being disciplined, abused, neglected or abandoned. And any type of discipline that would cause physical or emotional pain is considered unlawful.

Because of the lack of parental discipline, federal and state government along with private corporations have invested money in the prison system to disciple law breakers. These civil authorities will rather throw children in prison instead of allowing corrective discipline to be administered by law abiding parents. America has the highest capital of citizens in any nation incarcerated, and the reason for this is that corporations are profiting from the prison system.

The lack of corrective discipline has also taken root in the church. Nobody wants to be corrected. Their feelings are easily hurt. They pout, they sulk, they get an attitude or they try to get even. They say it's the devil; they leave the church, or they go around slandering the Pastor who corrected them.

When Jesus encountered a man in the synagogue with an unclean spirit, the man cried out, or the unclean spirit cried out, "Leave us alone." [Mark 1: 24] That is the same cry coming from the hearts of the rebellious in this age. They want to be left alone to express who they really are without any filter or with unbridled passion. But the Bible says, "It is a fearful thing to fall into the hands of the living God." Love and discipline must go hand in hand.

And have you forgotten the exhortation that addressed you as sons? My son, do not regard lightly the discipline of the Lord, nor be weary when reproved by him. For the Lord disciplines the one He loves, and chastises every son whom He receives.

It is for discipline that you have to endure. God is treating you as sons. For what son is there whom his father does not discipline?

If you are left without discipline, in which all have participated, then you are illegitimate children and not sons.

Besides this, we have had earthly fathers who disciplined us and we respected them. Shall we not much more be subject to the Father of spirits and live?

For they disciplined us for a short time as it seemed best to them, but He disciplines us for our good that we may share His holiness.

For the moment all discipline seems painful rather than pleasant, but later it yields the peaceful fruit of righteousness to those who have been trained by it.

-Hebrews 12:5-11.

Love is a strong force. In His wisdom Jesus said, "Love your enemies, do good unto those that despitefully use you and persecute you." (Luke 6:27) Love is part of our spiritual warfare armor. When any leader is under attack, love will sustain his or her spirit from being angry. Love will prevent a root of bitterness from lodging in his or her spirit. Love will cause him or her to walk in forgiveness.

We were all born as sinners and as sinners we were useless to the true and living God. We all followed the course or the dictates of the god of this world, the spirit that works in the children of disobedience. We were alienated from love, truth, righteousness, joy and faith, and were without hope in this world. But God was gracious, He saw our need for salvation and He met that need.

Love reached out to mankind while they were in darkness, dead in sin, and in the depths of despair and degradation and Love sent a Savior, a Deliverer, and Redeemer. Love saw that there was no intercessor, no man to stand in the gap, so Love's own right hand brought salvation unto mankind.

When a leader is deprived of the love of God, that leader will have the spirit of a dictator. A dictatorial spirit is very controlling, and void of empathy. Dictators make good generals in man's army, but not good shepherds over God's people. Dictators make rogue leaders over nations but they do not make good pastors, evangelists, teachers, prophets, or apostles, over the nation of God.

People void of the love of God are similar to the Pharisees. They are all about the law, rules, and regulations. The Pharisees wanted honor from men, but they did not want the honor that comes from God. They did not know God. They knew the letter of the Torah, but they did not know the God of the Torah.

When you exam the spirit of the Pharisees, you will realize that they were envious of Jesus's ministry of compassion to the people. The Pharisees were present at all of Jesus's meetings, not to receive an impartation of spiritual gifts or to receive truth. There were not present to donate to His ministry or to learn about the kingdom of God. They were looking for something to accuse Him of, because they planned to destroy Him. These were men of God; the spiritual leaders of the people, but Jesus warned His disciples.

Jesus said, "Beware of the leaven or the doctrine of the Pharisees which is hypocrisy.

- Luke 12:1.

It is important for leaders to know that membership in a church does not make one a part of the family of God. Everybody that attends church is not a child of God. Jesus said, "By their fruits ye shall know them."

There are three groups of people in church:
1. The Crowd: People who come to church on special occasions but they are not a part of the congregation.
2. The Congregation: There is a mixed multitude in the congregation those that are saved and those that are unsaved. They are all members of the local church.
3. The Believers: They are the born again individuals, who have entered the kingdom of God and are serving God in spirit and in truth.

The art of leadership, however, is not merely taught but caught. It must be caught, because leadership for God's people is first spiritual; God is a spirit. If you are striving for leadership, you must first serve under leadership. You must be a disciple, a follower, a trainee, an aide, an assistant, a minister in the service of others, in order to learn the art of leadership.

Joshua learned the art of leadership from Moses. Joshua had a different calling on his life. He was not a deliverer like Moses, he was not a monarch. What God needed was a man with courage, the right spirit, and tenacity to lead the armies of Israel into battle. Israel had to drive out the inhabitants of the land, so they could occupy their inheritance. Joshua served Moses and Moses set him before the people. After the death of Moses, the people received Joshua not as Moses' aide, but they received him as their new leader.

Leadership key #7
- **It is only through the transmission of divine anointing that leaders arise. But first you must be chosen by God.**

Let us look at the process:
> The Lord said to Moses, "Come up to me on the mountain and stay here, and I will give you the tablets of stone, with the law and commands I have written for their instructions." Then Moses set out with Joshua his aide, and Moses went up on the mountain of God.
> Exodus 24: 12-13.

1. Joshua served Moses: He was his aide. He ministered to Moses. All the time he was learning the art of leadership, and gaining the wisdom Moses received from being in God's presence.
2. What was imparted to Moses, was developed in Joshua.

And Joshua discomfited Amalek and his people with the edge of the sword. And the Lord said unto Moses, "Write this for a memorial in a book and rehearse it in the ears of Joshua; for I will utterly put out the remembrance of Amalek from under heaven."

- Exodus 17: 13, 14.

In this text we see Joshua being elevated from Moses' aide, to the role of captain of the army of Israel. Joshua was elevated because he served Moses diligently, courageously, and faithfully. He never competed with Moses for the attention of the people. Because of that God chose Joshua; he had the right spirit and the right attitude. God was so serious about obliterating the nation of Amalek, that he told Moses to write it in a book, and rehearse it in the ears of Joshua, why? Because God chose Joshua to be the captain that would lead the army of Israel into battle against the Amalekites, and after Moses' death, Joshua will be the one that would distribute the inheritance to the people.

But as long as Moses was alive, it was not the time for Joshua to go forth in his ministry of leading the people into their inheritance known as the "Promise land". He was next in line but if he had stepped out too soon, he would have caused confusion, division, and strife in the nation of God and to use today's terminology - he would have split the church.

Absalom did exactly the opposite. He plotted against his father, King David, and caused a civil war in Israel. He could not wait until David handed the reins of leadership over to him. Absalom did not understand David's special covenant relationship with God. God called David a man after His own heart. And succession to the Davidic throne depended on who God chose.

In the line of leadership succession under Moses, none of Moses' sons succeeded him.

1. First, we see Joshua serving Moses.
2. Secondly, we see Joshua serving the people in the strategic capacity as the captain of the armies of Israel.
3. Thirdly, we see Moses laying his hands on Joshua to impart his wisdom and his authority.

And the Lord said unto Moses, "Take Joshua the son of Nun, a man in whom is the spirit, and lay your hand upon him; and set him before Eleazar the priest, and before all the congregation, and give him a charge in their sight."

And you shall put some of your honor upon him, that all the congregation of the children of Israel may be obedient.

-Numbers 27: 18-20.

God is a God of order. God told Moses, "Lay your hand upon him." Joshua did not tell Moses, "I want to be a Pastor so lay your hand upon me; I am ready to go forth." Too many would be leaders do not want to submit themselves to the set governmental authority in their life, because they are too rebellious. Yet they want people to submit to their authority. According to the law of generation or reproduction, seed produces after its kind. A leader will produce people like himself; like priest, like people. What is on the leader will be developed in the people.

Every generation of new ministers must be taught that there is a sequence to elevation. If you miss the stages of development or the steps you need to take to get where God is taking you, you may find yourself out there on the battlefield with a title and a position, but without the necessary armor for war and void of wisdom or the grace to walk in the deeper things of God.

You cannot lead people to where you have never been yourself. If you have no exposure to the strategies and the craftiness of the enemy, how can you warn or protect those under your care?

Leadership Key #8
- **God Honors those that Serve Leadership.**

Joshua was not from the tribe of Levi, the governing priestly family. However, Moses' ministry mantle was passed unto Joshua because he was chosen by God to be Moses' successor. Even though Joshua was not related to Moses according to tribal bloodline, God chose him. What were his credentials?

1. He was called and chosen by God.
2. He served Moses.
3. He spent his time fasting on the mountain each time Moses was in the presence of God.
4. What God imparted to Moses was developed in Joshua.
5. Joshua was filled with the spirit.
6. God elevated him as the captain of the army of Israel.
7. He was faithful in his service to Moses, to the nation, and to God.

Why would any leader elevate someone who is disobedient, unfaithful, disloyal, rebellious, uncommitted, argumentative, and disrespectful? When a person is rebellious God puts a pause on their advancement in the kingdom. These qualities disqualify anyone for promotion, elevation, receiving a fresh anointing, and serving in a new capacity.

Joshua may not have realized it, but he was in training under Moses to eventually take Moses' position after he died. This is where a lot of potential leaders miss it. They do not want to serve; they want a label or a title, they want a position of honor, they want to preach, they want to be elevated without a period of preparation and service or a period of testing in the wilderness.

Those who never had a period of apprenticeship under any leader and were never taught the nuances of ministry, fail to understand that ministry is not all about preaching a message; there is the spiritual side to ministry, the business and professional side to ministry, the financial side to ministry, the evangelistic side to ministry, and the administrative and managerial side of ministry.

A leader must have administrative skills along with other skills in this technical age. Leaders must continue to be developed in their calling by aligning themselves to tried and tested ministry gifts and ministries that function on a kingdom level. Receiving greater levels of impartation, upgrading of the anointing and releasing of mantles is an ongoing process. In making a case for continued knowledge of the operations of the kingdom and how to adopt a kingdom mindset, leaders should gather more information from proven ministry leaders to be more efficient and effective.

One of the worst things that can happen to anyone is to be stuck behind a leader that has no sense of direction. He or she does not know where they are going or what they are doing, because of the lack of a vision and planning. His or her mind has not been renewed because they have not availed themselves of any opportunity to receive new revelation, or to tap into the new moves of the spirit taking place in the Body of Christ.

There are times leaders have to get out of their own environment to receive an impartation of what God has poured into others; all leaders need fresh bread, fresh manna, fresh revelation, and a fresh anointing. Every leader has to take responsibility for his or her own destiny. If the information you need for the season you are in is not in the house, then you have to go into another house where that information is being released to receive it. If your church is evangelistic and you want the prophetic experience in your house, then the leader should partner with a governmental prophet to impart that anointing and gift into the house.

Moses' ability to lead in the wilderness was predicated by his spending forty years in the wilderness before his assignment came from God. He could not lead the children of Israel into a theory, but into an experience.

Before anyone called of God places his or destiny in someone else's hand, he or she should first check the person's level of experience. Can they take you from strength to strength, level to level, glory to glory, victory to victory, or grace to grace? Can they teach you the deeper things of God? Can they enhance the call of God on your life?

If you claim a church or someone as your covering and you continue to be ignorant, void of Godly wisdom, and spiritual intelligence; is it because you are not being taught? Is your situation due to a lack of divine strength, or are you failing to apply the word, the techniques, or the ability God has given you in every area of your life? As believers we always need to evaluate the strength and level of the anointing on our spiritual covering, because we grow as they grow.

David had experience with a sling and stones. That was his level and weapon of choice. He proved that a sling works. While he was taking care of his father's sheep in the hills of Judah, he confronted a lion and a bear and killed them with the weapons he had. When he confronted the giant who challenged Israel, he did not confront him with the king's armor, instead he chose to fight the giant with the weapons with which he had experience and confidence. The level of his exposure in warfare was with a sling and stones.

On another note, what I have learned in ministry that it is not always what you know, who you serve, but who you are connected to that will get you to where God is taking you. On the flip side of that equation, it is possible that you can spend too much time following the wrong voice. The Bible says "My sheep know my voice." You have to know when the season for a relationship is over and when it is time to move on.

When you are seeking for a leadership covering, you have to choose a leader who can contribute to your prophetic destiny; Someone who can assist you with your spiritual development. Do not seek people who have no interest in the call of God on your life, whose only interest in you is to use you to promote their agenda and not the broader aspect of the kingdom of God.

> And Joshua, the son of Nun, was full of the spirit of wisdom; for Moses had laid his hands upon him; and the children of Israel hearkened unto him, and did as the Lord commanded Moses.
>
> - Deuteronomy 34:9.

Succession in ministry does not have to follow the example of the Levitical priesthood, where the generational anointing went to the sons in the family. Your successor in the kingdom of God does not have to be your natural children or a family member but the person selected by God.

Many leaders try to make the ministry a family business, so they place family members who are not qualified, called, or gifted by God into positions of leadership in the church. They try to hoard everything for themselves, while ignoring the call of God on the life of others who are faithful in the ministry. Family members and friends change the dynamics of a ministry because they cannot see you one way at home, and serve you another way at church.

If you are in a ministry that is given to nepotism and you are called into leadership, you may serve in that ministry for your initial training, but eventually you will have to leave. That style of ministry will not make room at the top for anyone outside of the family bloodline.

Leadership Key # 9
- **Governmental Leaders:**

Some people are called to a higher level of leadership than others in the Body of Christ. Every leader should know his or her level of ministry. There is an authority delegated to those on the level of government in the kingdom of God that has not been delegated to others.

> For unto us a child is born, to us a son is given and the government shall be upon his shoulders, and his name shall be called Wonderful, Counselor, Mighty God, Everlasting Father, and Prince of Peace.

> Of the increase of His government and of peace there will be no end on the throne of David and over His kingdom to establish it and to uphold it with justice and with righteousness from this time forth and forevermore. The zeal of the Lord of hosts will do this.
> -Isaiah 9:6-7.

Every nation needs some form of government. The children of Israel had to transition from slaves and servants to take on the responsibility of government in the wilderness. They needed a

166

leader with a governmental anointing. Moses spent the first forty years of his life living in the palace of the king of Egypt, preparing for his role as a leader in government.

He was educated on the level of a King. He learned the ways and the protocol of administration from a governmental prospective. He understood the dignity and the decorum of a monarch. He understood the importance of law and order. He was versed in the ethics of leadership. His exposure during the first forty years of his life, gave him the experience he needed for the role of a chief executive, ambassador of the kingdom of heaven and the chief dignitary over the nation of Israel. One cannot lead beyond one's experience, ability, or exposure.

When God sent Moses to Pharaoh, God knew that Pharaoh was considered and revered as a god in Egypt. Therefore God made Moses a god unto Pharaoh. They had the same rank. Moses was on the same governmental level with Pharaoh, but when seen from a spiritual perspective the ensuing struggle between them was a war of the gods. Pharaoh represented the kingdom of darkness and Moses represented the kingdom of heaven.

Moses' early years of training enabled him to occupy that strategic position as a government official who presided over the nation of Israel, under the canopy of the kingdom of Heaven. But he needed a cabinet of ministers or officials to assist him with the day-to-day affairs of the people.

When you are a part of an apostolic or prophetic company, you can be apostolic and not be an apostle. You can be prophetic and not be a prophet. These are governmental and foundational anointings that are transferred to the company of believers from the chief apostle. Even though God took of the spirit that was on Moses' and placed it on the seventy elders, Moses spirit gave them the ability to govern alongside Moses. it did not give them the same position and capacity that God gave Moses.

> And the Lord said unto Moses, gather unto me seventy men of the elders of Israel; whom thou knowest to be the elders of Israel, and officers over them; and bring them unto the Tabernacle of the congregation, that they may stand there with thee.

> And I will come down and talk with thee there; and I will take of the spirit which is upon thee, and will put it upon them; and they shall bear the burden of the people with thee, that thou bear it not thyself alone.
> -Numbers 11: 16, 17 KJV.

Under the Old Testament order, divine government rested on the shoulders of the priests, prophets, and kings. Anyone who was a man of God was a prophet. Therefore when God took of the spirit that was upon Moses and imparted it to seventy other men, they received an impartation of the spirit of Moses and they began to prophesy because Moses was a prophet. They also received a governmental anointing because they were tribal leaders.

> Behold, I will send you Elijah the prophet before the coming of the great and dreadful day of the Lord. And he shall turn the heart of the fathers to the children, and the heart of the children to the fathers, lest I come and smite the earth with a curse.
> - Malachi 4: 5-6 KJV.

Elijah had been dead for hundreds of years, before this prophecy was given. When God said, "I will send you Elijah the prophet," was He speaking about the man Elijah? Of course not, he was speaking about the spirit of Elijah.

Now if Elijah had been dead for several hundreds of years, how could someone receive the spirit of Elijah without the laying on of hands by Elijah? Governmental anointings come directly from God. Moses' and Elijah's governmental anointing came directly from God.

> And there appeared unto him an angel of the Lord standing on the right side of the altar of incense. And when Zechariah saw him, he was troubled, and fear fell upon him.
>
> But the angel said unto him, "Fear not, Zechariah, for thy prayer is heard; and thy wife Elizabeth shall bear thee a son, and thou shalt call his name John. And he shall go before him in the spirit and power of Elijah, to turn the hearts of the fathers to the children and the disobedient to the wisdom of the just, to make ready a people prepared for the Lord."
>
> -Luke 1: 11-17 KJV.

1. Some anointings are transferred.
2. Some are caught.
3. Some are given directly by God.

Nobody laid hands on Moses, Elijah, Elisha or John the Baptist. Because of their rank in the spirit, the power, anointing, and authority they operated in came directly from God.

When Elijah's completed his term of office as a governmental prophet to the nation of Israel; Elijah was escorted into heaven by a chariot and horses of fire. When his successor Elisha was surrounded by the great Syrian army, God showed Elisha his angelic army of chariots and horses of fire on the mountains surrounding his city. These two men represented the dispensation of the prophets. Elijah could call fire from heaven to consume his enemies, that was his weapon as a ranking military officer in Israel. His wars were fought in the spirit.

Moses was also a governmental prophet who presided over the nation. He represented the dispensation of the law. He taught the nation of Israel government, law, order, and structure.

Anarchy: Political disorder, disorder in any sphere of activity, lawlessness, civil disobedience.

With any secular government, anarchy has to be resolved by the government in power. People expect their government to resolve all their problems and when the government fails to do so, the people resort to anarchy.

In the church, anarchy occurs where there is immorality and instability in leadership. When there are complaints, dissention, strife, division, and misunderstanding among the membership, false accusations, and confusion results in people leaving the church.

The apostles in the early church had to deal with complaints, racial bias, false doctrine, and secular governmental reprisals against the church. The apostles used the wisdom of God to resolve the challenges the church faced.

Now in these days when the disciples were increasing in number, a complaint was made by the Hellenists' against the Hebrews because their widows were being neglected in the daily distribution.

And the twelve summoned the full number of the disciples and said, "It is not that we should give up preaching the word of God to serve tables."

Therefore, brothers, pick out from among you seven men of good repute, full of the Spirit of wisdom, whom we will appoint to this duty. But we will devote ourselves to prayer and to the ministry of the word.

And what they said pleased the whole gathering, and they chose Stephen, a man full of faith and of the Holy Spirit, and Philip, and Prochorus, and Nicanor, and Timon, and Parmenas, and Nicolaus, a proselyte of Antioch. These they set before the apostles, and they prayed and laid their hands on them.

And the word of God continued to increase, and the number of the disciples multiplied greatly in Jerusalem, and a great many of the priests became obedient to the faith.

-Acts 6: 1-7 ESV.

The Jerusalem Council of Apostles and Elders, the governing body of the church, had to resolve doctrinal differences between the Jews and Gentiles.

But some men came down from Judea and were teaching the brothers, "Unless you are circumcised according to the custom of Moses, you cannot be saved." And after that Paul and Barnabas had no small dissension and debate with them.

Paul and Barnabas and some of the others were appointed to go up to Jerusalem to the apostle and the elders about this question. When they came to Jerusalem, they were welcomed by the church and the apostles and the elders, and they declared all that God had done with them.

But some believers who belonged to the party of the Pharisees rose up and said, "It is necessary to circumcise them and to order them to keep the Law of Moses."

The apostles and elders were gathered together to consider this matter. And after there had been much debate, Peter stood up and said to them, "Brothers, you know that in the early days God made a choice among you, that by my mouth the Gentiles should hear the gospel and believe.

And God, who knows the heart, bore witness to them, by giving them the Holy Spirit just as He did to us. And He made no distinction between us and them, having cleansed their hearts by faith.

Now, therefore, why are you putting God to the test by placing a yoke on the neck of the disciples that neither our fathers nor we have been able to bear? But we believe that we will be saved through the grace of the Lord Jesus, just as they will.

And all the assembly fell silent, and they listened to Barnabas and Paul as they related what signs and wonders God had done through them among the Gentiles. After they finished speaking, James replied, "Brothers, listen to me. Simeon has related how God first visited the Gentiles, to take from them a people for His name. And with this the words of the prophets agree, just as it is written.

Therefore my judgment is that we should not trouble those of the Gentiles who turn to God, but should write to them to abstain from the things polluted by idols, and from sexual immorality, and from what has been strangled, and from blood. For from ancient generations Moses has had in every city those who proclaim him, for he is read every Sabbath in the synagogues.

-Acts 15:1, 2; 4-15; 19-21 ESV.

The Church in the wilderness had its share of complaints against their government. The people murmured and complained against God and Moses.

And the people complained in the hearing of the Lord about their misfortunes, and when the Lord heard it, His anger was kindled, and the fire of the Lord burned among them and consumed some outlying parts of the camp. Then the people cried out to Moses, and Moses prayed to the Lord, and the fire died down.

-Numbers 11: 1, ESV.

Moses was opposed by his brother Aaron, and sister Miriam.

Miriam and Aaron spoke against Moses because of the Cushite (black) woman whom he had married, for he had married Cushite woman. And they said, "Has the Lord indeed spoken only through Moses? Has He not spoken through us also?" And the Lord heard it.

-Numbers 12: 1-2. ESV

Anarchy in the camp was led by Korah against Moses:

Now Korah the son of Izhar, son of Kohath, son of Levi, and Dathan and Abiram the sons of Eliab, and On the son of Peleth, sons of Reuben, took men. And they rose up before Moses, with a number of the people of Israel, two hundred and fifty chiefs of the congregation, chosen from the assembly; well-known men.

They assembled themselves together against Moses and against Aaron and said to them, "You have gone too far! For all in the congregation are holy, every one of them, and the Lord is among them. Why then do you exalt yourselves above the assembly of the Lord?

When Moses heard it, he fell on his face, and he said to Korah and all his company, "In the morning the Lord will show who is His, and who is holy, and will bring him near to Him. The one whom He chooses He will bring near to Him.

- Numbers 16:1-5 ESV.

Leadership key # 10
- **Spirit Led Intercessions is The Essence of Ministry.**

John the Baptist was the last in the order of Old Testament prophets. His mission was to prepare the way for the Lord, prepare the way for the kingdom order. He was the fore-runner of Jesus; his assignment was that of a prophetic Herald. The Bible describes him as, 'the voice crying in the wilderness' his voice was making prophetic intercessions and declarations for the coming manifestation of the Messiah and the kingdom of God.

Everything coming into the earth from the kingdom of heaven needs a herald; someone to make prophetic declarations and intercession. Every ministry must be birthed by intercessions. Every new move of the spirit must be birthed by intercession, because the enemy brings reinforcements in his warfare against the plan of God. Therefore intercessions move the hand of God, causes divine intervention, and produces manifestation.

For God to manifest in the form of man in the earth, it took much intercession for this notable or memorial event to take place. God had prophetic intercessors like Anna the prophetess and Simon interceding for years in the temple at Jerusalem.

> And, behold there was a man in Jerusalem, whose name was Simeon; and the same man was just and devout, waiting for the consolation of Israel, and the Holy Ghost was upon him.
>
> And it was revealed unto him by the Holy Ghost, that he should not see death, before he had seen the Lord's Christ. And he came by the Spirit into the temple; and when the parents brought in the child Jesus, to do for him after the custom of the law.
>
> Then he took him up in his arms, and blessed God, and said. "Lord now let thy servant depart in peace, according to thy word. For mine eyes have seen thy salvation, which thou hast prepared before the face of all people."
>
> And there was one Anna, a prophetess, the daughter of Phanuel, of the tribe of Asher; she was of a great age, and had lived with a husband seven years from her virginity.
>
> And she was a widow of about four score and four years, which departed not from the temple, but served God with fastings and prayers night and day. And she coming in that instant gave thanks likewise unto the Lord, and spoke of Him to all them that looked for redemption in Jerusalem.
>
> -Luke 2: 25-36-38 ESV.

Intercessors cleared the way for the birth of Christ. Jesus was coming into an antagonistic environment and needed prayer cover. Without intercession the baby could have been killed by King Herod. Herod had the authority and soldiers at his disposal to look for the baby that was born 'king of the Jews' and when they found that baby, they had orders from the king, to kill that baby.

Every leader should know that they cannot start anything on a kingdom level on this earth without intercession and travail to God. The foundation must be laid with prayer to avoid the backlash of the enemy. Prayer is the foundation for success.

Spirit led intercession will produce manifestation. Every leader should be an intercessor. Intercession and spiritual travail are necessary for birthing a vision and bringing it into manifestation in the natural. Intercession precedes manifestation.

When Elisha asked for a double portion of Elijah's anointing, Elijah said, "You have asked for a hard thing, but if you see when I am taken up;" [If you see meant], if you can see the symbolic representation of my anointing. [The chariot of fire and the horses of fire], that means you are spiritually able, or capable to handle this level of anointing, but only God can decide if He will extend my ministry through you. Elisha however, never imparted that governmental anointing to anyone else before he died.

The Bible did not say so, but Elisha had to intercede all along the way as he served and followed the man of God. He had to pray and ask God for what he wanted. Elijah could not impart a double portion of that level of anointing to Elisha. Only God can decide who is mature enough, who is qualified and capable to carry that level of anointing. Elisha persisted with intercession. He learned from his leader that the fervent, effectual prayer of a righteous man makes power available. Persistence made the difference. He would not leave his leader's side, even though Elijah gave him the opportunity on several occasions.

2 Kings 2: 1-15 tells of his persistence and his reward. God will make an exception to His own rules, when He comes into contact with faith.

HIS PERSISTENCE:

> And it came to pass, when the Lord would take up Elijah into heaven by a whirlwind that Elijah went with Elisha from Gilgal. And Elijah said unto Elisha, stay here; the Lord has sent me to Bethel. And Elisha replied, "As surely as the Lord lives, and as you live, I will not leave you." So they went down to Bethel.

> Then Elijah said to him, "Stay here Elisha, the Lord has sent me to Jericho." And he replied, "As surely as the Lord lives and you live, I will not leave you." So they went to Jericho.

> And Elijah said to him, "Stay here, the Lord has sent me to the Jordan." And he replied, "As surely as the lord lives, and as you live, I will not leave you, so the two of them walked on.

One Must Be Present, Prayerful And Prepared For A Time Of Visitation.

> And Elijah took his cloak [mantle], rolled it up, and struck the water with it. The water divided to the right and to the left, and the two of them crossed over on dry ground.

> When they had crossed over, Elijah said unto Elisha; "Tell me, what I can do for you before I am taken from

you?" "Let me inherit a double portion of your spirit", Elisha replied. "You have asked a difficult thing," Elijah said, "Yet if you see me when I am taken from you, it will be yours – otherwise it will not".

And as they were walking along and talking together, suddenly a chariot of fire and horses of fire appeared and separated the two of them, and Elijah went up to heaven in a whirlwind. Elisha saw this, and cried out, "My father! My father! The chariot and horsemen of Israel!" And Elisha saw him no more, then he took hold of his own clothes, and tore them apart. And he took up the mantle of Elijah that fell from him, and went back, and stood by the bank of Jordan.

And he took the mantle that fell from him, and smote the waters, and said, "Where now is the Lord, the God of Elijah? He asked. And when he struck the waters, it divided to the right and to the left, and he crossed over.

The company of the prophets who were at Jericho said, "The spirit of Elijah is resting on Elisha." And they went to meet him and bowed to the ground before him.

- 2 Kings 2: 13-15.

Bowing themselves to the ground before him was an act of submission. They knew that with the mantle of Elijah resting on Elisha, he was now their spiritual father and leader.

Mantles are passed when there is relationship. Everyone in the Bible that inherited a ministry mantle served his or her leader in some capacity during his or her time of preparation in the embryotic stage of his or her ministry. This period of preparation is too vital to overlook. The ground has to be prepared with the necessary impartation of spiritual gifts, anointing, intercessions, the revelation of the Logos, the Rhema Word, and the power of the Holy Spirit.

Jesus was thirty years old when he began His ministry which lasted for three years. The preparation period took longer than the years spent in ministry. But the effectiveness of one's ministry is based on the period of preparation, known as the laying down of the foundation. The ministry of Jesus was effective, powerful, and life changing, due to the period of time spent on the foundation. His ministry changed the destiny of mankind.

Far too many leaders have stepped out too soon, and they were unprepared for the backlash they encountered. Jesus told the story of two men that built their house, one digged deep until he found bedrock then he laid his foundation. The other man in his haste to put up his building or to start his ministry laid his foundation on sand. They both encountered storms, wind, rain, the trials and circumstances of life, but the house built on sand fell, because it could not withstand the nature's fury. The house whose foundation was built on the rock endured (Matthew 7: 24-27).

Sand: Porous, loose, gritty particles of worn or disintegrated rock, varying in size. It is a shifting material which is affected by wind, and water. It cannot withstand floods; it is usually carried away by strong water currents and strong winds and is usually deposited along the shores of bodies of water, or desert places.

People confuse the manifestation of gifts of the spirit [1 Corinthians 12] with preparation for ministry. You may have one or more of these gifts mentioned, but the manifestation of spiritual gifts does not mean you are ready to deal with the spiritual forces that will surely come against you, in the form of demonic reprisals, and those human spirits that are jealous of anyone God is using to any extent. Leaders must seek God for divine strength to war and to stand in the evil day.

Leadership key #11
- You Will Receive An Impartation of The Anointing You Serve, Respect, and Admire.

While Elisha served Elijah, he observed his leadership skills, his level of governmental authority, his prayer life, the power he had as a general in the army of God, his level of anointing, and his relationship with God.

Far too many ministers in their developmental stages of ministry criticize and repudiate their leaders for their human errors and weaknesses. We must separate human weaknesses from immorality and a sinful lifestyle. There is a difference. All of God's people have human weaknesses whether we choose to acknowledge it or not. Some leaders are too emotional, some do not exercise wisdom, some may have a poor memory, some may not be too intelligent, etc. You may have a human weakness and still be anointed, prayerful, and powerful. Getting the job done is what matters.

You gravitate toward what you honor and respect. Elisha respected the anointing on Elijah's life. Therefore Elisha had an unusual request. "He wanted a double portion of Elijah's spirit." Elisha was his spiritual son. The son wanted what he saw operating in his father, and God gave him the desire of his heart. You cannot receive from a ministry gift if all you do is criticize and slander that person.

We can disqualify ourselves for promotion when we are not persistent, prepared, present, and prayerful. Elisha's mentor was a man of prayer, persistence, and faith. The apostle James said, "He was a man of like passions such as we are." He was a righteous man whose prayer life was strong, fervent, and effective, and it brought about the manifestation of the fire of God. His spiritual son, asked for and received a double portion of his leader's spirit. This was the anointing he served, honored, admired and respected.

Leadership Key #12
- **Leaders Must Guard their Spirit.**

The real you is spirit. God is a spirit. It is through the spirit that we relate to the cosmos. You have a physical body, an emotional body and an etheric body. When you were born all of these bodies were born simultaneously with you. Each body dwells in its respective realm, and as you grow, they grow simultaneously.

You cannot be an effective leader over God's people without God's spirit. Therefore it is imperative that one is born again, of the water and of the Spirit of God. Before the day of Pentecost, Jesus' disciples were not filled with the Spirit of God. The Spirit of God was given to the church on the Day of Pentecost. Before Pentecost they functioned as natural men, with their carnal understanding, having a passion for power and positions of importance in Christ's kingdom.

And the time approached for Him to be taken up to heaven, Jesus resolutely set out for Jerusalem. And He sent messengers on ahead, who went into a Samaritan village to get things ready for Him, but the people there did not welcome Him, because He was heading for Jerusalem.

When the disciples James and John saw this, they asked, "Lord, do you want us to call fire down from heaven to destroy them?" But Jesus turned and rebuked them, and they went to another village.

-Luke 9: 51-56

The KJV says, but He turned and rebuked them and said, "Ye know not what manner of spirit ye are of. For the son of man is not come to destroy men's lives, but to save them." And they went to another village.

In this scripture it states Jesus was set, resolute, and determined in His spirit to get to Jerusalem. He had an appointment there. The time was quickly approaching for Him to fulfill his assignment as the Lamb of God slain before the foundations of the world. This was the season of Passover and He was God's Passover Lamb. He could not be late for this divine appointment. His death could only take place in the chosen city of Jerusalem.

O Jerusalem, Jerusalem, you who kill the prophets and stone those sent to you, how often I have longed to gather your children together, as a hen gathers her chicks under her wings; but you were not willing.

-Matthew 23: 37.

In any case, I must keep going, today and tomorrow and the next day – for surely no prophet can die outside Jerusalem.

-Luke 13: 33.

Jerusalem was the hub of religious activity, for the temple of God was located in Jerusalem. This city was also the seat of government, the capital city, which had a reputation for killing prophets. At this time the city was under Roman occupation and only the Roman officials could give the order for capital punishment which was death.

James and John, the Sons of Thunder, as Jesus called them, (a name depicting their outrageous personality, bad temperament and anger), became enraged when Jesus was rejected by the Samaritans. And immediately they wanted to call fire from heaven to destroy the Samaritans in retaliation. The way a leader reacts or responds in a crisis or when his or her authority is challenged, lets you know the human disposition as well as the characteristics of his or her spirit.

The sons of Zebedee wanted to sit on Jesus's right hand and left when He came into His kingdom. Their behavior is typical of the indiscretions of those that lack understanding of the purpose of true ministry. James and John were self-centered, arrogant, inexperienced, and unwise. James became the first martyr among the apostles and his brother John went on to live longer than any of the other apostles, but he became a changed man in the ensuing years. His main message was love as the guiding principle for the church. He brought to light in his teachings how God demonstrated His love for sinners through Jesus.

As he grew older and wiser, his ministry took on a softer more mature tone; he imitated Jesus whom he referred to as "truth, light and life." As the author of the book of Revelation, God unveiled through John the unseen spiritual warfare the church is engaged in and the spiritual realities behind the church's trials and temptations. John affirmed the certainty of Christ's triumphant return to earth, giving the believer the strength and courage to endure suffering.

Leadership Key #13
- ### The Importance of Divine Timing

There is a time to every purpose under the heavens. The kingdom of heaven operates in seasons, and timing is very important to the culmination of God's plan on earth. When the set time or the fullness of time came, Christ entered the world to destroy the works of the devil.

Nothing on God's agenda happens before its time. Jesus Christ had a set time to come into the earth's realm. He had a set time to be crucified. He had a set time to depart, and the Holy Spirit had a set day and time to arrive.

> But when the fullness of time had come, God sent forth His son, born of woman, born under the law, to redeem those who were under the law, so that we might receive adoption as sons.
>
> – Galatians 4: 4, 5.

> When the Day of Pentecost arrived, they were all together in one place and suddenly there came from heaven a sound like a mighty rushing wind, and it filled the entire house where they were sitting.
>
> - Acts 2:1.

In the natural, when the season of winter comes, vegetation sleeps, migration of animals takes place, the seed is dormant in the ground waiting for spring to come to life. According to the seasonal cycle of the universe; Spring, Summer, Autumn and Winter shall never cease as long as the earth remains. These seasons coincide with the natural rhythm and cycle of life. Whether you are in the northern hemisphere, the southern hemisphere or in the equatorial regions of the earth, it is the law of the universe.

In Jesus' ministry, His due season to die was approaching and He had to be in Jerusalem to celebrate that last Passover with His disciples. He was the divine seed of God, that had to be in the ground at a specific season, and His allotted time to spend in *Sheol*, the grave, was three days and three nights.

For I delivered to you as of first importance what I also received; that Christ died for our sins in accordance with the Scriptures. That he was buried, that he was raised on the third day in accordance with the Scriptures.

-1 Corinthians 15: 3, 4.

Jesus was resolute about going to Jerusalem on time to celebrate this important Feast, *the last Supper*, with His disciples. He sent his advanced team ahead of Him to make preparations; but instead of them going straight to Jerusalem to find the upper room and to prepare for the feast, notorious James and John, the sons of Zebedee, made other arrangements for Jesus to make a detour through some of the villages of Samaria to do ministry.

Even though they walked with Jesus, and were subject to His tutelage, the disciples still did not know or fully understand his purpose or the importance of the hour. Every leader must follow the directives of the Holy Spirit, and not allow other people to make decisions for them that are inconsistent with the will of God and what God is doing in the present season.

The grace of God on a leader's life is frustrated when people on his or her team, have their own agenda, and will not follow the leader's directives, because they have another plan. Directives come from God to the leader. The vision comes from God to the leader. The anointing trickles down from the head down to the body.

Knowing people by their spirit is important. People with the wrong spirit and wrong agenda keep conflict in the church, because as oil and water do not mix, flesh and spirit do not mix. Many of these attachments will ride on your bus until a bigger bus comes along. It is called selfish ambition. People who want to be seen, who want attention, who are looking for significance, they always have an opinion as if they know better than everyone else, and they frustrate the unity among the workers because they are too busy promoting themselves.

Headship gifts must know how to place gifted people in the ministry, so that they can be an asset to the ministry, and not put the ministry in awkward situations, because they run ahead of everybody with their agenda like James and John.

The Samaritan people were going to make a demand on Jesus to minister, even after He had shifted His focus to be at the Feast of Passover on time. To handle the matter discreetly, Jesus did go through a few villages and did a minimal amount of ministry. However, after Jesus went back to heaven He did send a representative into Samaria.

Now those who were scattered went about preaching the word. Philip went down to the city of Samaria and proclaimed to them the Christ.

And the crowds with one accord paid attention to what was being said by Philip when they heard him and saw the signs that he did. For unclean spirits, crying out with a loud voice, came out of many who had them, and many who were paralyzed or lame were healed. So there was much joy in that city.

-Acts 8: 4-8.

What the disciple learned from this incident was, purpose demands timing, timing is seasonal, seasons change, and if you miss your season and your timing, you could abort your purpose.

The first Passover in Egypt changed the destiny of the descendants of Abraham. Now this last supper, this important Passover Feast that Jesus would spend on earth with His disciples would change the destiny of the Gentile world. Jesus was the Passover lamb that would die for all of mankind.

Pentecost occurred fifty days after Passover. After His resurrection Jesus spent forty days and nights with his disciples, teaching them things pertaining to the Kingdom of God. He ascended back to the father ten days before the Day of Pentecost, a day designated by God for the outpouring of the Holy Spirit. With his resurrected body He could no longer stay in the earth's realm.

> So it is with the resurrection of the dead, what is sown is perishable, what is raised is imperishable. It is sown in dishonor, it is raised in glory. It is sown in weakness, it is raised in power, It is sown a natural body, it is raised a spiritual body. If there is a natural body there is also a spiritual body.
> -1 Corinthians 15: 42-44.

Jesus told them, "It is expedient for you that I go away. If I do not go, the Comforter would not come." The Comforter had a set time to come, which was on the first Pentecost after the resurrection of Jesus Christ. This Pentecost had to be synchronized with the set time of Jesus' resurrection to fulfill prophecy.

Heaven has divine arrangements, purpose and timing to everything. God will not allow man to interfere with what the "Counsel of the Heavens" has determined. These are the things that the father has put in place before the foundations of the world.

Leadership key #14
- **Thou shalt not be Unwise**

Wisdom is founded in the fear of the Lord. Because of the fall of man, there is inherent in man a natural inclination to think foolishly. Jesus Christ came as the ultimate wisdom of God. Through Him the mind of man can be totally renewed to think higher thoughts through the mind of Christ. "Let this mind be in you which also was in Christ Jesus" (Philippians 2: 5).

My son, if you receive my words and treasure up my commandments with you, making your ear attentive to wisdom and inclining your heart to understanding; yes, if you call out for insight and raise your voice for understanding if you seek it like silver and search for it as for hidden treasures, then you will understand the fear of the Lord and find the knowledge of God.

For the Lord gives wisdom; from His mouth come knowledge and understanding; He stores up sound wisdom for the upright; He is a shield to those who walk in integrity, guarding the paths of justice and watching over the way of His saints.

-Proverbs 2: 1-8.

Every leader should seek for Wisdom on a daily basis. Wisdom guides and directs leaders in the decision-making process for every endeavor. When leaders are forced to make life changing decisions hastily, without seeking God for wisdom, they usually make decisions that they later regret, but refuse to admit they were wrong.

Bad decisions have caused leaders to put themselves and the church in compromising situations. Many churches have been shaken, split apart, abandoned, or had their candlestick removed [Rev. 2:5] due to charismatic leadership void of integrity and wisdom, who made bad decisions that affected the church community, and his or her family.

Every ministry gift is known by his or her level of wisdom and revelation. A person's level of spiritual maturity is very apparent when he or she is preaching or teaching the word of God. When a spirit of ignorance is present in a ministry gift, he or she counteracts his or her deficiency by becoming very religious, controlling, and unwise. Just as the church has embraced the fivefold ministry gifts, the church must also embrace and value the spirit of wisdom and revelation in the knowledge of God.

Who is wise and understanding among you? By his good conduct let him show his works in the meekness of wisdom. But if you have bitter jealousy and selfish ambition in your hearts, do not boast and be false to the truth.

This is not the wisdom that comes down from above, but is earthly, unspiritual, and demonic. For where jealousy and selfish ambition exist, there will be disorder and every vile practice.

But the wisdom from above is first pure, then peaceable, gentle, open to reason, full of mercy and good fruits, impartial and sincere. And a harvest of righteousness is sown in peace by those who make peace.

-James 3: 13-18.

Because the essence of leadership is spirit, any authority you operate in must come from the Spirit of God. When the Spirit of God comes upon a leader typically that individual rises from among his brethren and becomes salt to the earth.

Salt is a preservative, if salt has lost its saltiness it is good for nothing. It loses its purpose and function and is no longer relevant. As a leader you must make sure you maintain your saltiness, which is your relationship with Christ, by keeping sin out of your life. Sin contaminates decays, corrupts, and opens the door for demonic activity.

The Holy Spirit took a fisherman like Peter, who the Sanhedrin council determined was ignorant and unlearned, and lifted him from a secluded, self-centered lifestyle as a fisherman, and placed him in downtown Jerusalem where he fearlessly preached to the multitude on the day of Pentecost. Not only was he infused with power from on high, but he was infused with God's wisdom.

He became salt to the earth. When Peter stood before the council of the Sanhedrin he declared, "We would rather obey God than men." Peter transitioned from an ignorant, and unlearned fisherman to a governmental apostle who not only had the keys of the kingdom of Heaven, but he also had the rank and authority to raise the dead. He was blessed with kingdom, power, wisdom, and revelation because he was anointed with the spirit of Christ.

> And when they saw the boldness of Peter and John, and perceived that they were unlearned and ignorant men, they marveled and they took knowledge of them that they had been with Jesus.
>
> - Acts 4: 13.

You will receive the spirit of the person or people with whom you associate. All Christian leaders must choose their associates and companions in the gospel with great care. The law of reciprocity is a great law to measure relationships by. What am I doing to enhance you, and how are you benefitting from my relationship with you?

> Yet among the mature we do impart wisdom, although it is not wisdom of this age or of the rulers of this age, who are doomed to pass away.

But we impart a secret and hidden wisdom of God, which God decreed before the ages for our glory. None of the rulers of this age understood this, for if they had, they would not have crucified the Lord of glory.

-1 Corinthians 2: 6-8.

Daniel was a young man from the royal family and nobility that was initially trained in Israel before he was taken with the captives into Babylon. Babylon is a type of the religious, political, social and economic system of the world. He was among the young Hebrew men who were selected because he was skillful in wisdom, and endowed with knowledge. He understood learning and was competent to stand in the king's palace, to learn the language and literature of Babylon.

Daniel and his three companions trusted God and made a quality decision not to defile themselves with the king's food. This decision gave them favor with God and favor with the chief of the Eunuchs. For taking a stand in that environment God gave them learning and skill in all literature and wisdom, and Daniel had understanding in all visions and dreams. (Daniel 1: 17) God gave him the wisdom to function successfully at the highest level in government; as a president.

Daniel did not rely upon the wisdom of the Babylonians; he totally relied upon God's wisdom. When king Nebuchadnezzar had a dream there was no one in the kingdom, including the wise men of Babylon who functioned in the demonic realm as sorcerers that could interpret the king's dream. The king ordered all the wise men in the land to be killed. This was an opportunity for Daniel to seek his God and to declare God's wisdom which was far superior to the wisdom of the Babylonians. This wisdom was on a level that did not exist in the realm of Babylon; a wisdom that could only come from the God of wisdom.

This dimension of wisdom has returned to the church through the ministry of wise master builders, who are apostles and governmental prophets.

Therefore the wisdom of God also said, I will send them Prophets and Apostles, and some of them they will kill and persecute.

-Luke 11:49.

Therefore, indeed, I send you Prophets, wise men, [*Apostle*] and scribes; some of them you will kill and crucify, and some of them you will scourge in your synagogues and persecute from city to city.

-Matthew 23: 34.

God has given apostles the spirit of wisdom and revelation to decode the mysteries of Christ. Jesus told his apostles, "Unto you it is given to know the mysteries of the kingdom of God" (Matthew 13:11).

The foundation upon which the church is built is the revelation of Christ as it was laid down by the apostles and prophets. The church is built upon the wisdom of God, and it is the pillar and ground of the truth. New Testament apostles and governmental prophets are given divine insight into the mysteries of God. They are part of the fivefold ministry given to the church to make all men see the fellowship of the mystery which was hidden in Christ and decoded by the wisdom of God.

Leadership Key #15
- Controlling Powers Over The Spirit

When a spirit has no physical body through which to express itself, it is stuck in another dimension. But when it passes into a willing vessel - a man or woman, he or she becomes one with that spirit. Jesus said, "I and my father are one," because the Spirit of God was upon Him and had anointed Him to complete His assignment in the earth.

The reason God gave man a physical body is to be a vessel, a temple, a sanctuary or an abiding place for His spirit. Our spirit man is the direct channel between God and man. We receive instructions, direction, and purpose from Him through our spirit man. We follow the unction of the Holy Spirit in our spirit. From that vantage point He directs our lives from the guidance and warning we sense from Him.

The spirit man is what makes us who we are. It is the highest creative power inside us. We are spirit first, then body and soul. Our mind and our body are pieces of 'equipment' that are needed in order for our spirit to carry out the purpose of God in the earth. God does not talk to a piece of equipment – He speaks to our heart – our spirit man.

The plans of heaven come to us through our spirit. Our mind may find out a few seconds later and be able to interpret what our spirit has received. This is why our spirit sometimes knows something, but we are not able to put it into words – because our mind has not yet comprehended it.

Our spirit man is an individual. Each spirit man has a different call and a different purpose to contribute to the Body of Christ. Our spirit man is unlimited in potential as it feeds and nurtures itself from the Word of God.

> The spirit of man is the candle of the Lord
> – Proverbs 20:27

The area of spiritual control and manipulation is by far the most dangerous, because it treads on the spiritual principles of heaven. It is dangerous for both the controller and the one being controlled.

Spiritual manipulation is based on the soulish realm. It has nothing to do with the true spirituality, but uses a spiritual principle as its primary tool. This spiritual principle is often violated by leaders who have issues with control, rejection and jealousy.

> Obey your leader and submit to his or her authority. They keep watch over you as men who must give an account. Obey them so that their work will be a joy, not a burden, for that would be of no advantage to you.
>
> - Hebrews 13:17.

There are basically three types of control:
1. There is the natural control that people exert over others.
2. Self-control that must be exercised within the individual.
3. An abusive control that is exercised by one person over another.

Some means of control are more obvious than others, but if Satan can control a person, that person will be held in unnecessary bondage and hindered from fulfilling the purpose of God in his or her life.

We must understand these three types of control to accurately discern their influences.
- Parents exert a natural control over their small children as part of training them in the way they should go.
- Teachers must maintain control in the classroom in order to create a conducive learning environment.
- To some degree employers exert control over their employees to insure productivity for the company and the employees.

Natural control and self-control are godly traits, but the third type of control can destroy us, and that is abusive control. Abusive control can be defined as an attempt to dominate another person in order to fulfill one's own desires and to enhance personal security. This type of control is demonic.

Although the controller may appear to handle everything with ease and confidence, in reality he or she is in bondage to demons – scared, intimidated, insecure, and unfulfilled. He or she is terribly afraid of being rejected. Manipulation of others is a means for them to feel superior, in charge, and secure. The controller's goal is survival at any cost.

People who exercise abusive control seek to become the deciding factor in the lives of others. Such individuals replace the Word of God as the balance in the lives of those they dominate. They react negatively if they do not have control of all decisions made. There is no personal regard or consideration for the one being controlled and dominated.

Control is nothing more than spiritual manipulation to keep its victims in a subservient state of being. Spiritual manipulators have not developed godly character in a particular area. They are led by their lust or desire for control rather than by the spirit of God. We most often find these types of people in leadership.

Controlling Prayers: Another variation of spiritual manipulation is controlling prayers. Controlling prayers are born from worry, frustration, and flesh. A person who prays controlling prayers may act spiritual, but he or she prays from his or her desire rather than from his or her spirit, and he or she will not succeed.

Can Christian's pray controlling prayers? Certainly, they can! But if misused, these prayers are a form of witchcraft! Remember words are spiritual weapons.

A controlling prayer is a harmful, misuse of authority when it violates or dominates another person's will. It is composed of words with a spiritual force behind them, spoken to influence the course of another's life. The only time a controlling prayer should be used by a Christian is when the word of God is used against the enemy. Jesus explained this method of prayer in Matthew 16: 19.

> "And I will give unto you the keys of the Kingdom of heaven. Whatever you prohibit on earth will be prohibited in heaven; and whatsoever you permit on earth shall be permitted in heaven." [Complete Jewish Bible]

Abusive controlling people often pray his or her own fleshly desires for someone out of the human heart. In the same way, many people use prophesy to control people by prophesying out of the human heart, carnal mind and dictates of the flesh. They try to make the other individual obey their selfish desires, rather than the Lord's will for that person's life. The person praying may or may not understand that they are loosing evil influences which will affect the person's mental or spiritual stability.

The scriptures warn us;
> "By your words you will be justified and acquitted and by your words you will be condemned and sentenced."
>
> -Matthew 12: 37.

As leaders and as children of God we must realize that we can bless or curse with our words. Controlling prayers fall under the category of a curse, because they are words spoken against another person in an attempt to satisfy selfish human desires.

Selfish, controlling prayers can occur in any area of life when human desire is placed above the will of God. Spiritual manipulators twist scripture to give substance to their controlling prayers. Spiritual controllers think they know what is best for everyone involved. Because they do not have the heart of God, they cannot know the will of God.

Solution: True spirit-filled believers do not need to be concerned about controlling prayers if they are following the will of God. They should season themselves in the word, and develop Godly character. Through the word of God you can prevail over any soulish prayers that hinders. In other words through the word of God, you can prevail when someone tries to impose his or her will over your life.

Practice the word of God every day; develop sensitivity to the Holy Spirit. Commit to Godly character and integrity. These principles produce security in Christ Jesus and enables one to follow as the Spirit of God leads.

> As many as are led by the Spirit of God they are the Sons of God.
> - Romans 8:14.

Leadership Key #16
- Growing Into Sonship

Our focus should be on becoming Sons of God, growing into maturity as joint heirs of Jesus Christ, and becoming Christlike. Our authority comes from our relationship with Jesus Christ as joint heirs. When we have the attributes of Christ we can use His authority to defeat the ploys and schemes of the enemy. Our relationship with Christ is personal and it must be an individual pursuit to know God and to be found in Him.

Some are pursuing the gifts of the spirit because they want notoriety, flair, and flamboyance but not the pruning it takes to bring them into purpose. God's house must have order; therefore people must be taught how to conduct themselves in the House of God which is the pillar and ground of the truth.

Certain disciplines are required if we are to grow into sonship as a people chosen to handle eternal things. God has a prescribed way of doing things. The bible says the children of Israel knew the acts of God but they did not know the ways of God. As a leader you cannot take people to a place you have never been. You cannot teach things you do not know or have never experienced. You cannot function beyond the limits of your exposure.

Most leaders want God to use them to perform miracles, signs and wonders. Leaders want more and more anointing, more and more gifts because our flesh craves adulation, power, and the honor the flesh gets from people. But when there is a focus on satisfying the lusts of the flesh, we fail to focus on developing Godly character, and the heart of God. The flesh prevents us from ministering to people with the right spirit.

We are called Sons of God, but what does that mean? In our walk as believers, we grow in three stages of sonship:

1. Babes in Christ or infancy.
2. Children of God – a stage where we begin to understand more about God and the Spirit.
3. Mature sons and daughters of God have the ability to see the things the Father wants them to see and know. They have the ability to understand the heart of God. They can

perceive God's will because they know his ways and have his characteristics, attributes and the very things that make God who He is.

All of creation is awaiting the manifestation of the Sons of God. But it takes a process of time to grow into what God is calling us into. Our potential as leaders, entrepreneurs, writers, artists, apostles, prophets, pastors, evangelists, teachers, and other ministry callings. We are all children of God, but few become heirs of God, because God's heirs have passed through trials and the fires of adversity to learn and grow into the fullness of their status as co-equals with Jesus Christ.

The spirit seeks to manifest in your reality and it can only do so as you evolve from being your natural self into becoming a Son of God and a joint heir with Jesus Christ. We testify of being saved, sanctified, and filled with the Holy Spirit, but we have come to the realization that every believer must grow into the fullness of the stature of Jesus Christ to be a joint heir.

We are becoming, and when we get to that place of realization and manifestation of sonship, the universe will be at our command. The elements will be at our command. We will possess the divine nature and ability of God to speak to the darkness and say "Let there be."

Leadership Key #17
- ### Godly Leadership and Oppression

The line between evil oppression and true leadership is within the heart of the person in charge. When a person in authority begins to assume a "king-mentality" he starts to see his followers as his "subjects" existing for his own purposes. Then that leader will begin to control and intimidate the people, leading not out of the spirit of truth or love, but with fear and manipulation. That leader becomes a terror to the people mainly because he or she is no longer leading by the spirit.

> And the word of the Lord came to Samuel, "Saul has turned back from following me and has not performed by commandments." And Samuel was angry, and he cried to the Lord all night.
>
> 1 Samuel 15: 10, 11.

When we examine how Jesus managed His ministry, we must ask ourselves, "How can I use Jesus' ministry as my pattern?" There is a major difference between our own approach to ministry and Jesus's approach, which could explain why we are not achieving the same results, and not having the same impact on society like Jesus.

Jesus outlined His primary objective, which was to preach the gospel to the poor. He did not disciple the poor, but He chose twelve men to disciple them. If Jesus came to the earth today, many churches would not receive Him, because Jesus would not choose people that are religious leaders to be His disciples. He would choose men who would evoke criticism, because they do not subscribe to the religious mindset of today.

The main difference between the leadership skills of King Saul and King David was; King Saul was a selfish tyrant who oppressed those around him. In contrast, David used his anointing and skills as a warrior, and a worshipper of God to enhance the men that abdicated from the army of Saul and came to join his cause. They were discouraged, disgruntled, broken in spirit, in debt, oppressed, hopeless, and disappointed.

These men had been serving in Saul's army but had not received compensation or wages to support their family. They were tired of fighting the wars of a tyrant king. David encouraged them by providing for them. In doing so he brought them from the depths of despair to become transformed, valiant, courageous, skilled and mighty fighting men.

The key to David's success in rehabilitating these hardened warriors was his realization that they were valuable to him. They were fathers, brothers, sons, and husbands. David, a man after the heart of God, took responsibility for these men who had left all to follow David.

And David came to the two hundred men, which were so faint that they could not follow David, whom they had made also to abide at the brook Besor; and they went forth to meet David and to meet the people that were with him; and when David came near to the people, he saluted them.

Then answered all the wicked men and men of Belial, of those that went with David, and said, because they went not with us, we will not give them aught of the spoil that we have recovered, save to every man his wife and his children, that they may lead them away, and depart.

Then said David, "Ye shall not do so, my brethren, with that which the Lord hath given us, who hath preserved us, and delivered the company that came against us into our hand.

For who will hearken unto you in this matter? But as his part is that goes down to the battle, so shall his part be that tarries by the stuff; they shall part alike." And it was so from that day forward, that he made it a statute and an ordinance for Israel unto this day.

-1 Samuel 30: 21-25.

Inexperienced leaders seldom realize that they can do nothing by themselves. People are your greatest asset and they can also be your greatest source of pain. But if there were no people there would be no need for leaders. Leaders were God's answer to the cries of His people that were being oppressed.

> Nevertheless the Lord raised up judges, which delivered them out of the hand of those that spoiled them.

> And when the Lord raised them up judges, then the Lord was with the judge, and delivered them out of the hand of their enemies all the days of the judge.

> For it repented the Lord because of their groanings by reason of them that oppressed them and vexed them.
>
> - Judges 2: 16, 18.

Why did God raise up leaders for His people?

- God raised up leaders to keep order among the people.
- God raised up leaders in the time of war.
- God raised up leaders to deliver the people from oppressive kings.
- God raised up leaders to intercede to God on behalf of the people.
- God raised up leaders to govern the people.
- God raised up leaders to teach the people His word.
- God raised up leaders to lead the people into worship.
- God raised up leaders to develop ministers in their calling.
- God raised up leaders to bring about the manifestation of the kingdom of God.
- God raised up leaders to preach, teach, and demonstrate the word of God.
- God raised up leaders to be witnesses in the earth.
- God raised up leaders to show forth His glory among men.

- God raised up leaders as His voice in the earth.
- God raised up leaders to correct, warn, and teach the way of righteousness.
- God raised up leaders to bring about healing, deliverance from bondage, and oppression.

Leadership Key #18
The Essence of Leadership is Truth and Life.

Truth Life are derivatives of the Word of God. One of the characteristics of the Spirit of God is "Truth." Therefore every word spoken by the Spirit of God are words of truth. God's words are not conjecture, fables, and they are certainly are not lies. God never makes a mistake, nor does He have to apologize for misrepresenting himself because of what He said.

In the beginning God spoke and said, "Let there be" and whatever He declared came into manifestation. God spoke truth to a dead planet and He activated the cycle of the universe with the power of His word.

> In the beginning was the word, and the word was with God and the word was God.
>
> - John 1: 1.

The first thing God created in the beginning was life. He did so by reproducing himself, He begat life and He called life His son. Life was known as the Word of God.

Begat: procreate; produce, to bring into being:

> All things were made by Him; and without Him was not anything made that was made. In Him was life, and the life was the light of man.

And the word became flesh and dwelt among us, [and we beheld His glory, the glory of the only begotten of the Father] full of grace and truth.

-John 1: 2-3; 14.

To know God is to know Truth in the form of:
- The person of the word.
- The power of the word.
- The characteristics of the word.
- The symbolic features and expressions of the word.

In the beginning the word was spirit. The word became flesh to serve mankind. The word is spirit and life.

It is the spirit that quickens, the flesh profits nothing; the words that I speak unto you, they are spirit and they are life.

- John 6: 63.

When God created man in His image and likeness, God made man a spirit and wrapped him in flesh. As an earth dweller if you are to live in the fullness of God, you must be transformed to become the word. God wants His sons to have all the attributes that the word has; life, truth, spirit, light, love, power, and authority in both realms, natural and spiritual.

Let the word of Christ dwell in you richly in all wisdom; teaching, and admonishing one another in psalms and hymns and spiritual songs, singing with grace in your hearts to the Lord.

- Colossians 3: 16.

Our flesh has to die daily so that the spirit and word of life can take precedence in our being. God has invested Himself in leaders who he calls gift. They are assigned by God to bring about transformation, reconciliation, restoration, and deliverance to mankind.

Leaders must submit themselves to God daily, so that they can cultivate a personal and individual walk with God. Submission to God daily is essential to prevent leaders from being ensnared by the Spirit of Error, (1John 4:5, 6) which causes leaders to teach and preach with enticing words of man's wisdom, with humanistic intelligence which does not have the ability to transform lives. The power of transformation lies in the Spirit and power of the word of God.

> And I, when I came to you, brothers, did not come proclaiming to you the testimony of God with lofty speech or wisdom. For I decided to know nothing among you except Jesus Christ and Him crucified.

> And I was with you in weakness and in fear and much trembling. And my speech and my message were not in plausible words of wisdom, but in demonstration of the Spirit and of power, so that your faith might not rest in the wisdom of men but in the power of God.
>
> -1 Corinthians 2:4.

Truth is the very words of God. Every word uttered by God is truth. What gives the words of God their uniqueness is God's originative, generative, creative make-up. He is first. He made all things and He is the Creator. Therefore all He utters and performs become the standard by which all-subsequent activities and inspirations are measured.

No one was around when God brought Himself into existence; all life began with Him. God set the standard, devised the measurements and made up the rules when there was no one around but Himself. From these he designed and created all the works of His hands.

> Through faith we understand that the worlds were framed by the word of God, so that things which are seen were not made of things which do appear.
> -Hebrews 11:3.

God calls the combination of precepts, principles, statutes, commandments and laws that govern the universe and creatures, Truth. Angels and man are obliged to it and bound by it and in our realm truth qualifies our efforts.

> Behold you desire truth in the inward parts."
> -Psalm 51: 6.

Experientially, truth is the standard by which life's realities eventually line up with Faith, which is the first born of truth. For without faith nothing will produce because faith germinates the seeds of truth which is the word of God.

Truth is the seed and faith is the fruit, the substance that lines and shapes all that truth releases. So if truth is the seed and faith its fruit and faith works by love, then love is the architect of them both, because God is love.

All truth is Parallel: Where there is a truth in the natural there is a corresponding truth in the spirit. All truth has a vital side and a legal side. Where there is a vital truth, there is the practical aspect of walking in that truth. These two types of Biblical truth are crucial to Christian understanding and maturity.

Vital Truth: Necessary to the continuation of life; life sustaining; having immediate importance; essential; indispensable.

Vital truth is the most basic and essential type of truths upon which we build our lives. They are the first principles of the oracles of God, the most basic and most important revelations of God's word that are necessary for a life of stability in the Lord.

Jesus answered and said unto him, Verily, Verily, I say unto you, except a man be born again, he cannot see the kingdom of God.

-John 3: 3.

Follow peace with all men, and holiness without which no man shall see God.

-Hebrews 12: 14.

Legal Truth: is necessary for Christian maturity and is referred to as pivotal principles, or laws, which are determining factors.

A legal truth is one that determines the direction, or effect, or outcome of something. These are the spiritual laws upon which spiritual truths hinge. The legal aspects of truth mean; it has been established, authorized, and enforced by God's laws.

As long as the earth endures, seedtime and harvest, cold and heat, summer and winter, day and night will never cease.

-Genesis 8:22.

He also said, "This is what the kingdom of God is like. A man scatters in the ground. Night and day, whether he sleeps or gets up, the seed sprouts and grows, though he does not know how.

All by itself the soil produces grain – first the stalk, then the head, then the full kernel in the head. As soon as the grain is ripe, he puts the sickle to it, because the harvest has come."

-Mark 4: 26-29.

The Efficacy of Truth: Truth's power is to produce effects or intended results; its effectiveness, efficiency and ability is to produce a desired effect or product with a minimum of effort, expense, or waste.

God's truth has different forms of manifestation. When John the Baptist spoke a word that says, "The axe is laid at the root of the tree," he was speaking a word of judgment. Truth can take the form of words of comfort, exhortation, direction, instruction, a positional word, a word of release, or a governmental word to establish order or precedence. It can take a message of hope, deliverance, warning, a Rhema word to bring clarity, order and encouragement, or it can be a futuristic word.

The word manifests in different ways and forms depending on the anointing, the messenger and the message. The word is anointed and powerful enough to destroy the works of darkness. God uses His word to demonstrate His love, to break bondages, to set the captives free, to speak into people's destiny, and to bear witness of the power of God.

Some of the features and characteristics of the word are:
1. The sword of the Spirit
2. A hammer
3. A shield
4. An axe
5. An arrow
6. A trumpet
7. A lamp
8. Water
9. Fire
10. Bread
11. Light

12. Life
13. Stone

The word manifested in the volume of a book. It can be read and handled. The word came in human form it was seen, heard and touched.

> That which was from the beginning, which we have heard, which we have seen with our eyes, which we have looked upon of the Word of Life.
>
> -   1 John 1: 1.

As the natural body without the spirit is dead, so the word without the spirit is dead. While the spirit was brooding or nesting upon the waters, the word spoke, "Let there be." The manifestation of what was spoken came into existence by the power of the spirit. The spirit and the word agreed and together they created the universe.

> Through faith we understand that the worlds were framed by the word of God, so that things which are seen were not made of things which do appear.
>
> -Hebrews 11:3.

Why does the Word have a Spirit? Why does truth need a spirit? There is the word of truth and the spirit of truth. Truth originated in God. Jesus Christ is the embodiment of truth. He is the word that was made flesh and dwelt among us. He is also the way, the truth and the life. Jesus said, "If a man does not have the Spirit of Christ he is none of His."

The physical body is made of the tangible substance of the earth, the body is earthly. Without the human spirit the physical body is dead. So too the word without the Spirit is dead. In the word is the substance of what we hope for, which is faith. Faith comes by hearing the word of God. When the Word of God is spoken, faith is released. When the Spirit of faith is released it activates the power of truth, this enabling power makes mankind free.

The Word gives the framework or the structure for the Spirit to operate. The worlds were framed by the Word of God. Just as the body without the spirit is dead, the word without the spirit cannot produce spiritual evidence or manifestation. It becomes an inoperative word when it is void of the life of the spirit, because it cannot produce a kingdom experience. There is a definite distinction between God's word, man's word and the word of devils. God's Word is truth.

For this reason people who prophesy must be careful to speak what God says because God does not lie. This is why God is so incensed against false prophets, because their word comes from the heart and mind of man, and not from of the heart and mind of God.

> Thus saith the Lord of Hosts, hearken not unto the words of the prophets that prophesy unto you: they make you vain: they speak a vision of their own heart, and not out of the mouth of the Lord.
>
> -Jeremiah 23: 16.

Our point of reference is the Word of God, it is the standard by which we live and move and have our being. But our ability, capability, our unction, our revelation, wisdom, and our anointing comes from the Spirit of Truth.

There are many spirits speaking various types of messages to mankind; religious messages, political messages, various ideologies and philosophies. Some messages also come from secret societies, cults, anti-God groups, etc., and they all have a message.

God in His wisdom spoke to the gatekeepers of the Word of God to write the vision, write His messages, so that each generation can see, touch, and handle the Word of God as it comes in the volume of the book.

God wrote His message, the Ten Commandments on tablets of stone. Moses wrote the Torah and left it for the children of Israel to read and to take heed to the laws, statutes, and commandments of God. The apostles of the new order wrote epistles to the churches to read to bring clarity and understanding. Under the New Covenant the Spirit God writes God's word in our hearts that we might not sin against God.

Fivefold ministry gifts that preach, teach and prophesy must operate within the parameters of the word of God, and under the unction of the spirit of truth to be effective witnesses of the Lord Jesus Christ.

Leadership has been given the responsibility to handle the word of God truthfully and without deception. Deception can be found in many areas of ministry. In the pulpit, among fivefold ministry leaders, among those that prophesy, and among the laity. This happens when people chose to operate their gift instead of letting the Holy Spirit operate the gift.

> Now there are diversity of gifts, but the same Spirit. And there are differences of administrations, but the same Lord. And there are diversities of operations, but it is the same God which works in all.
> – 1 Corinthians 12: 4-6.

When a person brings his or her emotions, will, mindset, biases, prejudices, confusion and unbelief into releasing a prophetic word, then that word is tainted. When a person handles the word of God deceitfully they are operating with the spirit of deception and manipulation which is witchcraft.

> But we have renounced disgraceful, underhanded ways. We refuse to practice cunning or to tamper with God's word, but by the open statement of the truth we would commend ourselves to everyone's conscience in the sight of God.
>
> -2 Corinthians 4: 2.

The word is the 'Bread of Life,' Jesus said, "Man shall not live by bread alone but by every word that proceeds out of the mouth of God." (Matthew 4:4). The word of God releases the mind of God, the life of God, the power of God, and the light of God to the world. The Spirit and the Word operate as one, and complement each other. Every word spoken in the name of God should be released under the unction of the Spirit of God.

Jesus demonstrated in the natural what happens when the bread of life is distributed. He prayed and broke the natural bread and gave it to His disciples. The disciples gave the bread to the people. Five loaves and two fishes fed five thousand men not including women and children. That is the efficacy of the word. Its power and ability to multiply, because the word has the force of exuberant life.

On the first Pentecost after the resurrection of Jesus Christ, the church was in session in the upper room. There were one hundred and twenty disciples were assembled. After Peter preached the word, under the unction of the Holy Spirit, three thousand souls were added to the church. The word with all its characteristics and its exuberance working in conjunction with the spirit, demonstrated the power and the force of the kingdom.

The Essence of the Word Is Light: The light of the word is what separates the children of God from the children of darkness. When demons see a regenerated child of God, they see the glow of the glory of God as light. Adam's covering in the Garden of Eden was the glory of God, the light of God's holy fire. When he sinned he lost his covering and used fig leaves to cover himself and his wife.

Demons are afraid of God's holy fire. That is the treasure within the reborn human spirit. Demons also know when sin is in the life of a Christian, because sin cast a dark shadow in their light. And these shadows make a Christian powerless.

> For God, who commanded the light to shine out of darkness, hath shined in our hearts to give the light of the knowledge of the glory of God in the face of Jesus Christ. But we have this treasure in earthen vessels, that the excellency of the power may be of God, and not of us.
>
> -2 Corinthians 4: 6-7.

Dark shadows are spots of darkness on the garments of light in which the believer is clothed. The effects of those spots or blemishes are to darken the glow and alert the unseen world to the change in status of the servant of God. They have instructions of how to respond to such cases and are bound to God to handle it the way God has ordained.

Demons react with glee at the prospect of getting their shot at the servant of God. Angels must fade into the background until the matter between God and the believer is resolved; however long it takes.

For some messengers of God, their ego, blindness, presumption, pride, and the like causes the matter to take years before it is settled. Oftentimes when the servant refuses to repent or has made an emphatic decision to walk contrary to God, a change of helpers takes place in the spirit, because now the servant of God is in conflict with the word of God.

Those who are truly God's elect, who know the true anointing will discern when this change has taken place. The man or woman of God may continue in office, physically holding down a position in the church, however their godly seal will be broken and their covering removed.

Do not grieve the Holy Spirit of God, by whom you were sealed for the day of redemption.

-Ephesians 4: 30.

3. THE PURPOSE OF LEADERSHIP

Purpose is the key to life. Purpose gives mankind relevance, while significance is the motivator of all human behavior and conflict. God created man for a purpose. Man has a reason for being. Everyone must ask him or herself – Why am I here on planet earth and what is my purpose for being?

When a person does not know his or her purpose for being, his or her reason for existing, they live arbitrarily and contrary to the law of God, eventually they begin a downward cycle into the abyss of oblivion, being used as a pawn in the hand of man and Satan to commit crimes against God and mankind and to live outside of the presence of God.

But when a person understands that he or she is here for a purpose, and he and she knows what that purpose is, then and only then can he or she come into agreement with the universe and be identified for who he or she is and his or her contributions to mankind. We all have to leave a legacy behind for the next generation. We have to leave our footprints in the sands of time, so the generations to come would know that we were here. We must think in terms of what is our contribution to the planet.

When you look through the hall of faith and the annals of history, there are records of great men and women who made their contribution to making this world a better place, and their

215

footprints are here for generations of men to follow. Many of them had to overcome heartaches, struggles, pain, challenges, battles, rejection, and setbacks, but many persistently and diligently pursued their dreams, because when the vision came, they looked into the future and saw themselves completing their assignment, and against great odds they strove continually for its manifestation. That is what purpose is.

All of creation is awaiting the manifestation of the sons of God. They are awaiting the next pastor, the next evangelist, the next prophet, the next apostle, the next intercessor, the next teacher, the next administrator, the next miracle worker, the next man of faith. Creation wants to identify the God's sons. The universe wants to bear witness to their message and assist them in carrying out their assignment for the kingdom of God.

It is important that every son of God knows his or her purpose, and function in the kingdom of God. Knowing your purpose will allow every son of God to be aware of his or her responsibility to God's ultimate purpose. What is your purpose? Why be the usher when God has called you to be the Pastor. There are many people who have not been placed in the Body of Christ according to their calling, and that is why governmental apostles and prophets are necessary to the Body of Christ, to bring proper order and alignment of the sons of God.

I woke up one morning and the Holy Spirit said to me, "Wherever ignorant leaders are, the people walk in darkness."

The purpose of Godly leadership is to lead the people of God into their divine inheritance as the Holy Spirit leads. Those aspiring for leadership over God's people are not to use their position for the gratification of self, or the flesh, or to feel empowered, or for a family to feel they are set financially for the rest of their life, so let us eat, drink, and be merry.

I read an article which stated that in this generation, "Leadership is no longer about the honor of leading or labor; it is about the accumulation of wealth, prestige, and power."

Someone might wonder is the writer against wealth, prestige and power? The answer is, 'no' simply because you cannot get anything done in the kingdom of God without wealth. But what this writer is intending to let the reader know is; it is not by man's might, power, wealth or influence, but it is according to the purposes of God. It is what the Spirit of God initiates and empowers.

God has to be in all, for all, and through all that we do, so He can get the glory. I have seen many wealthy men of God fall into the clutches of the enemy, and in their fall, like Lucifer, they dragged many people down with them. Some never recovered and turned away from the Lord and from the church never to return.

The writer also asked the question, "Who are the leaders of men in our cities? His answer is a provocative one. He said, "They are the diligent." The virtue of diligence is of prime importance in the moral fabric of leaders.

In an effort to underscore the eternal nature of this reality, leaders of God's people must be diligent about God's business. Leaders are supposed to take God's people from glory to glory, and ultimately the exact expression of Jesus Christ because "when we see him we shall be like him."

> The plans of the diligent lead surely to plenty, but those of everyone who is hasty, surely to poverty.
> -Proverbs 21: 5 NKJV.

The virtue of diligence is part of a Christian's list of virtues. Diligence is the disposition to think and act with proper sense of urgency and zeal. The original meaning of the word is to make haste or to be eager.

The apostle Paul said,

"But as you abound in everything – in faith, in speech, in knowledge, in all diligence, and in your love for us – see that you abound in this grace also."

-2 Corinthians 6: 7 NKJV.

The apostle Peter echoes this Pauline sentiment and places diligence in both of his lists of virtues. (2 Peter 1:5-9).

Diligent leadership starts with a determined re-evaluation of what we value. When we are clear about what we prize above all then our leadership will be clear and effective. As Jesus said, where your treasure is, there your heart will be also (Matthew 6:21).

Transformational Leadership

This is the leader that enhances the motivation, morale, performance and moral compass of his or her followers. Transformational leaders, motivate their followers by what is referred to as "Motivational Inspiration." David found a way to motivate his men, who had defected from King Saul's army. They were discouraged, in debt, and disgruntled. But under David's leadership and anointing, these men were transformed into a superior fighting army that David led to fight the wars of Israel.

Then some of the children of Benjamin and Judah came to the stronghold to David. David went out to meet them and said to them, "If you come peaceably unto me to help me, mine heart shall be united to you, but if to betray me to my adversaries, since there is no wrong in my hands, may the God of our fathers look on it and decide.

Then the Spirit came upon Amasai who was chief of the thirty and said, "We are yours O David, and with you O son of Jesse, peace, peace be to him who helps you. Indeed your God helps you!" Then David received them, and made them captains of the band.

-1 Chronicles 12: 16-18.

Transformational leaders like David always find a way to give back. David had a spirit of generosity. David taught his men the importance of generosity. This lifestyle lesson was taught after David's camp was raided by the Amalekites. God told David to pursue after them.

And David recovered all that the Amalekites had taken and rescued his two wives. But nothing of theirs was missing, whether neither small nor great, sons nor daughters, spoil, or anything that they had taken for themselves. David brought it all back.

So David captured all the sheep and the cattle which they drove ahead of the other livestock, and they said, "This is David's spoil."

When David came to the two hundred men who were too exhausted to follow David, who had also been left at the brook Besor, they went out to meet David and the people who were with him, and when David came near to the people, he greeted them.

Then all the wicked men and worthless men among those who went with David said, "Because they did not go with us, we will not give them any of the spoil that we have recovered, except to every man his wife and his children that they may lead them away and depart.

Then David said, "You shall not do so, my brothers, with what the Lord has given us, who has kept us, and delivered unto our hand the band that came against us. And who will listen to you in this matter? For as his share is who goes down to the battle, so shall his share be who stays by the baggage, they shall share alike."

And it has been from that day forward, that he made it a stature and an ordinance for Israel to this day. And when David came to Ziklag, he sent of the spoil unto the elders of Judah, to his friends, saying, "Behold, a gift for you from the spoil of the enemies of the Lord."

-1 Samuel 30:18-26.

After Saul's death, David's generosity extended to the House of Saul. David said, "Is there yet any that is left of the house of Saul, that I may show him kindness for Jonathan's sake?"

And the king said, Is there not yet any of the house of Saul, that I may show the kindness of God unto him? And Ziba said unto the king, Jonathan hath yet a son, which is lame on his feet.

And the king said unto him, Where is he? And Ziba said unto the king, behold he is in the house of Machir, the son of Ammiel, in Lodebar. Then King David sent and fetched him out of the house of Machir, the son of Ammiel, from Lodebar.

Now when Mephiboseth, the son of Jonathan, the son of Saul, was come unto David, he fell on his face, and did reverence. And David said, Mephiboseth, and he answered, Behold thy servant. And David said unto him, "Fear not; for I will surely show thee kindness for Jonathan thy father's sake, and will restore thee all the land of Saul thy father; and thou shalt eat bread at my table continually."

-11 Samuel 9: 1-8.

As a transformational leader David demonstrated forgiveness and generosity. David put an end to the long war between the House of David and the House of Saul by showing the kindness of the love of God to a member of Saul's family.

Transformational leadership:
- Heals the breaches between the houses of God.
- Facilitates the spirit of unity among the brethren.
- Promotes forgiveness and the spirit of reconciliation.
- Builds memorials in the Spirit.

There was a certain man in Caesarea called Cornelius, a centurion of the band called the Italian band. A devout man and one that feared God with all his house, which gave much alms to the people, and prayed to God always.

He saw in a vision evidently about the ninth hour of the day an angel of God coming in to him, and saying unto him, Cornelius, and when he looked on him, he was afraid and said, what is it Lord?

And he said unto him, Thy prayers and thine alms are come up for a memorial before God.

-Acts 10: 1-4.

Ministry must be generational. There must be impartation into the next generation of leaders and reproduction of a new generation of leaders. Transformational leaders extend themselves into the next generation of leadership by reproducing themselves, activating, imparting gifts and their anointing unto others.

> One Generation shall praise thy works to another and shall declare thy mighty acts.
>
> -Psalm 145:4.

Jesus stated the purpose of His Mission on earth:

> The Spirit of the Lord is upon me, because He hath anointed me to preach the gospel to the poor. He hath sent me to heal the broken hearted, to preach deliverance to the captives, and recovering of sight to the blind; to set at liberty them that are bruised, to preach the acceptable year of the Lord.
>
> -Luke 4:18, 19.

If you are an entity in the earth, you are here for a purpose. When Jesus said," I will build my church." He built His church for a purpose.

The natural building is where the church assembles. The church is made up of people that are born again. There are the ecclesia, the called out ones. There are many people who are part of the visible congregation here on earth, but they are not a part of the church of Jesus Christ that is written in the heaven. This church is identified as Mount Zion.

> But ye are come unto Mount Zion and unto the city of the living God, the heavenly Jerusalem, and to an innumerable company of angels, to the general

assembly and church of the firstborn, which are written in heaven, and to God the judge of all, and to the spirits of just men made perfect. And to Jesus the mediator of the new covenant and to the blood of sprinkling that speaks better things than that of Abel.

-Hebrews 12: 22 -29.

As head of the church, Jesus defined the purpose of the church on earth by giving His church its commission.

Go ye therefore, and teach all nations, baptizing them in the name of the Father, and the Son, and the Holy Spirit. Teaching them to observe all things whatsoever I have commanded you; and lo, I am with you always, even unto the end of the world.

- Matthew 28: 19, 20.

Let us examine two words which give the great commission its relevance.
1. Teach
2. Disciple

In a nutshell, the Great Commission commands that we go to make disciples, it should be translated, "As you are going, make disciples of all nations." The word 'teach' in the original language means make disciples. When the word "teach" is used, it implies to impart instruction, or 'to make a learner' by simply giving out the gospel. But the word "disciple" implies both giving out the gospel and the response of the recipient.

To disciple involves a definite commitment by the one who is teaching and the one who is the disciple. Hence the great commission wants us to get more than "decisions." It wants us to make disciples.

To be a disciple means that you have made a commitment to Jesus Christ and you are in the process of following Jesus Christ. It includes an initial act of conversion and the continuing experience of sanctification, where the disciple takes off what is of the flesh and put on the characteristic of Jesus Christ.

When a person is called of God, he or she is impacted and driven by his or her God given purpose. His or her mind and spirit are elevated, and he or she functions from a dimension that is not of the earth. That dimension is the spirit dimension of the kingdom of God.

God's Purpose for Abraham: Abraham was called to be a Father of many nations. He is the father of faith. To fulfill his destiny, God called Abraham to leave his country and his kindred and go into a strange land. Abraham was the starting point of recovery.

> I will make you into a great nation and I will bless you; I will make your name great, and you will be a blessing.
>
> -Genesis 12: 2.

> By faith Abraham when he was called to go out into a place which he should after receive for an inheritance, obeyed; and he went out, not knowing where he was going.

> By faith he sojourned in the land of promise, as in a strange country, dwelling in tabernacles with Isaac and Jacob, the heirs with him of the same promise.
>
> -Hebrews: 11: 8 -10.

Abraham's faith had to be tested. To fulfill purpose a leader's faith and works must be tested.

224

God told Abraham to take his son Isaac into a mountain and offer him up there for a sacrifice. Abraham believed that God would raise his son up from the dead, and he obeyed God. That act of faith and courage was accounted to Abraham as righteousness.

God has given us levels of faith:
- The Gift of faith - 1 Corinthians 12: 9.
- The Law of faith – Romans 3:27.
- The Spirit of faith – 2 Corinthians 4: 13
- The Measure of faith – Romans 12: 3.
- The Righteousness of faith – Romans 4: 13; Romans 9: 30, Hebrews 11: 7.
- The Shield of faith – Ephesians 6: 16
- The Breastplate of faith and righteousness – 1 Thess. 5:8.
- The Walk of faith – 2 Corinthians 5: 7.

When Abraham heard God's word, he walked all the way from Ur of the Chaldees to the land of Canaan. He then walked all the way to the Mount Moriah the place that God designated for him to sacrifice his son. Because of Abraham's walk of faith, God said of him.

> Abraham will surely become a great and powerful nation, and all nations on earth will be blessed through him. For I have chosen him, so that he will direct his children and his household after him to keep the way of the Lord by doing what is right and just, so that the Lord will bring about what he has promised him.
> -Genesis 18:18, 19.

God saw the quality of the man He chose. This was a father that would direct his children, and his household to keep the way of the Lord. This was a man that would do what was right and just in the eyes of God. This was a man of faith and obedience.

He was chosen but he had to qualify himself for the promise by the test of faith and obedience. To earn the position of father of all nations he had to be a man of extreme faith; a man that was a leader in his own house, before he could be a leader of a nation. His legacy is still with us today. We have become children of Abraham because of his faith. He is the father of faith.

Leaders have to think futuristically. That takes vision, planning, and faith. Where I am going takes vision. What my next level is takes planning. What my next assignment is takes faith. Who are the people I am supposed to lead, develop, enhance, impart into, and be a blessing to, these answers are in God who has the blueprints for our life and service in the ministry.

Egotistical leaders are self-centered and often selfish. They have the attitude of King Nebuchadnezzar who had the opinion that it was he who built Babylon, the great city, all by himself. No one else could get the credit for the grandeur that was Babylon, not his predecessors and certainly not the actual builders. Leaders with that mentality don't develop leaders, they use people.

You cannot accomplish anything by yourself in this world. Leaders, think of what will happen if all the people walked away from your church. Your response will be interesting and the results would be devastating. People can be your biggest headache or they can be your biggest blessing, but it is all in the way leaders appreciate, enhance, and bless the people given to them by God. A leader cannot build anything without the assistance of people.

Jesus developed men who the Pharisees considered ignorant and unlearned and Jesus called them apostles. David developed men who were ignorant, frustrated, in debt, and deserters; and he equipped them to be better husbands, fathers and warriors who would become faithful men that would commit their life to assist David in becoming the king of Israel. That is what transformational leadership is all about.

Leadership Requires Vision, Faithfulness, Diligence And Ability:

> Then I said unto them, you see the distress we are in, how Jerusalem lies waste, and the gates are burned with fire; come, and let us build up the wall of Jerusalem that we be no more a reproach.
>
> Then I told them of the hand of my God which was good upon me; as also the king's words that he had spoken unto me. And they said, "Let us rise and build." So they strengthened their hands for this good work.
>
> -Nehemiah 2: 17, 18.

Nehemiah's assignment was to build the wall around the city. How did he accomplish that assignment? He did it by delegating responsibility to the people who were qualified to build. One of the worst things a leader can do is to delegate responsibility to people who just want a title, but do not want responsibility. Nehemiah needed men who knew how to build with their hands upon the wall and their swords at their side. They had tools for building and their swords for fighting.

Leaders must learn how to delegate authority to fulfill their purpose. Ten people can accomplish more and in less time than one person. The work of the kingdom is all about people working together to achieve a common goal. We call that goal an assignment or a mission. People are the earth's greatest resource. Moses needed skilled men to build the Tabernacle;

Nehemiah needed skilled men to build the wall and to put up the gates and doors in the wall around Jerusalem.

Even though Nehemiah was the visionary, he said "So we built the wall" he did not say, "I did it," this is my wall. I built this, it is my church, this is my ministry. The wall was built by the people of God. Nehemiah said, "We built the wall."

The Leader's Personality

True leadership is not just a position over people or a title.

a. Leadership is the art of developing greatness in people.

b. Leaders are forged out of the limitless power of God and the fires of adversity.

c. True leadership is all about serving, service to a community.

d. Godly leaders must have the ability to lead people by investing their life in guiding a group of people toward the worthy goal of Christlikeness. This is service.

The leader's personality is important. Personality is defined as that which constitutes a person. It includes every attribute: emotional, mental, physical, and spiritual. It is an intangible quality about one that makes one different from other people. It is a mysterious magnetism that either draws people or repels them. It has a powerful influence, and is far-reaching in its results either for good or evil.

Personality is character plus. It adds to character the ability to reproduce itself in others. There are people with fine Christian character, but poor expression of personality. Personality is that thing about a leader which projects to the back row of a group, and holds the attention of the most inattentive member.

What contributes to personality to make it attractive? Good habits, cleanliness in thought, words, action, conduct, and daily living. The outward manifestations speak of someone within.

Some traits are inherited, many are acquired. A Magnetic personality depends more on good health, mental awareness, and spiritual qualities than on physical beauty. But if you are a leader and nobody likes you, you cannot win friends and influence people with a negative personality. People may tolerate you, but when an opportunity to walk away presents itself they would leave your ministry because they find your personality offensive.

On the other hand some people outgrow a ministry. They have a call on their life and their due season has come to move on. When people leave your ministry they should not leave because of the offensive personality of the leadership. Jesus warned us that offenses would come, and many have left churches because of offense. But when a leader leaves a local church, it should be for a plausible reason.

a. It is their due season to leave.
b. Their training in that house is complete.
c. They have a new assignment at another house.
d. Their current affiliation has brought them as far as they can go in that house. (This is true in the case of someone called to be an apostle and in presently being raised in a Pastoral House).
e. They are being led by the Spirit of God into a new chapter of preparation to fulfill their destiny.

Problems arise when leaders try to hold on to people longer than they are willing to stay. No leader owns anybody. Every child of God has the God given right to be led by the Holy Spirit (Romans 8: 14). Releasing the saints to walk in their God ordained calling has been a challenge for many pastors who don't understand the law of reproduction. Training, developing and educating other leaders will solve that problem.

The Church is not a cult. Cult leaders own people like property. They control their every move, they isolate them from the influence of other people, they separated families, and they preach their brand of doctrine which always includes a message of isolation from society. When a cult brain washes people to believe the rest of society is wrong and they are the only ones that are right. This falls under the category of "Doctrines of devils."

A Cult can be defined as a sect: The Pharisees and Sadducees were religious sects in Jesus' day. Their system of religious worship included traditions of the elders and cultural customs which made the word of God void.

Leaders must continue to educate themselves, grow in wisdom and knowledge; they must impart revelation gained by their relationship with God. They must continue to study to show themselves approved unto God as a worker that is not ashamed to rightly divide the word of truth.

A disciple is not above his leader. A child is not greater than his parents. You will never be greater than the person who gave you life. You will never be greater than the person who birthed you in ministry, because the person who birthed you has reproduced him or herself in you. You are operating with their spirit. I have seen people in the spirit and knew right away who was their spiritual father or mother, because they looked exactly like that person in the spirit.

I experienced this one morning when I walked into a church. The Pastor had a seat by the entrance of the sanctuary where he and his wife sat to greet the people before and after the service. This

Sunday was no different. When I walked in they were sitting in that seat and I greeted them as usual.

To my shock and amazement when I entered the sanctuary I looked up at the pulpit area and the pastor was sitting in his chair on the platform. Who was the person I just greeted at the front door? I turned around immediately to see who was sitting at the door of the sanctuary. What I saw was the pastor's spirit which was dwelling in someone else. In the spirit that person looked exactly like the pastor, it was one of his spiritual sons.

Jesus said to Philip, "If you have seen me, you have seen the Father." Jesus is the exact imprint of the Father, the divine expression of God. God was in Christ reconciling the world unto himself.

The Bible calls us yoke fellows, which constitutes working together with someone in ministry; or ministries working together as a team. As it is in the natural so it is in the spirit. A team of horses can plow together in a synchronized manner. A team of dogs can pull a dog sled in a synchronized manner in the Alaskan wilderness. But you cannot put a horse and a donkey to plow together, you cannot put a lion and a gazelle to hunt together, a hyena and a sheep would not get along.

You cannot put a predatory animal that is at the head of the food chain to work with a lower specie animal. A gazelle knows that the lion will have him for lunch, and a gazelle would not take any assignment to work side by side with a lion. It is highly unlikely that a bear, tiger, or a lion can be the dominant specie in the same geographical jurisdiction, lions are territorial. There will be warfare until one emerges as the dominant specie.

Leaders with dominant personalities cannot work together. In Biblical times kings covenanted to support each other without allowing their sphere of authority to be compromised. Dominant personalities have to be in charge or they will not be interested. They do not want to invest time and energy into anything that they are not in charge of. Today dominant personalities can covenant to work together for kingdom expansion.

Peter and Paul were two high ranking apostles but they could not work together because of their dominant personalities. They were governmental apostles who had the same rank in the spirit, but they had to work separately in the kingdom.

1. Peter was given the keys to the kingdom, and opened the door to the Gentile world, but his ministerial sphere was to the Jews.

2. Paul was given revelation to write most of the New Testament, his apostolic ministry was to the Gentiles.

Iron sharpens Iron. Paul had the authority to check Peter when he saw that Peter was walking contrary by being a hypocrite.

> But when Peter was come to Antioch, I withstood him to the face, because he was to be blamed. For before that certain came from James, he did eat with the Gentiles; but when they were come, he withdrew and separated himself, fearing them which were of the circumcision. And other Jews dissembled likewise with him; insomuch that Barnabas also was carried away with their dissimulation [hypocrisy]

> And when I saw that they walked not uprightly according to the truth of the gospel, I said unto Peter before them all. "If thou being a Jew live after the manner of Gentiles and not as do the Jews, why compel the Gentiles to live as the Jews."

-Acts 2: 11-15.

Another problem arose with the Apostle Paul and Prophet Barnabas that warrants our attention.

> Now there were in the church that was at Antioch certain prophets and teachers; as Barnabas, and Simeon that was called Niger, and Lucius of Cyrene, and Manaen, which had been brought up with Herod the tetrarch, and Saul.

> As they ministered to the Lord, and fasted, the Holy Ghost said, "Separate me Barnabas and Saul for the work whereunto I have called them". And when they had fasted and prayed, and laid their hands on the, they sent them away.

> So they being sent forth by the Holy Ghost, departed unto Seleucia; and from thence they sailed to Cyprus. And when they were at Salamis, they preached the word of God in the synagogues of the Jews; and they had also John to their minister.

> Now when Paul and his company loosed from Paphos, they came to Perga in Pamphylia; and John departing from them returned to Jerusalem.

> -Acts 13: 1-3, 13.

John Mark was a young man with a lot of potential, but he was not ready for that level of ministry. They took John Mark along with them as their assistant so they could focus on prayer and the ministry of the word. His responsibilities were to take care of the needs of the apostle and prophet. He was their support minister, like a minister in training, or an armor bearer.

He readily consented to go on the mission trip until he saw the warfare. The missionary journey had just begun when John Mark saw the opposition of the Jews, the threats against their life, the demonic reprisals that Paul and Barnabus had to encounter while pioneering in a new field of labor. They had to break through demonic strongholds, religious mindsets and tradition. Seeing what the apostles were up against, John abandoned the mission when he got cold feet and he departed back to the safety of the local church.

Most people want the glamour and prestige of ministry. But not too many of them want the warfare that comes with the call. What he experienced on the mission field was not what he expected. He was willing to run with the horsemen but he was not battle ready.

After sometime Paul and Barnabus decided to go back on a second trip and Barnabas wanted to take John Mark who abandoned them on the first missionary journey. Paul strongly objected. These two dominant personalities would not submit to one another. They eventually separated and took different partners and different journeys to accomplish their mission.

> And some days after Paul said unto Barnabas, Let us go again and visit our brethren in every city where we have preached the word of the Lord, and see how they do.

> And Barnabas determined to take with them John, whose surname was Mark. But Paul thought not good to take him with them, who departed from them from Pamphylia, and went not with them to the work.

And the contention was so sharp between them, that they departed asunder one from the other; and so Barnabas took Mark, and sailed to Cyprus.

And Paul chose Silas, and departed, being recommended by the brethren unto the grace of God. And he went through Syria and Cilicia confirming the churches.

-Acts 15: 36 -40.

Personality Reflects a Person's Character: Barnabas was firm in his decision to take John Mark and to give him a second chance. Paul determined that if he abandoned the mission the first time, he would do it again because he was not ready for the mission field. As powerful as these two apostles were, their personalities and leadership style prevented them from working together. Barnabus disagreed with Paul and took John Mark along with him so he could develop the gifts in him and train him because Mark was a relative, a family member.

Aristarchus my fellow prisoner greets you, and Mark the cousin of Barnabas concerning whom you have received instructions –if he comes to you, welcome him.

-Colossians 4:16.

Later on, in his ministry Paul relented and requested the assistance of John Mark.

Luke alone is with me. Get Mark and bring him with you; for he is very helpful to me for the ministry.

-2 Timothy 4: 11.

Leaders sent to the mission field, have responsibilities above and beyond the average believers who remain at home in the local church. Cross cultural decisions have to be made, and choosing the right people for the ministry team is very important. A team leader should not allow a person struggling with any addictions or any substance abuse on a mission team.

I know of the case of a pastor who took a few members on a mission trip; after checking into the hotel a member of the team left the hotel without telling anyone where he was going. He went into the city to find a drug dealer so he could get drugs to keep him while he was on the mission trip with his pastor. After searching for him for many days, the team returned home without him; he showed up some days later and refused to give an explanation about his whereabouts.

No minister should take people that need deliverance on a mission trip to another nation. Teams members have to be spiritually, mentally, emotionally and physically able to do all that is required of them. Team members must also be willing to follow instructions and understand their place and purpose on the team, and know beforehand what is the team's mission and responsibilities.

Defining Personality: Personality can be defined as a dynamic and organized set of characteristics possessed by a person, that uniquely influences his or her cognitions, emotions, motivations, and behaviors in various situations.

Cognitions are his or her mental processes, paying attention, remembering, solving problems and making decisions. Leaders have to make decisions all the time, and they have to be mentally sound to do all that is required of them.

Personality can also refer to the pattern of thoughts, feelings and behaviors consistently exhibited by an individual over time that strongly influence our expectations, perceptions, values, attitudes, and predicts our reactions to people, problems, and stress.

Personality is not just who we are but it has to do with our psychological traits, which is an attempt to understand the unique aspect of a particular individual, his or her humanistic perspective, his or her biology, behavior, social skills, his or her dispositional traits, and his or her psychological development.

When choosing a leader one has to look beyond spiritual gifts, talents, glitz and glamour to dig deeper into what are some of the qualities in that person's character that will make them a good leader. Qualities such as integrity, faithfulness, wisdom, truthfulness, the fruit of the spirit, love, mercy, the ability to carry out the mission, good understanding, loyalty and commitment. God told Samuel, "Man looks on the outward appearance but God looks at the heart" 1 Samuel 16:7).

The Sin of Presumption: A notable crisis the church is faced with in this generation is the fact that people take upon themselves callings with the appropriate titles that was not given to them by God. Apostles are needed to deal with this egregious behavior among the people of God. Apostles are mandated by God to bring order to the Body of Christ. No one can give themselves a divine calling, only God is authorized to do so in His kingdom, but in the church people do it all the time.

When uninformed people wanting attention and significance, call themselves into the ministry and give themselves a title, they do not realize that they can never be rewarded by Christ for something He did not call them to. Every ministry mandate is a summons that comes from the high court of heaven. One day they would hear Jesus say, "I never knew you," People who call themselves lack depth, grace, capabilities, fortitude, strength, balance, and Holy Spirit assistance to function in a realm and position that puts them at risk to be assaulted and diminished by dark forces, without the assistance of angels.

Both the tares and the wheat are growing among us, and they all look at ministry as a smorgasbord or a buffet table they can choose from. Then they decide what they want to be, and assume the role, believing that a title gives them the right to act and participate in a calling of their own choosing.

True apostles have the authority from God to authenticate the calling of a believer. They are wise master builders gifted with perception and discernment to ascertain those who are truly called into higher service and to place them in their God ordained positions in the Body of Christ.

Qualities That Make Good Leaders: Of all the qualities that make up the personality of a Christian leader, none are more important than sympathy, compassion and an understanding heart. A leader should also cultivate a mental attitude of giving him or herself to others. If a congregation knows their leader is sympathetic and has an understanding of their problems, they will be unconsciously drawn toward the leader they admire. They will follow him, and cooperate with him. The leader needs to know that there are people counting on him, and that he has a powerful influence on those people.

Some years ago as I was reading my Bible and a scripture jumped out at me, and kept me in a state of pursuit after God for a very long time.

> And Enoch walked with God; and he was not; for God took him.
>
> -Genesis 5:24.

At that time I had no other translation with which to compare this scripture, so the word "walked" gave the text its flavor. I said, "If this man could walk with God, so can I. But how do I walk with God?" For years this was my prayer; "Lord show me and teach me how to walk with you. What do I do to walk with you?" I did not having the understanding that we walk by faith and not by sight.

What the Lord wanted me to understand about this text is that Enoch not only had a close relationship with God but Enoch had become one with God. That literally blew my mind. This text was all about his relationship, obedience, identity, and intimacy with the Father. Jesus said, "I and my Father are one. If you see me you have seen the Father." Here Jesus was declaring His identity and relationship with the Father.

Identity, Significance and Purpose: Adam had a unique kind of relationship with God; they had fellowship at an appointed time in the cool of the day, which could be early morning or late evening. In my case the cool of the day is early in the morning. Fellowship and relationship goes hand-in-hand. Anytime relationship is broken there goes fellowship.

The most significant thing that Adam lost when he fell, was his godlike identity as a son of God. This is what gave Adam his significance and purpose. Satan took this away from Adam when he coerced Adam into disobeying God. Satan then became his master and Adam became his slave. The godlike identity that Adam lost is what man craves for; this is what gives man his significance, identity and purpose. Adam caused mankind to be changed from sons of God to slaves of Satan. After the blood of Jesus Christ exonerates man, he reverts back from being a slave to becoming a son of the Most High God.

On the Mount of Temptation Satan said to Jesus, "If you are the Son of God command these stones to be made bread; if you are the Son of God throw yourself down off the pinnacle of the temple." Satan approached Jesus with the same subtle, nonchalant, conniving, indifferent manner that he approached Adam and Eve with in the Garden. Trying to down play the significance of their identity as sons of God as though identity was an unimportant factor in a son's relationship with the Father; a relationship that had to be maintained by obedience. (Genesis 3:1-9). As a son Jesus knew who He was; God, the Father, was in Him reconciling the world back to Himself. As leaders, God is in us and has given us a ministry of reconciliation.

Jesus, came to earth as the son of man, the second Adam; yet He was the Son of God and creator of the universe. Why would the Creator of the universe, the King of kings obey the commands of a created, fallen being? Jesus knew who Satan was, He knew Satan's agenda.. As the son of man, he had to be tempted in every area that man is tempted of the devil, He had to overcome temptation, death, the grave and hell to be our advocate, high priest, redeemer and the liberator of mankind.

> Now we are the sons of God but it does not yet appear
> what we shall be.
>
> -1 John 4:2.

I had an experience with a demon that stood to resist me; I said, "Do you know who I am? I am a son of God, I am a joint heir with Jesus Christ, I am a servant of God, I have the spirit of Jesus Christ living in me, and I am a worker together with Jesus Christ." On hearing me make a declaration of my identity, my "I AM's", he fell out of the atmosphere onto the floor, looked and me and walked away.

When Peter got the revelation that Jesus Christ was the son of the living God, Jesus in turn identified Peter as Simon, Bar-Jona, son of Jona, and said to him, "Upon this rock," rock of revelation and identification, "I will build my church.

When sons of God know their identity in Christ, only then can they align themselves with the purpose of God. Divine purpose brings forth the manifestations God desires for His people. His desire is that you become a conduit of ideas that come to you directly from God, that will cause you to be transformed by the renewing of your mind.

Nothing is static. God is constantly revealing aspects of Himself, and we must conform to His will as he reveals Himself to us individually, and to the Body of Christ. This is why change is the essence of life. We are becoming. God is moving and we are changing. We are in a constant state of preparation to fulfill our individual destinies, and for the return of Christ. The Bride of Christ must prepare herself, she has to get ready. "The Spirit and the Bride says, "Come."

Eventually she has to conclude her mission and purpose on earth. Christ has to present the kingdom to the Father and the bride has to join Christ at the marriage supper of the Lamb. Jesus said it quite well "It Is Finished." And just like Jesus said it, every son must finish or complete his assignment before standing before the judgment seat of Christ for his earned reward.

4. BUILDING WITH A VISION

To begin the process of construction, every architect and master builder knows that he or she must have blue prints or a pattern to follow. A pattern and a plan is what we call a vision.

A foundation is essential to a building project. The building is erected upon a foundation. A solid foundation is fundamental to the stability of the structure built upon it. So too is the cornerstone. It is very crucial to the solidity of the foundation. Without the cornerstone, the foundation itself is not stable or strong, the cornerstone is essential.

In building a ministry or church, the cornerstone refers to the Biblical principles, or the doctrinal truths that the ministry is built upon. Structurally speaking, the cornerstone is not synonymous to the foundation but rather a special and unique part of the foundation. It is laid long before the process of laying the foundation for a ministry begins.

Definition: A cornerstone is at the corner of a building uniting two intersecting walls. They are laid so as to give strength to the two walls with which they were connected. The strength of the building depends on the cornerstone. At the cornerstone the whole structure is united, strengthened, and held together. It can be called the foundation of the foundation.

The Apostle Paul: Late in his life the apostle found himself having to explain and defend his ministry, because of accusations brought against him by the Jews. In his defense to King Agrippa he began by describing the foundation he once built his life upon, when he was still called Saul, and before he met the Lord Jesus Christ on the road to Damascus. He said:

> "My manner of life from my youth, which was spent from the beginning among my own nation at Jerusalem, all the Jews know. They knew me from the first, if they were willing to testify, that according to the strictest sect of our religion I lived a Pharisee ....indeed, I myself thought I must do many things contrary to the name of Jesus of Nazareth.
>
> This I also did in Jerusalem and many of the saints I shut up in prison, having received authority from the chief priests; and when they were put to death, I cast my vote against them. And I punished them often in every synagogue and compelled them to blaspheme; and being exceedingly enraged against them, I persecuted them even to foreign cities."
>
> -Acts 26:4-5: 9-11.

Saul's pre-Christian foundation was extreme adherence to the law even to the point of persecuting those who no longer adhered to that law. When he met Christ not only was his name changed from Saul to Paul, but his foundation changed as well.

On the road to Damascus, Saul met Christ and was given a new cornerstone upon which he was to build the foundation of his life. No longer was he to pursue 'the persecution of Christians', now, as a Christian himself, he was called to pursue the salvation of both Jews and Gentiles.

Because of the vision from the Lord on the road to Damascus, his foundation, his name, and the direction of his life changed, and the Lord transformed him from a persecutor to a disciple, a destroyer to an apostolic builder.

You'll know a vision is from God when it fits with His Scripture; when it furthers His kingdom, and when His glory is the chief goal. Later on, Paul having insight into his vision as a builder in the kingdom says:

> "According to the grace of God which was given to me, like a skilled master builder, I laid the foundation, and someone else is building upon it. Let each one take care how he builds upon it. For no one can lay a foundation other than that which is laid, which is Jesus Christ."
>
> -1 Corinthians 3:10, 11.

When God gives a leader a vision to build Him a House, the materials he uses in construction will determine his reward. The cornerstone of the House of God cannot be man's philosophy, ideas or opinions, political agendas, the manifesto of anti-Christ governments or doctrines of devils that do not embrace Jesus Christ as Lord. But the wise master builder must use God's Word, God's vision, and plan of reconciliation and redemption as building blocks for kingdom manifestation.

> Now if anyone builds on the foundation gold, silver, precious stone, wood, hay, straw, each one's work will become manifest; for the Day will disclose it, because it will be revealed by fire, and the fire will test what sort of work each one has done.

> If the work anyone has built on the foundation survives, he shall receive a reward. If any man's work

is burnt up, he will suffer loss, though he himself will be saved, but only as through fire.

-1 Corinthians 3: 12-15.

The admonition comes to us from the word of God, that in building, we must not only be sure that we are building according to the pattern given in the vision, but the materials we use in construction, and how we build has eternal rewards or consequences.

The people we lead must be led to Christ. They must become rooted, grounded and established in Christ's doctrine, He is the chief cornerstone. The Christ spirit has to be resident in those that are the sons of God. It is the Spirit of Christ and the Word of God that qualifies them to be sons. The spirit of truth and the word of truth; this makes them a joint heir with Christ.

Behold, I am laying in Zion a stone, a cornerstone chosen and precious, and whoever believes in him will not be put to shame.

-1 Peter 2: 6.

There are two vital aspects of a vision we want to consider. Both of which involves the plan, the purpose, the pattern, the strategy, and the structure of the vision.

- Birthing the vision.
- Building the vision

Spiritually, a vision is manifested through intercession and supplication. Prayer is a necessary component for birthing a vision and bringing it into manifestation in the natural. Intercession precedes and produces manifestation.

"Who had heard of such a thing? Who hath seen such things? Shall the earth be made to bring forth in one day? Or shall a nation be born at once?" For as soon as Zion travailed, she brought forth her children."

-Isaiah 66: 8

It is against the laws of nature for such a thing to happen, such a thing does not follow the natural progression of life, so the prophet is asking, "Who had heard of such a thing? It is against the laws of nature. Can the earth produce in one day? The answer is, "no".

But God who created the laws of the universe made an exception with Zion, also known as the Church of the living God, the heavenly Jerusalem, the general assembly of the first born who is enrolled in heaven. (Hebrews 12:22)

On the day of Pentecost, Peter preached to the people who were assembled in Jerusalem for the feast of Pentecost. There were people from every nation of the known world and three thousand souls were won to the Lord (Acts 2).

God's Vision for a Sanctuary in the Wilderness: God instructed Moses to erect a tabernacle to contain His presence among His people continually. Israel was sentenced to wander for forty years in the wilderness making it imperative that they maintain their worship to the true and living God. Their worship roots were embedded in the Egyptian culture; and Idolatry was a constant problem. The Tabernacle was to be built according to the pattern of the sanctuary in heaven. God gave Moses a vision of the sanctuary and no structure of this type was ever erected before in the history of man. The design, the colors, the materials to be used all came from God.

> Then have them make a sanctuary for me, and I will dwell among them. Make this tabernacle and all its furnishings exactly like the pattern I will show you.
>
> -Exodus 25: 8.

After Moses the visionary died, God told Joshua, Moses successor, "Moses my servant is dead, now you arise and take yourself and these people over Jordan" (Joshua 1:2).

A new season had come; it was a new day for Israel. Change was inevitable, for there was a new generation with a mindset that was different from their parents who died in the wilderness. This new generation grew up in the wilderness, they did not grow up in Egypt. Their root system was not developed in Egypt therefore they were not attached to the Egyptian culture.

To fix the ills of the nation with an Egyptian mindset, the generation that came out of Egypt was sentenced to die in the wilderness. Their death was the beginning of the new season, a new generation under new leadership. They would enter the Promised Land, and settle in the inheritance God promised Abraham to give to his descendants.

The new leader was a young man with a foundation in the Egyptian culture, but because he was trained by Moses, he had a different spirit. God gave him the responsibility to divide the land and give to each tribe their portion of the inheritance.

Moses brought them out, and led them through the wilderness. Now the mantle of leadership was passed onto Joshua. First, he had to take them across Jordan. The river Jordan was the line of demarcation from the old into the new. The men had to be circumcised before entering the promise-land, signifying that God has rolled away the reproach of Egypt off of them. They kept the Passover the day they crossed over Jordan and the next day the manna ceased, and a new day and a new season began. The nation of Israel began to eat of the fruit of the land of Canaan.

As Joshua took over the reins of leadership, God told Joshua:

> No man shall be able to stand before you all the days of your life. Just as I was with Moses, so I will be with you. I will not leave you or forsake you.

> Be strong and courageous, for you shall cause this people to inherit the land that I swore to their fathers to give them.

> Only be strong and very courageous, being careful to do according to all the law that Moses my servant commanded you. Do not turn from it to the right hand or to the left, that you may have good success wherever you go.
>
> -Joshua 1:5-7.

Whenever Problems Arise In Building Or Birthing A Ministry, It Is Often Due To The Lack Of These Elements:

A lack of Wisdom: A position or title does not make one a wise leader, there is an art and skill to leadership. True leadership develops people. Leadership is not about bossing people around and being controlling. "Do as I say and not as I do." That is not leadership. True leadership must be endowed with godly wisdom and understanding. Every flock of sheep needs a shepherd. Without a shepherd they will be prey to predators and thieves. Godly wisdom makes the leader aware, discerning, sensitive, prudent, skillful, diligent, persistent, and discretionary.

A Lack of Vision or Limited Vision: A lack of vision collectively means a lack of foresight, a lack of perception, a lack of prophetic insight, a lack of forecasting, a lack of anticipation, a lack of planning.

- A lack of Generational planning.
- A lack of Understanding of how Money works.
- A lack of Order and Discipline.
- A lack of Character.
- A lack of Faith.
- A lack of Prophetic direction.
- A lack of Worship.
- A lack of Prayer.
- A lack of Generosity – a lack of giving.
- A lack of Unity – where there is no unity or agreement there will be discord which is one of the things God hates.
- A lack of Competence – meaning a lack of gifted or skilled people.

A vision is something that was birthing in your spirit; something that God showed you or is showing you. A picture that God keeps bringing before you. For some it is a burden. You feel the weight of responsibility. It makes you cry, and your soul is in constant travail until you give birth to the vision. For some it's the same message, the same dream, the same idea over and over until a plan is implemented.

When the Holy Spirit impregnates you with a vision, you carry that vision in your spirit, sometimes you will have dreams and in the dream you will see yourself ministering in places where you have never been, or in an unfinished building you never knew you had begun building. God gives you glimpses of your future in dreams, and after a while, or at the set time God will arrange an opportunity.

In 1993 God gave me a dream. I dreamt I had an unfinished house in Trinidad. There were people in the front portion of the house worshiping God. My mother was one of the people in the house. They were having church services, but the building was incomplete.

The pastor was showing me around the building along with one of my brothers while the service was in progress. I was shocked to know that I had an unfinished house in Trinidad, because it is not in my nature to leave things unfinished. There were no cupboards in the kitchen, the floors were undone, there were no appliances, the house needed furniture, painting, and decorations, etc.

When we passed through the kitchen into the back yard, and I heard the sound of an aircraft overhead, and I looked up. There was a plane coming to fetch me, to take me back to America. I said to the Pastor, my flight is here and I have to leave for the airport to catch my flight, but I will be back to finish the house. The dream ended."

Curious to know what God was showing me, I returned to Trinidad the following year. My sister took me to meet a Pastor at his home. At the front portion of the building, they held church services, while the Pastor and his family lived in the back. The building was unfinished as I saw in the vision, I stood outside looking at the building in amazement; this was the beginning of a kingdom building project God was giving to me, but the vision was for an appointed time, I saw the place of its commencement but had no idea where it would take me.

That pastor has since gone home to be with the Lord, and that church is now in the hands of a new generation of leaders that I don't have relationship or fellowship with; yet I have been traveling back and forth to the nation of Trinidad ministering since that eventful day in 1993 according to the leading of the Lord. Since that time to now, God has expanded the vision and has given us a mandate to the nation.

Some of the Old Testament prophets spoke about a burden in the valley of vision. Nehemiah had a burden. His spirit was troubled when he heard about the plight of the people in Jerusalem. The situation was dire. It broke his heart, and so he prayed, fasted and mourned before the God of heaven.

> In the month of Kislev in the twentieth year, while I was in the citadel of Susa; Hanani, one of my brothers came from Judah with some other men and I questioned them about the Jewish remnant that survived the exile, and also about Jerusalem.
>
> They said unto me, those who survived the exile and are back in the province are in great trouble and disgrace. The wall of Jerusalem is broken down, and its gates have been burned with fire.
>
> When I heard these things, I sat down and wept. For some days I mourned and fasted and prayed before the God of heaven.
>
> -Nehemiah 1: 1-3.
>
> Then I said to them, you see the trouble we are in; Jerusalem lies in ruins, and its gates have been burned with fire; Come, let us rebuild the wall of Jerusalem," and we will no longer be in disgrace.
>
> I also told them about the gracious hand of my God upon me and what the king had said to me. They

replied, "Let us start rebuilding," so they began this good work.

-Nehemiah 2: 17-18.

Nehemiah's work was a rebuilding project. The original wall was torn down, and it had to be rebuilt after the original pattern.

A vision is for an appointed time. God has a time for every purpose under the heavens. When we wait on God, at the appointed time heaven and earth comes into agreement with the will of God. Jesus told us to pray that "The will of God be done on earth as it is in heaven."

God is a God of planning, creativity, design and purpose. When the set time comes for a vision to manifest, He puts the people, the opportunity, and the plan in place, and everything works together for good to them that love God and to them that are called according to His purpose.

When Jesus came to the region of Caesarea Philippi, he asked his disciples, "Who do people say the Son of Man is? They replied, "Some say John the Baptist; others say Elijah, and still other, Jeremiah or one of the prophets." "But what about you?" he asked. "Who do you say I am?"

Simon Peter answered, "You are the Christ, the Son of the living God." Jesus replied, "Blessed are you, Simon son of Jonah, for this was not revealed to you by man, but by my Father in heaven.

And I tell you that you are Peter, and on this rock I will build my church, and he gates of Hades will not overcome it.

-Matthew 16:13-17.

The revelation that Jesus was the Christ, the son of the living God was given to Peter. In response to Peter identifying Christ by revelation, Jesus then said to him, "I also know who you are. You are Simon son of Jonas and upon this rock I will build my church."

Then Jesus said, "Upon this revelation, you know me as the Son of the living God, and I know who you are." I will build my church. This knowledge of who Christ is – determines the nature of the relationship man has with Christ. Not only was Jesus going to build His church upon this revelation, but He also said to Peter, "I will give you the keys to the kingdom of heaven." Keys mean authority. Peter, you are the one that I am authorizing to open the door for the release of the kingdom of Heaven.

In Peter's world, the Jews had nothing to do with Gentiles. But in the kingdom of heaven Calvary will change all of that. God's vision for mankind – included both Jews and Gentiles. Through the church He would reconcile both Jew and Gentile to God. Reconciliation would bring an end to the hostility between Jews and Gentiles. He preached peace to those who were afar off – the Gentiles – and peace to those who were near – the Jews – near meaning bloodline descendants and seed of Abraham.

When God Gives You A Vision, It Is To Fulfill A Need Among His People.

We live in a technical age, and there are prophetic voices in the technical arena that predict what your grandchildren will be using in the next fifteen to twenty five years. They predict the type of technical devices that would be relevant in the next generation. These new advances in technology do not hit the market overnight. It takes years of strategic planning and scientific development.

Marketing plans are in place long before these devices hit the marketplace. When they reach the marketplace young consumers start lining up at the stores, days before the day of release arrives. They sleep in front of the store, because they want to be the first to have the new technology. These technical visionaries use their creative genius to birth ideas or concepts they have seen in their imagination, and they know what would be relevant in the next generation.

When they come into a creative zone, inspiration and creativity starts flowing; they spend sleepless nights and days creating, taking the vision from an idea and a concept, to a project; drawing the vision, building prototypes, shaping, testing, then producing. All this is involved before it goes into manufacturing, and onto the marketplace. That process takes time.

As a Creator, God is the architect of everything. There are creative things that were in the mind of God before the foundation of the earth. He has building plans, ideas, concepts and projects that He wants His children to implement, because God is a creative genius and He downloads into man His creative ideas and concepts that we call vision.

When God wanted to recover the earth, His vision was to birth a nation of kings and priests. That vision started with one man. Abraham is the starting point of recovery. God wanted a bloodline from which his son Jesus Christ would come into the earth. Therefore He covenanted with Abraham.

> Abram believed the Lord, and He credited it to Him
> as righteousness. He also said to him, "I am the Lord,
> who brought you out of Ur of the Chaldeans to give
> you this land to take possession of."

"Know for certain that your descendants will be strangers in a country not their own, and they will be enslaved and mistreated four hundred years. But I will punish the nation they serve as slaves, and afterward they will come out with great possessions.

-Genesis 15: 6- 19.

God is a visionary. A visionary has intelligent foresight and perception; they can see something unfolding in the future long before it becomes visible to the natural eye. Armed with foreknowledge and insight, a visionary always has a futuristic plan and purpose. In the continuum of time God gives birth to His visions, plans and ideas. He is a Master Builder who builds according to a pattern based upon a principle.

To fulfill His vision and prophetic word to Abraham, God sent one of the sons of Jacob into Egypt in advance of a world-wide famine which would eventually be the catalyst for the rest of the family taking residence in Egypt according to the prophetic word to Abraham. Seventy souls of Abraham's descendants went down into Egypt, and it took four hundred years in the womb of Egypt for the nation of Israel to be birthed.

When God delivered them from Pharaoh, and from the bondage of slavery, He met with them at Mount Sinai and covenanted with them. He gave them laws, commandments, statues and precepts to govern their lives. This united the twelve tribes as one nation under God.

A vision is wrapped around a purpose. Dreams and night visions are ways through which God communicates to all men. God gave gifts, talents and capabilities to mankind, saved and unsaved. God uses chosen ones to fulfill His ultimate purpose in the earth. He will use ungodly people even though they do not know Him, to build or to birth something that He placed in their imagination.

Most likely you had an employer who was unsaved, but had a vision to build a successful business; and God opened a door of opportunity for a child of God to be employed. Employed people pay tithes and give offerings to support the work of the kingdom of God.

The Seed Principle is both a Spiritual and a Natural law:

In the natural, when a seed is planted in soil or the earth, it goes into darkness. The root system is developed in darkness or in obscurity. Transformation of that seed takes place in darkness, the process of metamorphosis takes place in darkness.

Everything that manifests in the earth and spirit begins with a seed. Ideas, thoughts and concepts whether good or evil are seeds that have to be developed. Building projects, ministry gifts, businesses, churches, families, all began with a seed. The same operations and development take place in the natural as well as in the spirit. Man plants and waters the seed but God gives the increase.

> And He said, "The kingdom of God is as if a man should scatter seed on the ground. He sleeps and rises night and day; the seed sprouts and grows, though he knows not how.
>
> The earth produces by itself, first the blade, then the ear, then the full grain in the ear. But when the grain is ripe, at once he puts in the sickle, because the harvest has come.
>
> -Mark 4: 26-29.

A vision takes the form of a seed. It is developed in the darkness of obscurity. Nobody knows who you are; nobody has ever heard about you. Little by little according to divine timing the vision is implemented, level by level, stage by stage, before it grows into full manifestation. This is when the harvest comes when the vision begins to bear fruit. No vision bears fruit overnight. From the seed to the time of harvest the process takes time. It takes patience, faith, and diligence to manifest a vision.

Another Important Element In Producing A Vision Is The Soil:

Mark 4: 13-20 gives us an explanation in the parable of the sower and the seed, and it shows us different scenarios of why the seed fails to produce a harvest or why the vision fails to manifest.

1. Some people are like seed along the path, where the word is sown. As soon as they hear it, Satan comes and takes away the word that was sown in them.
2. Others, like seed sown on rocky places, hear the word and at once receive it with joy, but since they have no root, they last only a short time. When trouble or persecution comes because of the word, they quickly fall away.
3. Still others, like seed sown among thorns, hear the word, but the worries of this life, the deceitfulness of wealth and the desires for other things come in and choke the word, making it unfruitful.
4. Others, like seed sown on good soil, hear the word, accept it, and produce a crop – thirty, sixty, or even a hundred times what was sown.

The sower and the seed is the mother of all parables, and it lets us know that some people are such poor quality soil that they cannot produce anything.

- They don't want to give birth to anything. It is too much work. They want to inherit or take-over someone's vision or building project.
- They don't want to pay the price, or make the necessary sacrifices, financially or otherwise to produce their vision.
- Many have aborted their vision, because they have allowed people or the enemy to distract them, and others came in as wolves in sheep clothing and stole their vision.
- Then there are those who are called of God, but have not been planted in a vineyard or house that can reproduce kingdom quality leaders with a kingdom mentality.
- Many lack understanding of the call of God.
- Then there are those called ones who have no tangible fruit, because they are distracted by the cares of this life, and they lack diligence in watering the vision in order to produce a harvest.
- Those that fail in the process are like the fig tree that Jesus stumbled upon, with lots of leaves but no fruit (Mark 11:13-20). They chose the prestige of ministry, the adoration of man, the outward appearance of success, while they are accomplishing nothing with regard to the assignment that God gave to them.

Transformation and development takes place between you and God in your secret place of communication. Only God can tell you when you are ready. When the season for harvest arrives, you have to be ready to market the vision.

If your vision is to build a house of God, for the worship of God and for the edification of His people. When you stand before His people to minister the word, they will have expectations. God sends forth His word to heal, to bring enlightenment, to impart wisdom and understanding, but most of all for His people to know His ways and to know Him personally and intimately.

If they have an ear to hear, the people will want to hear the substance of the word. They want truth, not speculation or man's opinion. If the soil is good, the word will produce fruit. Good soil will receive a greater level of information, revelation, and impartation through the word; and if the water level of the word is low, anyone who can discern spiritually would know that the soil is not ready to produce a harvest.

When the Tabernacle of God was in Shiloh, Eli was the High Priest, and his two sons Hophni and Phineas were priests of the Lord, but these men were wicked men. The nation was experiencing its darkest hour, with civil unrest and lawlessness in the house of God. The Bible says, "In those days the word of God was rare, there was no open vision." There was no prophetic voice to the nation. And the lamp in the Tabernacle had gone out.

But God had a young man named Samuel, who was the seed for the new season of kingdom manifestation; He was being trained for the next dispensation in Israel. In the midst of this darkness, God called the boy Samuel and revealed himself to Samuel. His development as a prophet took place in the darkness of the corruption taking place in the House of Eli.

God began sending His word to Samuel, and in the process of time, the word of Samuel came to Israel, and all Israel knew that God had ordained him to be a Prophet. Samuel gave birth to the first school for the prophets of Israel. With this school of prophets in place, Israel would never be left without a prophetic voice to the nation. God birthed this vision through Samuel.

Samuel gave birth to the vision of a prophetic school. Elijah and Elisha continued his legacy and had schools for prophets in Gilgal, Bethel, Jericho, and Jordan because prophets needed to be schooled. The Old Testament prophetic ministry was to be a part of the foundation for the New Testament building. The House of God is built upon the foundation of the Prophets and Apostles.

> For through Him we both have access in one Spirit to the Father. So then you are no longer strangers and aliens, but you are fellow citizens with the saints and members of the household of God, built on the foundation of the apostles and prophets, Christ Jesus Himself being the cornerstone, in whom the whole structure, being joined together, grows into a holy temple in the Lord.
>
> -Ephesians 2:18-21.

In the Old Testament anyone called into ministry in Israel, was a prophet. The word of the Lord came to them and they spoke under the unction of the Spirit of Prophecy. But in the school of the prophets, Master Prophets like Samuel, Elijah, and Elisha taught the prophets principles that assisted them in developing the gift. Untrained prophets seldom know how to use their gift wisely.

Samuel, Elijah, and Elisha were governmental prophets or prophetic fathers who presided over the nation of Israel. In the school of the prophets, they chose to impart their mantle, wisdom, knowledge, expertise and understanding of the spiritual dimension to junior prophets.

The Evidence of a Vision:
- The tangible evidence of a vision or dream is its manifestation.
- Vision entails building and birthing. But there must be a plan in place, if not, the vision will fail to manifest.

God had a vision of restoration, deliverance and reconciliation for mankind and a plan for the implementation of His vision. God started with Abraham, Isaac, Jacob and then the nation of Israel. He then chose the tribe of Judah, and from the tribe of Judah He chose Mary and Joseph, and Mary gave birth to God's seed of restoration, deliverance, and reconciliation.

God operates in seasons and in the continuum of time. There is a time to every divine purpose under the heavens. He reveals His will, His plans and purpose when the set time has come for manifestation. Jesus Christ came in the fullness of time, to put God's vision of salvation into operation. God's plan involved building a house and birthing a new generation.

> But you are a chosen race, a royal priesthood, a holy nation, a people for His own possession, that you may proclaim the excellencies of Him who called you out of darkness into His marvelous light.
>
> Once you were not a people, but now you are God's people; once you had not received mercy, but now you have received mercy.
>
> -1 Peter 2: 9, 10.

Even though Jesus was the Christ, the Son of the living God, and Creator of the universe, He had to subject Himself to the laws of nature. The earth was created for man. To come into the earth environment, He had to spend nine months in the womb of a woman. A womb is the only legal doorway of entry into the earth environment for a human being.

God had to submit Himself to the laws that existed in the universe. As creator Jesus was the word that built and sustained all created things. But as the second Adam, as man, He had to submit Himself to the very laws that He put in place to sustain the universe.

Demonic strategy is always to possess a human; they want to be here legally. But Jesus gave the church power to trample upon serpentine spirits and scorpions and over all the power of the enemy, because they are here illegally; except when man gives them the authorization to be here.

When man worships idols, or participates in Occultism, man gives authority to devils to be present in his environment, and to carry out diabolic acts against mankind, and against God's plan.

Premature Birthing of a Vision: In the natural some babies were born prematurely, before some of their body parts were fully developed. Some had physical, mental, or emotional challenges. Some lived, some died, and some outgrew their deficiencies and lived a normal, healthy life.

There is a parallel truth here. Many ministry gifts or ministries were birthed prematurely or they were activated too soon and did not experience normal development. Some ministry gifts are running without a vision, running without a plan, running without a message. They are not ready mentally, morally, and most of the time they are not spiritually developed.

It is dangerous to awaken a gift too soon, especially when there is no evidence of good character, morals, virtue, godliness or righteousness in a person. Prophesy is futuristic, when a person receives a prophetic word about God's plan for their life, the rule is, they have to live a life consistent with the word of God before the prophetic word comes to pass. God's promises are conditional, a person can abort the promises of God by being rebellious, contrary, immoral, disobedient and living outside of the presence of God.

The prophet Ezekiel was called a Watchman, and as a Watchman he had certain responsibilities to the people and to God. One was to warn the righteous and warn the wicked. If not, their blood would be on him. Similarly, when people show no fruit of the spirit, no consistency by living the principles of the word, if the leadership of the church, shows lack of wisdom, judgment and discernment, and allow that candidate who has not been proven, to take their place as a minister in the house of God, then their blood and the blood of all the souls that they hinder will be on that leader.

Son of man, I have made you a Watchman for the house of Israel. Whenever you hear a word from my mouth, you shall give them warning from me.

If I say to the wicked, "You shall surely die, and you give him no warning, nor speak to warn the wicked from his wicked way, in order to save his life, that wicked person shall die for his iniquity, but his blood I will require at your hand."

But if you warn the wicked, and he does not turn from his wickedness, or from his wicked way, he shall die for his iniquity, but you will have delivered you soul."

Again, if a righteous person turns from his righteousness and commits injustice, and I lay a stumbling block before him, he shall die. Because you have not warned him, he shall die for his sin, and his righteous deeds that he has done shall not be remembered, but his blood I will require at your hand.

But if you warn the righteous person not to sin, and he does not sin, he shall surely live, because he took warning, and you will have delivered your soul.

-Ezekiel 3: 17-21.

Paul's Revelation of God's Vision: God had a vision to build a house so that both Jews and Gentiles could be fellow heirs of the same body and promises of God. The Apostle Paul had a revelation of God's vision:

How that by revelation He made known to me the mystery; [as I wrote before in few words; whereby, when ye read, ye may understand my knowledge in the mystery] which in other ages was not made known unto the sons of men, as it is now revealed unto his holy apostles and prophets by the spirit; that the Gentiles should be fellow heirs of the same body, and partakers of his promise in Christ by the gospel."

-Ephesians 3: 3-6.

The foundation is the same as the root system of a tree or a plant. It might take years to develop the root system of a mighty tree, or a great ministry. The weight of the building is put on the foundation. Similarly, the weight and strength of the vision has to be placed on the foundation, as the weight and strength of a tree is carried by the strength of the roots.

For through Him we both have access in one spirit to the Father. So then you are no longer strangers and aliens, but you are fellow citizens with the saints and members of the household of God, built on the foundation of the apostles and prophets, Christ Jesus Himself being the cornerstone.

In whom the whole structure, being joined together, grows into a holy temple in the Lord. In him you also are built together into a dwelling place for God by the spirit.

- Ephesians 2: 18-22.

From time to time the vision has to be re-evaluated. God wants us to bear kingdom fruit; only kingdom fruit remains or endures. You may have to enlarge the vision and take it from the city to the nation and then to the world. You may have to employ people with capabilities, skills, and professionalism to take the vision to the next dimension.

Evaluating Your Relationships: You may have to evaluate your relationships from time to time and ask yourself - what is this relationship all about? Are we going in the same prophetic direction? When God is calling you higher, you cannot take people with you who cannot contribute to where you are going. Abraham had to separate himself from chaos.

He told his nephew Lot, "Let there be no strife between you and me. If you take the east I will go to the west." Lot chose the well watered plains of the east and pitched his tent towards Sodom and Abraham went in the opposite direction.

But the difference was, God had a covenant with Abraham, not with Lot. Lot was a beneficiary of the Abrahamic covenant by association. Lot was wealthy because Abraham was wealthy. When they separated, we all know what became of Lot. I am sure he prospered for a while, because he became one of the elders that sat at the gate of the city of Sodom. But look at his legacy, look how his life ended; look at the mess he left behind. Abraham had to intercede for Sodom when God came to destroy the city because Lot lived there.

We have to be careful with whom and what we attach ourselves, and from whom we detach ourselves. Some people detach themselves from a life source. Abraham was a life source. He was a covenant man, and God called him Abraham because he was the father of many nations. Nations and kings were in his loins. He carried a generational blessing to the nations of the world. It was unwise for Lot to detach himself from Abraham.

I was sharing with my daughter recently about relationships. After she returned home from a reunion and birthday celebration with some of her high school friends, she was frustrated. It seemed to her that her friends never grew up. I said to her, "The friendships that I value are those that help me to continue to learn and to grow. They add content to me because of their experience and spiritual caliber. You must choose your relationships based on who you are, and where you are going.

Relationships Have To Be Defined Within The Context Of God's Vision, Plan, And Purpose.

Nehemiah's Burden:

> Then I said to them, "You see the trouble we are in, how Jerusalem lies in ruins with its gates burned. Come, let us build the wall of Jerusalem, that we may no longer suffer derision. (reproach)

> And I told them of the hand of my God that had been upon me for good, and also of the words that the king had spoken to me. And they said, "Let us rise up and build," So they strengthened their hands for the good work.

> But when Sanballat the Horonite, and Tobiah the Ammonite servant, and Geshem the Arab heard of it, they jeered at us and despised us and said, "What is

this thing that you are doing? Are you rebelling against the king?

Then I replied to them, "The God of heaven will make us prosper, and we His servants will arise and build, but you have no portion or right or claim in Jerusalem."

-Nehemiah 2; 17-20.

Nehemiah could only build the wall with people he could relate his vision to. He could not relate his vision to Sanballat or Tobiah. Nehemiah saw a need among God's people, but what made the difference was his close proximity to the king who was not of the seed of Abraham.

Nehemiah had the right connections for the fulfillment of the vision God gave him. He was the king's cupbearer; he had a relationship with God and his relationship with the king gave him the favor and resources he needed to complete the vision. God will anoint an unjust person to prosper, then use his or her wealth to fund the kingdom, to accomplish His will in the earth.

Thus says the Lord to his anointed, to Cyrus, whose right hand I have grasped; to subdue nations before him and to loose the belts of kings; to open doors before him that gates may not be closed.

I will go before you and level the exalted places; I will break in pieces the doors of bronze and cut through the bars of iron. I will give you the treasures of darkness and the hoards in secret places, that you may know that it is I, the Lord, the God of Israel, who call you by your name.

For the sake of my servant Jacob, and Israel my chosen, I call you by your name. I name you, though you do not know me. I am the Lord, and there is no other, besides me there is no other God; I equip you, though you do not know me, that people may know, from the rising of the sun and from the west, that there is none besides me. I am the Lord, and there is no other, I form the light and create darkness, I make well-being and create calamity. I am the Lord, who does all these things.

-Isaiah 45: 1-5.

As a visionary you must know when God connects you to that key person who will bring your vision to a place of realization, and manifestation.

When God gives you prophetic insight into the next season of your life and ministry, it is time for change. Abraham had to leave Ur of the Chaldees and Haran to go into Canaan to fulfill his destiny and the will of God for his life. But he did not get wealthy until he went into Egypt. The King and the noble men of Egypt gave Abraham his wealth.

When Abram entered Egypt, the Egyptians saw that the woman was very beautiful. And when the princes of Pharaoh saw her, they praised her to Pharaoh. And the woman was taken into Pharaoh's house.

And for her sake he dealt well with Abram; and he had sheep, oxen, male donkeys, male servants, female servants, female donkeys, camels.

But the Lord afflicted Pharaoh and his house with great plagues because of Sarai, Abram's wife. So Pharaoh called Abram and said, "What is this you have done to me? Why did you say, "She is my sister," so that I took her for my wife? Now then, here is your wife; take her, and go."

And Pharaoh gave men orders concerning him, and they sent him away with his wife and all that he had.
–Genesis 12: 14-20.

When heaven demands change, God will change your ministry mantle. God will change your spirit. God will change your heart and God will even change your geographical location. God will increase your capacity, while He is stretching your faith, increasing your grace and elevating your measure of understanding to a kingdom dimension. God will give you a new direction, and connect you to the right people. God will increase your anointing, and God will upgrade you.

When The Wind Of Change Is Blowing, If You Want To Be Relevant In The Next Season You Must Embrace Change.

I was sitting on my sofa reading my bible when I saw a mantle in the spirit. On my return from my ministry trip, I saw the mantle again, this time it was bigger. God had upgraded my ministry mantle to carry the weight of new responsibilities. An increase in the size of the mantle enables one to carry the weight of the new anointing and responsibilities in proportion with the upgrade or the new level of ministry.

Anytime you are planting in the kingdom of God, if the fruit of what you are doing fails to manifest, it is a sign that there is a problem. One of the areas you must check is the quality of the soil you are planting in. If it is poor quality soil like wayside soil, then the soil needs to be upgraded. Wayside soil, thorny soil, and stony soil are all unproductive. They cannot grow a vision. The seed you are planting may be quality seed, but the soil is not quality soil. The wise sower then has to look for good soil to sow his seed, a place where the soil is receptive to the quality of the revelation and ministry you are releasing. Sometimes the sower has to move on to find greener pastures.

The apostle Paul called himself a "Wise Master Builder." He built with the word. He extended the kingdom message by sowing a quality word of revelation which was the building blocks for the Spirit of the kingdom being released within people, and the establishing of churches wherever he and his team went.

In this season of kingdom manifestation, the principles, guidelines, systems, authority, fruitfulness, and dominion of the kingdom must be taught by the visionary who must operate from the deeper mind of God. God must be above all, in all, through all, and that comes from intimacy with God. Intimacy causes one to be impregnated by the Holy Spirit with the mind of Christ and the God-given abilities and gifts to release the vision.

When the vision takes on the dynamics of the kingdom of God, the old principles by which you lived and operated your ministry must change. God has to change your heart. He has to put a different mantle and anointing on you. He has to upgrade or renew your mind to accommodate a kingdom mentality and spirit.

You have to go to another dimension in the spirit where keys are given, Peter received keys to the kingdom, David had keys to the kingdom. When God gives you keys to heavenly knowledge, revelation, divine wisdom, and understanding, it comes with certain things; a new mantle, a fresh anointing, fresh grace, and an updated vision to implement what God is calling you to.

David had three levels of anointing:
- Samuel anointed him to be king. [1 Sam. 16:13]

- The elders of Judah anointed him to be king over Judah. [2 Sam. 2:3]
- The elders of Israel anointed him to be king over Israel. [2 Sam. 5: 3]

David was also a worshipper and a warrior who fought the wars of God. It was not until he was king over Israel that David wanted to build a house for God. As king over Israel, David had the anointing, the position, the authority, the favor of God, and the wealth to undertake that extremely extravagant and expensive project.

God told David, "His son Solomon would build the house." God is a designer, an architect and a builder. He gave the blueprints of the house to David because it was David's heart's desire to build a house for the presence of God. But the design for such a palatial house could only come from the mind of God.

God gave David the blueprints for the type of house that would be suitable for the king of kings; a house that a God of His magnitude and magnificence as the Creator of the universe, would dwell in. The vision of the house came with instructions, structure, and order. David wrote the vision down and gave it to Solomon with a charge. The vision was birthed by David but built by Solomon.

David's Address to the Nation's Leaders:

David summoned all the officials of Israel to assemble at Jerusalem. The officers over the tribes, the commanders of the divisions in the service of the king, the commanders of thousands and commanders of hundreds, and the officials in charge of all the property and livestock belonging to the king and his sons, together with the palace officials; the mighty men and all the brave warriors.

King David rose to his feet and said, "Listen to me, my brothers and my people. I had it in my heart to build a house as a place of rest for the Ark of the covenant of the Lord, for the footstool of our God, and I made plans to build it, but God said to me, "You are not to build a house for my name, because you are a warrior and have shed blood.

God's Choice of a Successor to David:

Of all my sons – and the Lord has given me many – he has chosen Solomon to sit on the throne of the kingdom of the Lord over Israel. He said to me, "Solomon your son is the one who will build my house and my courts, for I have chosen him to be my son, and I will be his father. I will establish his kingdom forever if he is unswerving in carrying out my commands and laws, as is being done at this time.

David's Charge to Solomon:

And you, my son Solomon, acknowledge the God of your father, and serve Him with wholehearted devotion and with a willing mind, for the Lord searches every heart and understands every motive behind the thoughts.

If you seek Him, He will be found by you; but if you forsake Him, He will reject you forever. Consider now, for the Lord has chosen you to build a temple as a sanctuary. Be strong and do the work.

1 Chronicles 28: 1-3; 5-9.

God Chooses His Sons to Build His House:

- Moses was commanded to build a tabernacle or a sanctuary for God according to the vision God showed him in the mountain of God. Moses was God's son.

- David had a desire to build God a house. God gave him the pattern of the house, but God wanted Solomon, David's son, to build the house. David and Solomon were God's sons.

- Jesus who was of the lineage of David also declared, that He would build a house for God. Jesus was God's son.

Moses, David, Solomon and Jesus were monarchs. They had the status of kings with a governmental anointing. But the house that Jesus built was different in that it had natural building blocks (people, lively stones). But the true nature of the house is spiritual. All the saints that have gone on before make up this spiritual house along with those that are alive in the earth, whose spirit has been born again and have experienced transformation, having passed from spiritual death to spiritual life.

> You also, like living stones, are being built into a spiritual house to be a holy priesthood, offering spiritual sacrifices acceptable to God through Jesus Christ.
>
> For the scripture says, "See, I lay a stone in Zion, a chosen and precious cornerstone, and the one who trusts in Him will never be put to shame."
>
> - 1 Peter 2: 5-6.

In the Spirit, the Church is called Mt Zion:
> But you are come to Mount Zion, to the heavenly Jerusalem, the city of the living God. You have come to thousands upon thousands of angels in joyful assembly. To the church of the first born, whose names are written in heaven?

You have come to God, the judge of all men, to the spirits of righteous men made perfect. To Jesus the mediator of a new covenant and to the sprinkling blood that speaks a better word than the blood of Abel.

- Hebrews 13: 22-23.

When David became king, the city and seat of government was called Zion, the city of David. Zion was a fortress. David built in Zion the Tabernacle of David, a tent to house the Ark of the covenant, which represented God's government. As David aligned himself with the kingdom of Heaven, he placed singers and worshippers around the Tabernacle of David to worship God continually day and night. (1 Chronicles 16:1-7;

Building Demands Persistence, Diligence, Keen Insight, Competence, and Wisdom.

After the seventy year exile, the Temple had to be rebuilt. Zechariah, the prophet lived at a time when Jerusalem was being rebuilt, but the Temple still laid in ruins. It had to be rebuilt to keep the people from falling into spiritual chaos and fragmentation. Through this great effort to rebuild the Temple the spiritual life of the nation would be strengthened and preserved, and through this revitalized people of the covenant, the Messiah would come.

Haggai and Zechariah sought to awaken the nation from its indifference. The people responded, and the building was completed in 516.BC. Zechariah also had a deep interest in the family of David, and the preservation of this royal line. He believed in the great prophecies concerning the Messiah, who would be a son of David. This is why he looked with such hope to Zerubbabel, the governor of Judah, a descendant of David.

Zerubbabel never fulfilled the magnificent hopes which Zechariah had for him but he was an instrument in God's ongoing purpose. He strengthened the spirits of the discouraged Israelites and kept alive the hope of the promised "Son of David." The nation continued to have this hope that one day a son of David would come and restore the kingdom back to Israel.

At the ascension of Jesus which marked the end of His earthly ministry, knowing Jesus was the Messiah, the son of God, and the son of David, the disciples asked Jesus, "Will you at this time restore again the kingdom to Israel?"

They did not understand that even though Jesus was of the lineage of David, the one who the Bible calls a root out of dry ground (Isaiah 53:2). Jesus did not come to restore the natural kingdom of David. He said, "My kingdom is not of this world." Entrance into his kingdom is through the born again experience. His kingdom is God's rule, authority and principles; righteousness, peace, and joy in the Holy Spirit. We have this treasure in our earthly bodies. Kingdom building is a New Testament enterprise. The building is done with the revelation of Christ in the word of God.

> Jesus answered and said unto him, verily, verily I say unto you, except a man be born again, he cannot see the kingdom of God.
>
> - John 3:3.

The Apostle Paul called himself a wise master builder. He built the kingdom in the hearts of the people. He built with the word of wisdom and revelation. Jesus said, upon this rock I will build my church.

> Then Barnabas went to Tarsus to look for Saul, and when he found him, he brought him to Antioch. So

for a whole year Barnabus and Saul met with the church and taught great numbers of people. The disciples were called Christians first at Antioch.

- Acts 11:25, 26

The apostle Paul said, "You will understand my knowledge in the mystery of Christ which was given to me by revelation." The apostles were building the church without the benefit of the New Testament. Revelation came from the Law and the Prophets. But the mystery of Christ, His resurrection and the kingdom had to be revealed by the Spirit of God. Men spoke from God as they were carried along by the Holy Spirit (2 Peter 1:21).

> For this reason I, Paul, a prisoner for Christ Jesus on behalf of you Gentiles, assume that you have heard of the stewardship of God's grace that was given to me for you. How the mystery was made known to me by revelation, as I have written briefly.

> When you read this, you can perceive my insight into the mystery of Christ, which was not made known to the sons of men in other generations as it has now been revealed to his holy apostles and prophets by the Spirit.

> This mystery is that the Gentiles are fellow heirs, members of the same body and partakers of the promise in Christ Jesus through the gospel.
> -Ephesians 3: 1-6.

Every New Testament Ministry Has To Feel The Impact Of The Cross.

There are Old Testament principles that the cross abolished. Figurative laws were reverted into New Testament applications,

276

and the apostles had to teach these New Testament applications under the unction of the Holy Spirit.

Old Testament principles when they hit the cross shifted: Ceremonies like circumcision of the flesh became circumcision of the heart. The old Levitical priesthood was abolished, and Christ became our eternal High Priest under a new order; the order of an endless life. The cross abolished animal sacrifices and Jesus became God's atoning sacrifice for the sins of the world.

One law that was unchanged when it went to the cross was the law of seed time and harvest, cold and heat, summer and winter, day and night. That law will remain the same as long as the earth endures. Seed time and harvest was not affected by the cross.

Discerning the Time of Visitation: In building and birthing a vision sometimes the season will demand change, and if the leadership does not recognize that the season for change has come, they will remain stuck in a legalistic, dispensational time warp. That is what happened to Israel.

There were people in Israel praying for the Messiah to come and the restoration of the kingdom to Israel. Anna the prophetess, and Simeon came into the temple to greet the Christ child when his parents brought him in eight days after he was born. They knew that child was the Messiah, but where were the other prophets in Israel?

The Messiah came and they did not know it. They thought Jesus was just another prophet. The legalistic Jews did not receive Him; the nation did not know the time of their visitation. Similarly, a local church or a ministry gift can miss his or her time of visitation, mainly because some leaders have the spirit of the Pharisees. They want to control the move of God.

Controlling leaders like the Pharisees are often plagued by the spirit of jealousy, and think that God must always accommodate their point of view. When a person or a local church misses his or her time of visitation or elevation due to ignorance or disobedience, there are consequences.

Israel spent forty unnecessary years in the wilderness wandering. Their disobedience, murmuring, complaining and idolatry caused God to place a sentence of death on them. That generation would never see the Promised Land, and would never inherit the Abrahamic blessings.

Are You Building Something That God Did Not Tell You To Build?

I was ministering to a congregation when a woman came forward and asked me to pray for her ministry. I said, "What is the name of your ministry?" After giving me the name, the Spirit of the Lord said to me, "We have a dilemma here, there is no ministry with that name written in the kingdom of heaven." She said, "But God gave me that name." I said, "Maybe He did, but for something else. There is no ministry with that name recorded in heaven."

The vision and blueprints for every ministry given to man by God is recorded in the heavens. In the same way in every city or town the blueprints and records of every building, house or property is recorded at the town hall or the city hall, along with the name of the present owner, the year the property was built, the dimensions of the property, the history of ownership, any improvements that were made to the structure, the construction materials, the price paid for the property by the current owner, and any other relevant information that pertains to the property. And there is such a thing as property taxes that every citizen with property must pay. We have the same equivalent in the enterprise of God. His buildings have to be bought and maintained by His people (Malachi 3: 8-10).

Building in an Antagonist Environment: A vision starts as a seed and goes from level to level, developmental stage to developmental stage. As it ages, you will be able to look back years later, and be amazed at how the vision has developed, if you are building after the plan God gave you.

God continually adds to the vision, allowing it to enlarge, and stretch out, so that it can produces a greater harvest. The vision can become a great tree (symbolic language), and others will be able to eat of the fruit of the tree. When a vision grows to that dimension it will have the capacity to help others with their vision, by sowing seed into their building project. In that way there can be a continuous flow of generational seeds and blessings.

However, sometimes the seed is planted in an antagonistic environment, and that happens for various reasons, mainly because of the way people think if their minds have not experienced transformation, if that is the case, whatever comes out from the heart of God and deposited in that environment will not be received. When that happens a spirit of abortion is resident in that environment.

It is not inconceivable to think that in the Body of Christ a vision be can be aborted if it is birthed in an antagonistic environment. The visionary will have to make a decision whether to obey God or change his or her affiliation and environment.

After Israel left Egypt and covenanted with God to be a nation, their thought patterns and behavior never changed because they were rooted in the Egyptian culture; that was all they knew. The Egyptian culture was rooted in ritualistic idolatry.

The wilderness was a new environment but their behavior never changed. Their root system was developed in Egypt. God delivered them from the land of Egypt, from the power of darkness, affliction, imprisonment, and bondage. But the culture of Egypt was so embedded in them, that the spirit of Egypt was constantly dragging them back to where God delivered them from; and they brought the culture of Egypt with them in their heart into their new environment.

God made them multi-millionaires when they left Egypt, but with all their wealth their mindset never changed, because their generational roots and paganistic system of worship is something they cherished. They complained, murmured, and provoked God until God wiped out that generation and only those twenty years and younger lived to enter the promise land.

In this season of kingdom advancement, many denominations are trying to move forward in the spirit of kingdom building, while trying to maintain their religious traditions. Change will take them out of their comfort zone, and many leaders do not want to offend the faithful few. They do not want people getting angry and leaving the church so they continue with religious programs, elementary sermons void of revelation and inspiration, with no insight into the mind, will, purpose and the current move of God.

The Challenge of Growing a Vision: The biggest challenge in ministry is taking a small vision and growing it up to an experience, which does not happen overnight. Why it is such a challenge? It could be the mindset of the people; cultural customs, religious tradition, the lack of financial support, and the lack of competent leaders or skilled people.

But as a new generation of leaders take their place in the kingdom. We are seeing that the problem with the church is our root system. God has to pull our minds out of somewhere dark and inhibiting in order to bless the new generation that is crossing over Jordan to enter their inheritance. And this is why transformation is so essential. We have to adapt to a kingdom mentality and culture. In the kingdom of God prayer is not an event, it is the culture of the kingdom.

Inheriting the Limitations of the Womb That Gave You Birth:

When a vision is a fetus, you have to keep feeding it. Sometimes your vision does not have a definition; you don't know what you are giving birth to. You don't know what this baby will be like when it grows up, but as you continue to pray the revelation will come.

Rebekah, Isaac's wife, had no idea of what she was carrying in her womb, but when she went to God, He told her there were two nations in her womb. The seed for two nations were in her womb.

After you give birth to your vision, there is the pediatrics of the vision. You have to grow the vision up, and bring it to adulthood so it can bring forth fruit.

There were two men born with an impediment. One was a man that Jesus healed who was born blind, and the other was a man who was born crippled that was laid at the beautiful temple gate each day. The apostle John and Peter healed the man. They were both born with an impediment they acquired in their mother's womb.

The womb is symbolic of the place where your ministry is developed before it manifests. Figuratively speaking, sometimes you inherit the limitations of the womb that gave you birth; meaning when you are carrying a vision you have to be careful of what you are releasing with your mouth, because you are either releasing a judgment or a blessing that would come back to you in your future. You will inherit the negativity of your religious culture and it will reproduce itself in your ministry.

Pharaoh ordered the midwives to kill the sons of Israel that were born in Egypt. Herod ordered that all babies two years old and under to be killed. The sons were the seed for the next generation. Both Pharaoh and Herod were trying to abort God's vision.

When Jesus came into the earth He was born into an antagonistic environment when the nation was under the rule of Rome. King Herod was a wicked man, a murderer. God told Joseph to take His seed, Jesus, into Egypt until the death of Herod. At that time Egypt had become a safe place to hide the Son of God.

Similarly, you will be met with resistance by leaders with the spirit of Pharaoh and Herod. The Pharisees and Sadducees were religious. They operated under the guise of religion, but their heart was no different, they too were murderers. They passed judgment on Jesus because they envied Him and because they wanted to pull Him back into the letter of the law.

But Jesus knew His purpose. He understood the Father's vision and what His assignment was. He knew his assignment was to fulfill the law and to meet God's demands for justice, so mankind could be exonerated from the curse of sin and death.

He had to be the atoning sacrifice for mankind; to undo the works of Adam who released judgment on all of mankind. As Savior and Redeemer, Jesus came to reverse that judgment. Therefore He could not operate with the religious system that was in place, because it was designed to pass condemnation instead of releasing blessings.

There is therefore no condemnation to them that are in Christ Jesus who walk not after the flesh but after the Spirit.

- Romans 8:1.

A New Generation of Leaders: This is a different era and we have a new generation of leaders in the Body of Christ with a different mindset, and a different tone. They don't want to experience demonic struggles and demonic pain. They want to experience liberty, anointing, success without sweat, and the powers of the world to come without paying the price for anything. They have a sense of entitlement. They want their gifts to open doors for them, and they want to be successful in ministry without doing the work of laying a foundation.

And the people served the Lord all the days of Joshua, and all the days of the elders who outlived Joshua who had seen all the great work that the Lord had done for Israel. And all that generation also were gathered to their fathers. And there arose another generation after them who did not know the Lord or the work that he had done for Israel.

-Judges 2: 6-7, 10.

Similarly, as a new generation of Israelites rose up after Joshua and all the elders of Israel from the previous generation had passed away, this new generation did not know anything about Egyptian bondage or life in the wilderness. Wearing the same shoes and clothes in the wilderness for forty years, and eating manna every day, that was not their experience.

They inherited the benefits that God gave to their parents, the promises God made to Abraham, Isaac, and Jacob. They had land, houses, and cattle; the riches of what the earth produced. Everything was handed to them and there was no reason to be thankful or grateful. They felt a sense of entitlement like most privileged kids often do.

Because they did not know struggle or warfare their heart turned away from God, as they looked at the heathen nations around them, they began to emulate their form of worship and lifestyle. They forsook their God and forgot about His statues, precepts, laws, commandments, and the constitution God gave them to live by and to govern the nation. They began to adopt the paganistic lifestyle and religion of the heathen who worshipped idols and practiced sorcery and other forms of witchcraft.

Every new generation is faced with the same options. New leaders, who have not experienced warfare, do not want to struggle to build or birth anything. Some of them are educated with Biblical knowledge at seminary schools of religious thought that birthed in them Biblical principles and religious philosophy. When they graduated from Seminary they were given a church to pastor and because they never experienced birthing, they too have a sense of entitlement. They expect to reap where they did not sow, they want to be in charge of a vision they did not invest money, time, effort, or prayer in building.

They want to take over what some visionaries remained on their knees for sleepless nights to give birth to; what they contended with the devil for; what they invested in and made financial sacrifices to obtain. They want a ready-made ministry, and they don't want to pay for anything. As far as they are concerned ministry is a job for which there must be great rewards of prestige, money, privileges, honor, and people's allegiance. And leaders with this mentally are always selfish, self-centered, prideful, and ungrateful.

They want your church, they want your ministry, they want your money, they want your blessings and they want your allegiance to Christ to be turnover to them. They want to manage your life and your ministry. They want to tell you what to do and how to do it. They want your worship; they want to be your God.

So we have a culture in the church that has given rise to predators. People looking for opportunity to steal, disarm, and insert themselves into ministries with the hope that they will take it over. Especially ministries or churches that are headed by women, they will act as if they are a friend of the ministry, when all the while they are planning a coup or to annex that ministry to theirs so they could reap the fruits of it.

Before his departure the apostle Paul gave an admonition to the church at Ephesus:

> "Pay careful attention to yourselves and to the flock, in which the Holy Spirit has made you overseers, to care for the church of God, which he obtained with his own blood.
>
> I know that after my departure fierce wolves will come in among you, not sparing the flock, and from among your own selves will arise men speaking twisted things, to draw away the disciples after them.
>
> Therefore be alert, remembering that for three years I did not cease night and day to admonish everyone with tears. And now I commend you to God and to the word of His grace, which is able to build you up and to give you the inheritance among all those who are sanctified.
>
> -Acts 20: 28-32.

I. APOSTOLIC DEFINITION

And He went up into a mountain and called to Him those whom He desired, and they came to Him. And He appointed twelve (whom He also named apostles) so that they might be with Him and He might send them out to preach and have authority to cast out demons.

-Mark 3: 13-15.

Every nation has some form of government. The church is a holy nation. Apostles are governmental and foundational gifts to the New Testament church. They along with governmental prophets are part of the foundational structure of the church.

For unto us a child is born, to us a son is given and the government shall be upon his shoulders, and his name shall be called Wonderful, Counselor, Mighty God, Everlasting Father, Prince of Peace.

Of the increase of his government and of peace there will be no end, on the throne of David and over his kingdom, to establish it and to uphold it with justice and with righteousness from this time forth and forevermore. The zeal of the Lord of Hosts will do this.

-Isaiah 9: 6, 7.

The first twelve apostles formed the apostolic foundation of the New Testament church. The church is built upon the foundation of the apostles and prophets. Jesus Christ is an apostle and He is the chief cornerstone of the church.

> And he carried me away in the spirit to a great, high mountain, and showed me the holy city Jerusalem coming down out of heaven from God.
>
> It had a great, high wall with twelve gates, and at the gates twelve angels, and on the gates the names of the twelve tribes of the sons of Israel were inscribed.
>
> And the wall of the city had twelve foundations, and on them were the twelve names of the twelve apostles of the Lamb.
>
> -Revelation 21: 10, 12, 14.

The word apostle came from the Greek word *Apostolos* which means a delegate, an ambassador, one that is sent from one place to another to accomplish a special mission. Apostles therefore are sent ones with a pioneering anointing. They are faithful to transmit or reflect the intentions of the sender. This is the primary attitude of a true apostle. They carry a stronger anointing and carry a greater degree of power and authority.

The wide range of authority given to an apostle enables him or her to release people into their God ordained calling and function in the Body of Christ. Unlike the pastor, apostles have the authority to release apostolic and prophetic gifts, and other supernatural ministries in the local church.

If the church is to transition into an apostolic position, the minds of the people must be renewed for the people to receive a revelation of the present plans and purposes of God. Apostles and governmental prophets have been given insight into the mysteries of the kingdom of Heaven. Jesus told His apostles, "It is given unto you to know the mysteries of the kingdom of Heaven."

Pastoral Mindset vs. the Apostolic: The apostolic anointing differs significantly from the pastoral anointing in that it is a pioneering gift which executes and releases new things and new ministries. The pastoral gift thinks in terms of gathering, protecting, maintaining order, restricting and controlling. Many would-be apostles and governmental prophets under a pastoral ministry will find themselves restricted and held back, and will be frustrated because the anointing on a pastoral house is not sufficient to activate spiritual gifts of a higher dimension and releasing them into their divine destiny.

What can a pastor do with someone who has the governmental anointing of an apostle or a prophet? For the most part that pastor will restrict that anointing from being released in the house, because of fear of losing control. Most leaders have been trained to think pastorally, and even though they sense an apostolic call, they cannot identify with it, and some because of tradition, do not know how to make the transition into the apostolic mindset.

The pastoral mindset has hindered many that have higher callings from transitioning into the apostolic call. You cannot fulfill an apostolic calling with a pastoral mindset. A pastoral mindset confines the leader to the local church to meet the needs of members. However, many pastors are being challenged to embrace and walk in the apostolic anointing. The pastoral mindset has its limitations, and an apostle cannot fulfill an apostolic calling with a pastoral mind-set because of its customs, limitations, and tradition. The apostolic mentality is quite different from the pastoral mentality.

Apostolic Dimensions: Apostolic is not a denomination. An apostle is one of the fivefold ministry gifts given by Christ to the Church. Apostles are God's first appointment as members of the Body of Christ. To understand the church as the building of God, you have to see the apostles as a foundational ministry. A foundation in any structure is indispensable. It provides strength, stability, and is the key to expansion.

The apostle serves with the prophet to lay the foundation to serve the building of God, while the entire building receives its alignment and positioning from the cornerstone, Jesus Christ.

> And God has appointed these in the church: first apostles, second prophets, and third teachers, after that miracles, then gifts of healings, help, administrations, varieties of tongues, workers of miracles. Do all have gifts of healings? Do all speak with tongues? Do all interpret?
>
> -1 Corinthians 12: 28-30.

> Having been built on the foundation of the apostles and prophets, Jesus Christ Himself being the chief cornerstone.
>
> -Ephesians 2: 20.

Apostles do not mature overnight; every ministry gift matures and develops gradually. The function of an apostle and prophet has been so abused; some have even called themselves to these offices. But how is a person identified as an apostle?

- An Apostle needs to know God's call.
- God never leaves Himself without a witness; therefore, the call needs to be confirmed.
- Then the call needs to be recognized by the church.

After recognizing the call, room must be made for the spiritual development of the ministry. Peter is an example of a man who began his apostleship full of instability and irrationality, but eventually he grew into a powerful, able man of God, whose maturity was glorious. Even in his instability, Peter was an apostle under construction.

The Lord builds upon the potential of a person. Even though they may be called an apostle, the immature seed of apostleship is present deep within his or her spirit. God calls apostles long before anyone recognizes them, long before the details of their development are identified and processed. No apostle is alike. They are a diverse group, and no single apostle sets the water mark for the ministry of apostles.

Outside affirmation is essential to identifying the call. Eventually the call would progress into a clear prophetic summons and sanction. We do so by selecting, ordaining, and setting legitimate apostles into office as given in the account of the church at Antioch when Paul and Barnabus were singled out by the voice of God for the work God called them to do. Apostolic selection is a spirit-led activity that is done publicly and in the arena of prayer and worship. To proceed in apostolic ministry without the prophetic presbytery, and public affirmation and ordination is entirely out of order.

The laying on of the hands of the presbytery and the impartation of the divine anointing is vital. This is the final seal upon the calling and commissioning of an apostle. The gift will come intuitively and will ultimately progress to an impartation of supernatural power.

As there are a variety of operations in the ministry of prophets, pastors, evangelists and teachers; so too does the apostle minister in a variety of functions and spheres. Not all apostles have the same ministry or activity. Therefore, comparing one apostle with another is not wise.

> Now there are diversities of gifts, but the same Spirit. There are differences in ministries but the same Lord. And there are diversities of activities, but it is the same God who works in all.
>
> -1 Corinthians 12:4-6.

Apostles must be conscious of the measure of their jurisdictional authority, they are limited by the sphere that God has assigned them to, in order to become everything that God wants them to become. Paul was an apostle to the Gentiles. Peter was an apostle to the Jews. The twelve were sent to the lost sheep of the house of Israel. At that time they were forbidden to go to the Samaritans [Matthew 10:5].

Apostles can prophesy, evangelize, teach, and even pastor a church. Some are more prophetic, some are more evangelistic, and some are more pastoral. The fivefold ministry gifts were given to edify and perfect the church and each gift has its own function. But the apostolic anointing flows through order. Only when the church is in the right order it will be successful. Many local churches are suffering because of the lack of order. They do not understand the order of God.

Apostolic Diversity

▪ THE LOCAL CHURCH APOSTLE — He or she has pioneered a local church, or opened the door to start a church in a community or city. Local apostles are limited to the locality or city where they have pioneered the work, mainly because they do not have the strength to go beyond the realms or scope of that particular community. Their seat of authority is the local church. But the apostolic anointing will allow him or her to govern that particular community or city in the realm of the spirit. The apostolic anointing will also enable the apostle to assist the people in their jurisdiction because of the governmental authority given to the apostle by God.

Everyone who starts a church is not an apostle. No one should take on responsibilities that God did not give to them. No one wants to wear the label as a false ministry gift operating outside of his or her sphere of authority. The enemy quickly recognizes people operating under a false anointing, because in the realm of the spirit they would not be identified or recognized and a spirit of error or deception would attach itself to the person.

- REGIONAL OR NATIONAL APOSTLES – Apostles that fit into this category have a measure of authority within a region, a territory or a large city. Only God can determine the regional boundaries by which this measure of authority is given. The apostle also has authority over the territorial spirits in that region. This does not mean that the regional apostle has authority over territorial spirits in other regions. As a regional apostle, God may give an apostle the authority to be a gatekeeper over an entire continent or nation.

- INTERNATIONAL APOSTLES – God does not give one apostle to a nation. He gives several apostles to a nation. The larger the sphere the more apostolic activity there is. Several apostles would be birthed to that nation. An International Apostle is known by his revelation, authority, anointing, gifts, and measure of rule. Without revelation an apostle cannot have authority, because authority is determined by the light of revelation the apostle receives from God. Every revelation has an amount of light that is released. If one walks in the maximum light of that revelation then one will walk in total authority according to that revelation.

It is by the authority of your revelation that one is known in total strength by the demonic forces and territorial principalities that oversee a nation. Therefore, International Apostles must operate in the ministry of deliverance. He or she is a principality in the kingdom of God; an equivalent of a principality in the kingdom of darkness. He or she must have ministry gifts and walk in a level of anointing so that the ministry can meet the needs of the people.

An International apostle must understand the cultural diversity of the kingdom of God and become all things to all men so they can win some. This statement was used by the apostle Paul who was an apostle to the Gentile nations. With the special ability given by God an apostle can exercise general leadership over churches. He or she exercises extraordinary authority in spiritual matters that is spontaneously recognized and appreciated by those churches and ministry leaders that acknowledge him or her as their leader.

These ministry leaders from various nationalities can go to their covering apostle for counsel and help. They are peacemakers equipped with the wisdom of God; they are troubleshooters and problem solvers. They may make demands that sound autocratic but when the anointing and authority is recognized, their wisdom is gladly accepted.

What Defines an Apostle? - The apostolic calling is a summons to called ones that issue from the Father through Jesus Christ. Apostles are sent. Jesus is the chief apostle, He was sent by God, the Father into the earth. Jesus is the Apostle and High Priest of our confession (Hebrews 3:1).

The summons of God to the apostolic is the voice of God alive in our spirits issued from the Father through Jesus Christ, calling us higher. It is both an invitation and a command to go forth, build, plant, preach the good news of the kingdom, and engage the enemy, by releasing those held in captivity and taking territory which, by the enemy's own admission belong to him.

> And the devil took him up into an exceeding high mountain and showed him all the kingdoms of the world in a moment of time, and said to Him, "To you I will give all this authority and their glory, for it has been delivered to me, and I give it to whoever I will. If you, then, will worship me, it will all be yours."
>
> -Luke 4: 5, 6.

Because of the likelihood of the office coming into abuse by unqualified persons who assume the position for which they are not called, we need further insight into what is required of apostles. Here is a brief summary that would help us to understand the work of apostles:

1. Apostles are required to have a definite and personal call from God to the office of an apostle.
2. Apostles must have specific fruit to which they can point to demonstrate their apostleship. "By their fruit you shall know them."
3. Apostles must be totally submitted to Christ and be led by the Holy Spirit. If not, they may fall like Judas.
4. The work of an apostle will always be in the areas of equipping, training, and leading others into mature ministry.
5. Apostles are elders and they model maturity of character. They must meet the requirements of morality, righteousness, and truth.
6. Character is what validates the apostolic ministry. Character includes integrity, honesty, honor, courage, strength, respectability, uprightness, morality, goodness, truthfulness, and sincerity.

7. The lifestyle of an apostle must reflect the character of Jesus Christ. Character affects the way the ministry of an apostle is received.

8. Apostles walk in tremendous power and authority. They are known for their acts, including miracles, signs and wonders, healings, church planting, evangelism, preaching and teaching.

9. Apostles have two primary means of communicating truth.

• A vocal ministry
• A written ministry

Apostles can spend hours teaching, preaching and prophesying. This is the verbal part of the work of an apostle. Apostles also distributed epistles and messages to the churches when they could not be there in person. They kept in touch through paper and ink. In today's economy the internet is another way that apostles can communicate with their peers and constituents.

Effective communication is essential to the work of an apostle. God requires truth and wisdom to be the vocal expression of an apostle. The church today has other vehicles of communication that the early church never had, such as; radio, telephone, internet, live streaming, on-line conferences and workshops, etc. Believers can tune into ministries that are broadcasting live on radio and television. Believers sow into ministries, send in prayer requests, and listen to sermons over the internet. The word is on tape; revelation is written in books. Knowledge has increased according to the prophecy of Daniel 12:4.

And the word of God increased and the number of the disciples multiplied in Jerusalem greatly; and a great company of the priests were obedient to the faith.

-Acts 6:7.

Apostles acknowledge the principles of increase which are rewards for obedience, persistence, faith, and investing oneself in the work of the ministry. Whenever God is involved, His desire is to bless what we plant, so that our garden, vineyard or ministries can be fruitful. As the word increases so does our ministry increase and become fruitful. God gives the increase as we follow His lead. Sowing the word and reaping a harvest is an essential part of authentic apostolic ministry.

Fruitfulness is a kingdom requisite. Apostles adhere to the divine order of increase which is "Be fruitful and multiply." Apostles plant and water because they want to present a harvest to the Lord. Planting is seasonal and timing is essential. The Holy Spirit reserves the right to direct His apostles. He is not obligated to bless what He does not initiate. Apostles do not build buildings, they permeated cities with the Word of God, they plant and organize congregations and move them into rental or purchased buildings, and we call that entity, a church.

But the work does not stop there; Apostles have to constantly nourish and sustain what they have planted, using the washing of the water of the word, skillfully imparting truth, correction, irrigating souls with wisdom and revelation until Christ is formed in them. Then they put leaders in place, to watch over the souls; leaders who will continue to feed and water what they have planted. Paul taught the church at Antioch for an entire year. (Acts 11:26) He remained at Corinth for eighteen months, using the water of the word to nourish the disciples. He remained in Ephesus for three years teaching day and night (Ephesus 20:31).

Once a church becomes capable of sustaining itself, the apostle if he or she is not the founder can move on. A strong apostolic church can reproduce itself by producing future apostles, prophets, and pastors. Strong apostolic churches are able to furnish the finances necessary to support new works and those itinerant apostles on the mission field.

Apostolic Wisdom: Apostles decode the hidden wisdom of God. Every apostle is known by his revelation. The release of the hidden wisdom of God through apostles is an offensive strike against the forces of darkness, because apostolic wisdom reveals the deeper mind of God at work in the universe.

> Therefore the wisdom of God also said, "I will send them prophets and apostles.
> -Luke 11:49.

Apostolic wisdom is not found in the wisdom of man. Apostles are filled with the spirit of wisdom and revelation. It is this wisdom that enables apostles to be expounders of truth, and to build according to the pattern revealed to them by God.

When Jesus spoke to the multitudes He spoke in parables, but He revealed the mysteries of the kingdom; the hidden wisdom of God to His apostles. With the restoration of the apostles to the church, God is releasing a deeper dimension of truth, and divine wisdom to the church. The church is the agency of the kingdom. God's wisdom is foolishness to the natural man.

Proverbs 8: describes how God used wisdom when He created the universe. This chapter explains how things exist, function and have been maintained from the foundation of the world by wisdom. In the scriptures, every time the Lord was about to initiate and establish His work, the spirit of wisdom was sent first.

> Then the Lord spoke to Moses saying, "See, I have called by name Bezaleel the son of Uri, the son of Hur, of the tribe of Judah.

And I have filled him with the Spirit of God in wisdom, in understanding, in knowledge, and in all manner of workmanship, to design artistic works, to work in gold, in silver, in bronze, in cutting jewels for setting, in carving wood, and to work in all manner of workmanship.

And I, indeed I, have appointed with him Aholiab the son of Ahisamach, of the tribe of Dan; and I have put wisdom in the hearts of all the gifted artisans, that they may make all that I have commanded you"

-Exodus 31: 1-6.

The Wise Man Daniel: Even though the prophet Daniel was learned in all the wisdom of the Chaldeans, he did not rely on the wisdom of Babylon to function. He totally relied upon God's wisdom. God gave him, along with his companions, skill in all literature and wisdom; and Daniel had understanding in all visions and dreams (Daniel 1:17).

There is a man in your kingdom in whom is the Spirit of the Holy God. And in the days of your father, light and understanding and wisdom, like the wisdom of the gods, were found in him; and King Nebuchadnezzar, your father, the king- made him chief of the Magicians, Astrologers, Chaldeans, and Soothsayers.

In as much as an excellent spirit, knowledge, understanding, interpreting dreams, solving riddles, and explaining enigmas were found in this Daniel whom the king named Belteshazzar, now let Daniel be called and he will give the interpretation.

–Daniel 5:11-12.

God's wisdom in Daniel allowed him to decode the mysteries of God in dreams and visions. This level of wisdom did not exist in Babylon and it became the catalyst for Daniel's promotion. The demonic wisdom used by the wise men of Babylon was useless; they had no clue about the operations of the higher dimension of the kingdom of God.

Paul's Apostolic Prayer for the Church at Ephesus:
> "Therefore I also, after I heard of your faith in the Lord Jesus and your love for all saints, do not cease to give thanks for you, making mention of you in my prayers; that the God of our Lord Jesus Christ, the Father of glory, may give to you the spirit of wisdom and revelation in the knowledge of Him, the eyes of your understanding being enlightened.

> That you may know what is the hope of His calling, what are the riches of the glory of His inheritance in the saints, and what is the exceeding greatness of His power toward us who believe, according to the working of His mighty power which He worked in Christ when He raised Him from the dead and seated Him at His right hand in heavenly places, far above all principality and power and might and dominion, and every name that is named, not only in this age but also in that which is to come.

> And He put all things under his feet, and gave Him to be head over all things to the church, which is His body, the fullness of Him who fills all in all."
> -Ephesians 1:15-23.

Jurisdiction Determines the Measure of Authority: We must also take into consideration the spiritual development of the apostolic gift. Every ministerial gift takes time for growth and development. Apostles mature gradually; so does every other ministry gift.

When Christ referred to his disciples as apostles they were still immature. Peter was still unstable and irrational; he was in the developmental stages but an apostle regardless. Jesus told him, "When you are converted strengthen the brethren." God saw the potential in Peter. Though the seed was in him there was a need for the process of kingdom development; it took time for his authority and function to be fully developed.

There are limits to an apostle's authority. An apostle's authority does not function everywhere. It only functions within the apostle's jurisdiction or sphere of authority. Apostles may have divinely imparted authority, but outside of God's determined sphere they don't have any authority. Also it must be understood that all apostles do not have the same ministry or activity.

The apostle Paul implies that apostles should not boast beyond their measure of authority, but within the limits of their jurisdiction, and not in other men's labors (2 Corinthians 10 & 11). Apostles can never become everything God wants them to be, if they are not fully aware of their sphere of authority to which God has assigned them.

Some apostles may never have the opportunity to convene a national apostolic council in any given nation. Their measure of rule may only be to a local church, a city, a particular group of people, or to a particular nation or continent. Knowing the scope of the apostolic calling is of great importance to an apostle, because some apostles have no authority outside of their jurisdiction. Paul's assignment was to the Gentiles.

Apostles are Wise Master Builders: Wise Master Builders are spiritual architects. They build by revelation and not by tradition. Every true apostle is known by his or her revelation of the mysteries of God. Apostles use a kingdom strategy for building just like God who is an architect. God built and sustains all things by His powerful word. All life exists because of His word. Apostles use the strategy of building with the word, block by block, revelation upon revelation, line upon line, precept upon precept, here a little and there a little.

The Apostle Peter says, "We as lively stones are built up into a spiritual house to offer up sacrifices of praise and adoration unto God." The building of God or the house of God is not built with natural stone, brick, clay or wood or with natural hands. Through the revelation of the word of God, apostles build the kingdom of God in the heart and lives of the people of God, expanding their spiritual apparatus and capabilities to receive more from God.

The apostle Paul so rightly said, "I long to see you that I may impart unto you some spiritual gift that you may be established (*become strong*) (Romans 1:11).

Apostles are sent by the Kingdom of Heaven: The apostolic anointing is a sending anointing. The Holy Spirit was sent on the day of Pentecost on an assignment. The Holy Spirit is a sending spirit. Jesus was sent by God to the earth on the greatest apostolic assignment; to redeem lost souls held in captivity by the powers of darkness. Jesus is an apostle. Jesus sent His apostles on an assignment into the entire world to preach the message of the kingdom and to teach them to observe all the things He taught them.

The apostolic ministry of the church was activated on the day of Pentecost when the Holy Spirit arrived. The apostolic role of the Holy Spirit is:

- To establish territorial jurisdiction for the apostle to operate with full authority on the level given to the apostle by God. Some are called to nations, some to cities, some to regions and some to local assemblies.

- To legislate the different degrees of apostolic anointing with the corresponding mantles, and measures of authority.

- To legislate apostolic authority to people, places and churches where there is relationship.

An apostle does not have the authority to go into every church to correct and set things in order. The authority of the apostle Paul could only operate in churches he had established and set in order, or churches who had received his ministry. Paul did not try to exercise any authority in Jerusalem where James and the apostolic council of elders had their seat of authority. He did not try to usurp authority or to stretch himself into another person's jurisdiction or boast beyond his measure of authority or grace (2 Corinthians 10:13).

Ambassadorial Apostles: When an apostle serves as an ambassador they are defined as an itinerant minister. Itinerant apostles nurture apostolic movements on a large scale. They can do so on a national or international level. They are able to call together leaders in the region, to establish a relational structure, to neutralize whatever negative church politics that hinders the cohesiveness in that region. They often serve to promote apostolic movements in different parts of the world. Not only is an ambassadorial apostle able to convene regional, national and international conferences, and apostolic summits, but they are able and available to set in order existing ministries, churches and apostolic movements.

Mobilization Apostles: There are apostles that provide a specific function in the Body of Christ. They do not oversee or provide covering to churches. Instead they provide apostolic covering over individuals or groups within a certain kind of specialized ministry. An example of this kind of specialized ministry is the National Council of Intercessors. The apostle over this group can be a member of a local church who is subject to a pastor, but serve as a covering apostle for this group of leaders and intercessors.

They may be under a personal covering of another leader, like a pastor, yet in a particular ministry or within a particular group; they might look to a functional apostle for direction, discipling, and accountability.

Territorial Apostles: Some apostles have their primary apostolic function determined by a certain geographical territory. These territorial apostles have been given a great deal of authority within a certain nation, city, region, or territory. God does not give one apostle to a nation, a city, a territory or a region. There may be several apostles serving in that same geographical area, however, they may have different responsibilities for that area. It is important that these territorial apostles be recognized and affirmed by the leaders in that particular society.

Apostolic Teams: Most itinerant apostles travel with a team, or try to develop a team to support them in the work of the ministry. This is very vital and most essential not only to the work but also for the chief apostle. Members of that team must be trained, called, able men and women, who are willing to support the work prayerfully, financially, and otherwise. With this level of leadership more can be done to greatly expand the network and the possibility of including more churches in the overall vision and mission.

With team ministry, personal relationships are important to the function and flow of the network. Jesus, Paul and Peter all employed apostolic teams. Jesus began with twelve apostles, Paul had many more in his team than Jesus because of the territorial assignment he was given. He was an apostle to the Gentiles; while Peter's apostolic assignment was to one nation - the Jews.

Apostolic Ministry is a Ministry of Warfare: An apostle is given power against unclean spirits and is sent with specific instructions about the realm of darkness. An apostle is called into military service. Apostle Paul spoke of the weapons of our warfare, they are not carnal weapons but they are mighty through God meaning they are spiritual weapons, not weapons after the flesh. Therefore, it is important that an apostle keep his spirit under control so that he or she does not respond to opposition after the dictates of the flesh by being judgmental, critical, or bitter.

> We are afflicted in every way, but not crushed, perplexed, but not despairing, persecuted, but not forsaken, struck down, but not destroyed. Always carrying about in the body the dying of Jesus, so that the life of Jesus may be manifested in our body.
> -2 Corinthians 4: 8-10.

God is a God of war and the warfare ministries of apostles are as follows:
- Protector
- Defender
- Deliverer
- Covering
- Helper
- Shield
- Refuge

- Fortress
- Watchman
- Gatekeeper
- One that leads prisoners out of captivity
- One that Judges and makes war. (Old Testament type of Judge.)

Many apostles have been given other mantles alongside their gift and office of an apostle. For example, I have the gift of teaching, which is my primary ministry. I am therefore a teacher/apostle. With the help of the Holy Spirit we have raised up a mentoring, counseling, and teaching ministry for those called into leadership. We also cover a network of ministers and para-church ministries within a cultural and regional sphere.

The Pauline Pattern: They lead networks, oversee churches and para-church ministries, and individuals look to the apostle for spiritual mentoring and covering. These chief apostles or executives are given a sphere or jurisdiction which includes a number of churches, and some para-church ministries.

Fathering Another Aspect of Apostolic Ministry: James, the brother of Jesus, was an apostolic father and the overseer of the council at Jerusalem. He was a man well respected and held in honor among the other apostles and the church. An apostolic father is the type of man that younger apostles can refer to for wisdom and godly counsel, spiritual direction, and prayer.

In his role as chief counsel, or chief executive, James had full apostolic authority in the Jerusalem council. Men that lead large denominations or organizations are a type of James the brother of Jesus. The other apostles came to Jerusalem at his invitation. James did not take a vote or table the matter for further discussion at a later date. He issued an apostolic directive for both Jews and Gentiles and ordered that letters be sent to all the churches informing them of the council's directive.

Apostolic Networks: are the new wineskin into which God is pouring new wine. The pastors and leaders of parachurch ministries within the network look to the apostle for their spiritual covering. Pastors also receive their ordination to ministry at the hands of the apostle. The apostle is their covering. The covering apostle has permission to speak into the lives of the pastors, both for encouragement and for rebuke when necessary. The covenant relationship is perpetuated by the pastors giving a tithe of their personal income to the apostle.

Apostolic Authority: While Jesus was busy carrying out the responsibilities of His ministry a question arose among His disciples, "Who is the greatest?" Jesus perceived their thoughts; however, the sons of Zebedee's mother came to Jesus with this special request. Her desire was for her two sons to sit one on the right and one on the left side of Jesus when He came into His kingdom. Jesus interjected, "You don't know what you are asking? "Can you drink of the cup that I drink of? And can you be baptized with the baptism that I am baptized with?" Ignorantly, they answered, "Yes we can." Jesus then explained, "What you are asking for is not mine to decide, those positions will be given to those for whom they have been prepared. However, since you said, "You can drink of the cup and be baptized with the same baptism that I am baptized with; you will truly drink of that cup and experience the same baptism."

Jesus realized they needed a lesson on the nature of their ministry, and their authority as apostles. To make this lesson plain He contrasted the authority in the Kingdom of God with the world; they were not the same. Greatness in the kingdom of God was a result of sincere servitude, not carnal competition. Christ went on to reveal to them that even though He was Lord over all, He came to serve. An apostle is a servant, sent by the kingdom of Heaven with a commission, mandated responsibility and authority to carry out the assignment within the scope of the mission (Matthew 20:20-28; Mark 10:35-45).

Since the day that James and John made that selfish request the question of authority has always been contemplated in every phase of leadership, and the scope of apostolic authority is no different. Certainly, apostles are called to exercise authority, but Christ had made it clear that this authority was to be earned humbly. The thoughts and intents of the heart had to be motivated properly because the rewards are given sovereignly.

How much authority do apostles have? How are the lines of apostolic authority structured, and how much authority should they use? In the early church leadership shifted several times among apostolic figures. Each one was raised up by God for a particular season of influence and purpose of God for their lives and the church. The flexibility within the leadership of the apostles demonstrates what apostolic authority is not; it is not successional, meaning it cannot be imparted at the will of man; it is not hierarchical, meaning it is not composed of numerous layers of authority. Apostolic leadership and submission among other apostles is relational, and subject to change as the situation and the will of God may dictate.

Apostles found their identity in being a bond servant of Jesus Christ. Paul said, "He was called to be an apostle, separated unto the gospel of Jesus Christ" (Romans 1:1). Paul found his purpose and identity in doing the will of God. All his rights and privileges were forfeited and his assignment by Christ took preeminence. Therefore an apostle is first and foremost a servant. The quality of humility and the servant's attitude must be deeply rooted in his inner man.

Principles of Apostolic Authority: The local church at Antioch was a sending church. Neither Paul nor Barnabus founded that church, but they were submissive to that church. Paul always started his missionary journeys from Antioch. Paul and Barnabas did not leave Antioch until they were properly sent by the Holy Spirit through the local church leadership (Acts 13:1-3). In this context we see the apostle's submission to the local church. We don't see where they ever usurped any authority or tried to use their apostolic mantle to rule the local church in any ministry context.

Cooperation and not Domination. Apostles should never see themselves as people who want to control people's lives. Submission to authority is a matter of free will. People must choose to cooperate. Jesus spoke of the deeds of the Nicolaitans, a thing which He hated. Though not much is known of this sect, from the root word *nikao* comes the word "to conquer" hence the Nicolaitans were people conquerors. They dominated and controlled the saints. There is so much of that spirit in the church today. The spirit of control is a dominating spirit, it intimidates unsuspecting people to bring them into submission, It takes advantage of the ignorant, it lords itself over God's people by force, disrespecting, argumentative and judgmental; its intent is to produce fear and a slave-like mentality.

Paul understood as he wrote to the believers at Corinth, "Not that we have dominion over your faith, but are fellow workers for your joy; for by faith you stand" (2 Corinthians 1:24). Paul understood that the saints at Corinth, needed correction and discipline for a behavior and a lifestyle change. But they were not placed in a position of dependence upon his faith, but to stand on their own faith. As an example, a teacher and an apostolic leader, Paul said, "Follow me as I follow Christ." Paul's role was to help them run the race looking unto Jesus the author and the finisher of their faith. The people as well as the apostle,

308

pastor, and local church leaders are interdependent on each other. None can be complete without each other.

Voluntary Submission: When the believers and their leaders are in proper relationship to each other, both genuine respect and true submission will be present. Apostles like Paul exercised great influence over believers in his role as an apostolic father. However, apostles could not and should not demand submission and cooperation from the people, but they could receive it from them when it is willingly extended. As the people voluntarily submit, the apostles lead and govern. This is the true pattern for submission and godly authority in the home, the church, and the government. A leader cannot lead unless people willingly follow, nor can an apostle demand a response because he or she is an apostle. Apostles are servants who minister to those who will freely receive their authority.

> And as they went through the cities, they delivered to
> them the decrees to keep, which were determined by
> the apostles and elders at Jerusalem. So the churches
> were strengthened in faith, and increased in numbers
> daily"
>
> -Acts 16: 4, 5.

The Autonomy of the Local Church: There are levels of authority in the natural as well as in the spirit. On the local church level, authority is given to the Pastors and Elders who govern the work of God and administrate within the confines of the local church assembly. However, beyond the local church the apostle oversees the work for the purposes of the gospel within a particular sphere of either geographical or cultural influence.

Apostles work well with local churches they have planted, and also work with ministries in a variety of functions within the geographical area that have submitted to their authority. In the

Jerusalem church the apostles and local leaders stood together with James, the chief apostle, who issued authoritative decrees for the Gentile church to observe and follow.

In this unanimous corporation, the apostles never overode the local authority. The principle of local autonomy and self-rule remained intact, while the authority of the apostles in council at Jerusalem together was governing the broader scope of the work of God beyond the local church.

Mutual Accountability: Apostles are accountable to one another and to God. In the military, every segment of each branch of the military is accountable to a higher authority. So it is with the army of God. This level of apostolic accountability stems out of relationships and submission to one another in love. But my question is, who are the generals accountable to? The answer is God, the Lord of Hosts.

At the apostles' council of Acts 15, the apostles came together in the spirit of mutual accountability to settle disputes and doctrinal problems. They gathered and submitted to the admonition and counsel of one another. Some had to change and conform to the decisions agreed upon by their apostolic peers. Paul's open rebuke of Peter (Galatians 2) reveals that apostles were free, if not obligated, to chasten each other for any wrong doing.

Apostolic Authority And Functions Relative To Their Respective Ability And Personality:

It is important to keep in mind that all apostles are not the same. Peter, Paul, and John are the three best known of the early apostles. Nevertheless they were different. Peter was given the keys to the kingdom, therefore he was a breakthrough person, a pioneer; he was evangelistic, and the first one to cast the net into the sea. His secular gifting was also applicable to his spiritual gifting.

Paul was essentially a builder, his secular gifting was tent making. Paul was a master tent builder and a master builder in the kingdom of God. His revelation about the Body of Christ stems around God's building. The foundation, the chief cornerstone, structure, order, and bringing Christians into the deeper knowledge of Christ and His Church.

John's personality was quite different. He was the one who laid on Jesus' bosom. When the spirit of error threatened the church, John was a restorer, bringing the people back to their original position in Christ and the original thought of God. He was given the messages to the seven churches in Asia because he was a restorer. He restored the believers to the heart of God.

Whenever Christ-centered authority is in place, people must submit to each other in the spirit of love and unity. The local church must remain strong and independent, yet totally open to spiritual guidance, instructions, and the influence of the apostle. Spiritual leaders must be open to accountability to each other and accountability to the word and Spirit of God for the good of the believers. It is from this vantage point that unity will spread among leaders of diverse backgrounds, cultures, and nationalities.

Apostolic Functions are as Follows:
- Apostles unfold the mysteries of God.
- Apostles restore the rights of believers.
- Apostles bring and restore order.
- Apostles come against illegal covenants.
- Apostles unfold mysteries and distribute gifts.
- Apostles break the spirit of witchcraft and destroy curses.
- Apostles open the heavens, rebukes brass heavens.

- Apostles open spiritual jails, and shut the gates of Hell.
- Apostles open the spiritual eyes of the blind.
- Apostles understand present truth, or present revelation.
- Apostles know a season of visitation.
- Apostles know the seasons of God.
- Apostles bring spiritual and physical healing.
- Apostles bring order in regards to the kingdom of God.
- Apostles bring deliverance, the removing of demonic spirits.
- Apostles release those held in demonic captivity.
- Apostles open doors.
- Apostles are pioneers, forerunners, pacesetters, and sent ones.
- Apostles settle doctrinal questions and disputes.
- Apostles lead the church in spiritual warfare.
- Apostles make decrees and declarations.
- Apostles set overseers and pastors over the work of God.
- Apostles set Bishops over the work of several churches.
- Apostles develop leaders.
- Apostles plant churches.
- Apostles oversee and strengthen churches.
- Apostles provide spiritual covering for other leaders.
- Apostles impart and activate spiritual gifts.
- Apostles have actually seen Jesus personally.
- Apostles perform supernatural signs and wonders.
- Apostles judge witchcraft.
- Apostles provide spiritual fathering and mothering to their children in the faith.
- Apostolic operations include deliverance of people, land, and buildings occupied by demonic entities.
- Apostles set deacons and elders into their office on the local church level.
- Apostles bring vision, strategy, structure, government, direction, correction, order, and give life to the vision.

Apostolic Character: There must be a balance between the gift and character. Character is the seat of one's moral being. It is the inner life of man which reflects either the traits of sinful nature or the traits of divine nature as it is influenced by the word of God. Character is displayed in the actions of a person under pressure. And is the sum total of all the negative and positive qualities in a person's life, manifested in their thoughts, values, motives, attitudes, feelings, and actions.

Definition: Character is a distinctive trait, quality, attribute, characteristic, nature, moral strength, self-discipline, a pattern of behavior or personality found in an individual, moral constitution, moral strength, and constitution.

In Hebrews 1:3 –the writer states that Christ is the very character of God, the very stamp of God's nature. And the one in whom God stamped or imprinted His being.

> He is the radiance of His glory and the exact representation of His nature, and upholds all things by the word of His power.
>
> -Hebrews 1:3.

True apostles must display Christlikeness. Qualities in the nature of Christ Jesus their Lord. True authentic apostolic ministry begins with a person's heart and character. The Bible warns us that false apostles will arise along with false prophets, teachers, pastors etc. The dark kingdom always tries to emulate God's kingdom, and deploy people with corrupt morals and values into the business of the kingdom for gain. These are days in which it will be imperative to assess the validity of one who calls themselves an apostle. A proliferation of flaky apostolic imposters is on the rise and it is expected that these deceitful workers will transform themselves into apostles of Christ.

Apostles are not self-appointed. An apostle is a leader that has been endowed by God with gifts, talents, supernatural ability and authority. He or she is sent by God with authority to establish the work of the kingdom, to provide governmental order within a local church or within a certain sphere of ministry. They follow the leading of the Holy Spirit who is a sending spirit, to release what the spirit is saying to the churches. They set men and women in place for growth and the maturity of the local church.

False apostles, false teachers, false prophets, and false pastors are self-appointed or they may be appointed by someone else who is in fact ignorant, and operating out of self-will or covetousness instead of the mind, will, and purpose of God. Someone who wants to set him or herself up as a covering; someone operating is a sphere of authority that was not given to him or her by the kingdom of Heaven. Hence the reason for Jesus saying to those who did works in His name without the corresponding relationship and obedience, "I never knew you."

The apostle Peter gave a warning to the church in general about false prophets and teachers (2 Peter 2). Jesus gave a warning about false apostles in His admonition to the church at Ephesus (Revelation 2:2). Jude, the brother of James, the chief apostle at Jerusalem also wrote a warning to the church in general (Jude 1). Before his departure, apostle Paul warned the church at Ephesus that after his departure, grievous or fierce wolves will enter in not sparing the flock (Acts 20:29).

The gift of an apostle is given by the grace of God, but identified by character, works and divine endowments. God's decision to make an individual an apostle must be recognized and affirmed by the mouth of two or three witnesses. This is a rule, that God would do nothing in the earth without revealing it to His servants the prophets. Someone has to bear witness to the call and gift of God in and on a person's life. To be out of the will of God is a dangerous place to be. When the gift is identified and recognized, then the office is conferred upon the individual by the governmental leaders in the church. This is not an ordination; it is the commissioning of someone who is already ordained.

Unfortunately, most leaders in the Body of Christ look at the outside appearance for identifying marks of an apostle, because people want to make a quick association with the title, but the apostolic is first an inward quality. We must look at character; the things that define an apostle are on the inside. This is an essential truth; to be apostolic is a matter of character above any other single quality.

> Truly the signs of an apostle were wrought among you in all patience, in signs, and wonders, and mighty deeds.
>
> -2 Corinthians 12: 12.

What Character Is Not: Don't be alarmed when someone shows you who they really are. Character is what a person is at the present time, not what they will become. When trials, tribulations and afflictions come into a person's life, the real person surfaces. A person may behave one way while they are enjoying the blessings of God, but their character can change drastically under the pressure of trials and afflictions.

True character does not appear without pressure. It is the pressure of trials, afflictions, and temptations that we all must experience, that produce patience and character. Anyone that lives godly in this world will suffer affliction and persecution. The common irritations of everyday living expose the weaknesses in every person's life. It tells how they respond to disappointments and tribulations. Character is formed under fire and the qualities that surface are a part of that person's character and identity.

Character is not only what a person sees on the outside, but what they do not see. God told Samuel, "Man looks on the outward appearance but God looks on the heart." A person cannot hide his or her weaknesses from the Lord. A person can do outward religious works, and still be ungodly, immoral, and wicked. Charitable works are not always a sign of good character.

Character is discerned by the way one respect him or herself; the way he or she respects authority, honor his or her father and mother, treat his or her fellowman, and abide by the law that says, "Do unto others as you will have them do unto you." Character determines the way you honor and respect people.

The Law of Holiness:

> This is the law of the house; upon the top of the mountain the whole limit thereof round about shall be most holy. Behold, this is the law of the house.
>
> – Ezekiel 43: 12.

Serving the Lord in the beauty of holiness is a kingdom requirement. Holiness is the true nature of God, along with truth, love, wisdom and righteousness. The only way the church can defeat the powers of darkness is with holiness. It is the one thing the devil fears most.

Those called to the apostolic ministry will only survive if they abide in perfect holiness before God. It is the only way spirits that have infested the church can be exposed and driven out from the midst of God's people. There must be a return to sanctification, purity, and holiness.

> As obedient children, do not be conformed to the former lusts which were ours in your ignorance. But like the holy one who called you, be holy yourselves

also in all your behavior, because it is written, "You shall be holy, for I am holy."

-1 Peter 1:14-16.

The Anointing Is Tied To Character: A Christian leader must develop his or her character in order to achieve God's goal for his or her life. His personal relationship with the Lord is built upon intimacy with God, a godly character as well as a depth in God's word and prayer. The habits, lifestyle, and patterns which the leader develops will have a major influence upon the ministry he or she has received from the Lord. He or she must live how the word admonishes every child of God to live.

Because of the spirit of influence, a leader's companions, mentors, or associates also help to define his or her character. There is an old proverb that says, "Show me your friends and I will tell you who you are." King Saul was not a prophet, but when he came into the midst of the company of prophets he prophesied.

> After that you will come to the hill of God where the garrison of the Philistines is; and when you come to the city, you will meet a company of prophets coming down from the high place with harp, tambourine, flute, and lyre before them, prophesying. Then the Spirit of the Lord will come upon you mightily, and you will show yourself to be a prophet with them and you will be turned into another man.
>
> -1 Samuel 10: 5, 6.

A leader must first put his house in order. A leader's family life will always be called into question. It will be judged by the other families that are in his congregation. Without character he will not have a successful family life. His marital life will only succeed as he matures and develops character.

Character plays an important part in financial matters. A leader's integrity, prudence, wisdom, business acumen, responsibility, and discretion play an important part in a leader's life and the way money matters are handled. If a leader does not know how to be prudent with money, God will not commit to him true riches.

A major issue for the Lord under the Old Covenant was wealth. He laid down principles and guidelines for the kings of Israel concerning wealth. (Deuteronomy 17:14-20). In today's economy too many leaders are in personal debt because of greed. Debt is also a spirit. The Old Testament kings parallel the New Testament apostles so it would be worthwhile to go back to the rules and regulations set by God for the Old Testament kings and make a study of these rules.

7. PRINCIPLES OF THE HARVEST

The Law of Generation or Reproduction states that every tree yields fruit after its kind (Genesis 1:11). Christ Jesus is the holy seed of God; the word that was made flesh and dwelt among us. As believers, those that have been declared the righteousness of God in Christ Jesus, we are symbolized in scriptures as trees of the planting of the Lord (Isaiah 61:3).

Every leader must realize that he or she is going to reproduce him or herself in those under them. When the apostles were arrested and appeared before the council of the Sanhedrin, they noted that these were ignorant and unlearned men, but they discerned their spirit and realized that these men had been with Jesus (Acts 4:13).

Leaders must understand that the anointing can be imparted and mantles can be transferred. The inspired teachings, truth and revelation of the scriptures impact the lives of others. Therefore, leaders that have been chosen by God to disciple, teach, and train people, should examine their own lives in the light of God's word constantly, and have an ear to hear whatever correction the spirit is bringing to their consciousness about themselves. It is by our fruit that we will be identified.

> You have not chosen me, but I have chosen you and
> have ordained you, that you should go and bring forth

fruit, and that your fruit should remain; that whatsoever you shall ask of my father in my name, He may give it to you.

-John 15: 16

There are some key words that stand out in this text, they are: chosen, ordained, fruit, remain, ask and give. Using these key words I want to lay a foundation for some principles of the harvest by diligently analyzing a statement in the text, "Go and bring forth fruit that your fruit should remain."

Jesus would often use the language of creation in his teachings. For in his teachings, the Creator is telling man to look at his creation; for He is speaking a language to us by created things and creatures. Created things were used as symbols of kingdom truth.

The key principle in interpreting the symbols Jesus used in His parables is this: If a scripture does not make literal or actual sense, then it can only be interpreted as having symbolic sense. So to understand the essence of a parable, we have to first understand the characteristic of the symbol.

The three fundamental elements of symbolic interpretation are:
- The significance of a symbol: This is based upon the literal or actual nature and characteristics of the symbol.
- A symbol is meant to: Represent something essentially different from itself.
- The link between that which is used as a symbol and that which is symbolized is: The characteristics that are common to both.

The whole universe speaks the language of creation. We can see this clearly in Psalm 19:

The heavens declare the glory of God; the skies proclaim the work of His hands. Day after day they pour forth speech; night after night they display knowledge.

There is no speech or language where their voice is not heard. Their voice goes out into all the earth, their words to the ends of the world.

-Psalm 19: 1-4.

This principle is laid down by the apostle Paul (1 Corinthians 15: 46). The spiritual did not come first, but the natural, and after that the spiritual.

The Creator is telling man - look at His creation, for within created things and creatures, God has hidden truth. For He takes the language of creation and it becomes the language of the symbol, which in turn becomes the language of redemption.

In the midst of having a discourse with His leaders about "The Sower and the Seed," they asked Jesus, "Why do you speak to the people in parables? He gave them an explanation in Matthew 13: 10-11. "The knowledge of the secrets of the kingdom of Heaven has been given to you, but not to them."

The king James version says, "It is given to you to understand the mysteries of the kingdom of heaven, but it was not given to them."

His apostolic leaders were chosen to receive a level of divine truth, spiritual wisdom, and revelation that the masses were not able to receive because it was not given to them. Jesus had a different method by which He taught the masses.

Symbolic language was God's secret code for veiling or revealing truth according to the attitude of the listener. This method of teaching Jesus used was the 'parabolic method.'

After speaking to the multitude Jesus would reveal to His apostles the hidden mysteries of the parable which was the secrets of the kingdom of heaven. He also taught them the method of interpretation.

In Matthew 13:9 Jesus concluded His lesson by saying: "He who has ears let him hear." Why did Jesus use this statement? Because all of creation can hear. Creation bears witness to the word of the Lord, and creation complies with the release of God's word. All of creation knows that no word of God returns to Him void.

There are instances in the scriptures where prophets prophesied to the earth, and said, O earth, earth, earth, hear the word of the Lord (Jeremiah 22:29). They also prophesied to the elements. Elijah called fire from heaven and fire fell (2 Kings 1:10). Joshua commanded the sun to "stand still" and it stood still (Joshua 10:12-14). Why? Because all of creation can hear.

> And some of the Pharisees from among the multitude said unto him, "Master rebuke your disciples. And He answered and said unto them, "I tell you that, if these should hold their peace, the stones would immediately cry out."
>
> -Luke 19:39-40.

The Lord through the mouth of the prophet Jeremiah called upon the earth to bear witness to the Word of the Lord.

> Hear, O earth; behold I will bring evil upon this people, even the fruit of their thoughts, because they

have not hearkened unto my words, nor to my law, but rejected it.

> \- Jeremiah 6:19.

Everything in the universe and in the kingdom of God starts with a seed. God put a universal law in place called "Seedtime and Harvest"; this law encompasses both realms – Spirit and Natural.

> As long as the earth endures, seedtime and harvest, cold and heat, summer and winter, day and night will never cease.
>
> -Genesis 8:22.

The apostle Paul said, "If we sowed spiritual things in you, is it too much if we reap natural things from you?" (1 Corinthians 9:11) To bear fruit, seed must be planted. However in our text, Jesus was not speaking to His apostles about reproducing themselves naturally, but reproducing themselves spiritually, by reproducing kingdom fruit. Kingdom fruit will remain, endure, or last for eternity; the directive was, 'that you will produce fruit that will endure.'

The universal principle of sowing and reaping is also a kingdom requisite. In the parables of Jesus the language of creation was used, but within the context of the lesson – the symbolic elements, when perceived and understood, were relaying the message of redemption.

As we look at our text Jesus was saying to the leaders of His Church, "I chose you, I appointed you - the purpose for which you were chosen and appointed is this, to bring forth fruit that would endure; and conditional upon you bringing forth that quality of fruit, whatsoever you ask of the Father in my name, He will give it to you."

As a fruit lover, the idea of fruit not decaying, or fruit lasting or fruit enduring, lets me know that Jesus was not talking about natural fruit. Natural fruit is corruptible, it will rot, it will decay and it eventually has to be thrown out if not used.

> We are born again not of corruptible seed but incorruptible, by the word of God, which lives and abides forever.
>
> -1 Peter 1: 23.

The word of God is incorruptible – it is seed that remains, seed that will not decay, seed that will endure, seed that produces abundantly, seed that produces the life of God.

> But as many as received Him, to them gave He power to become the sons of God, even to them that believe on His name.
>
> –John 1:12.

> Beloved now are we the children of God, and it has not appeared as yet what we shall be. We know that when He appears, we shall be like Him, because we will see Him just as He is. And every man who has this hope fixed on him purifies himself, even as he is pure.
>
> - 1 John 3: 2, 3.

There is natural seed and there is spiritual seed. Every human on the face of the earth is seed. Jesus was God's seed. The Law of Generation or reproduction says "Every seed must produce after its kind." Humans were born of the will of man therefore humans produce humans. This law applies to other kingdoms as well. Animals reproduce animals according to their species. Vegetation reproduces vegetation after its kind.

Because every human has an appointment with death the natural seed of man cannot endure, it is designated as corruptible seed. However, Jesus Christ, God's son, came as the second Adam, a quickening spirit, a life giving spirit. He did not come to give eternal life to corruptible flesh; He came to give life to the spirit of man that's dead because of sin.

> And you hath he quickened [made alive] who were dead in trespasses and sins.
>
> -Ephesians 2: 2.

To produce spiritual fruit one has to partake of the life of Christ. The kingdom directive is, "You must be born again" not you must be a church member. Many church members are void of an experience with Christ that makes Him their Savior and Lord.

Salvation does not begin and end with a person coming to the altar and saying the sinner's prayer. Christianity is a lifestyle, it is a daily walk with God. It is through Him we live and move and have our being. We surrender our fleshly life and we take on His higher life of the spirit.

> Jesus answered, Verily, Verily, I say unto thee, except a man is born of water and of the spirit, he cannot enter into the kingdom of God.
>
> -John 3: 5.

God's kingdom is an everlasting kingdom, a kingdom that endures forever – His kingdom is of a spiritual essence therefore, It is only in the kingdom of God that incorruptible fruit can be produced.

> Verily, Verily, I say unto you, Except a corn of wheat – or a kernel of wheat - falls into the ground and dies, it remains only a single seed - it abides alone; but if it

dies, – it sprouts and reproduces itself many times, it brings forth much fruit.

-John 12: 24.

According to the law of generation or reproduction, it takes one seed to produce much fruit, in which there are many more seeds. This law applies to the kingdom of God also, for it is the way seed is reproduced in the kingdom.

So is the kingdom of God, as if a man should cast seed into the ground. And should sleep, and rise night and day, and the seed should spring and grow up, he knows not how.

For the earth brings forth fruit of herself; first the blade, then the ear, after that the full corn in the ear; But when the fruit is brought forth immediately he puts in the sickle because the harvest is come.

-Mark 4: 24-26.

God gave all seed an assignment. When seed is planted in the right environment which is the earth or the womb, that seed goes through a process of change called metamorphosis or transformation which develops the new embryo and prepares it to mature and multiply by producing other seeds.

This is what Jesus was referring to when he said, "Except a grain of wheat falls to the ground and dies it abides alone." God sent His seed, who is His son, into the earth on assignment to taste death for every man. In his death He produced life for many who were born again of the water and the spirit.

But we see Jesus, who was made a little lower than the angels, for the suffering of death, crowned with glory and honor, that He by the grace of God should taste death for every man.

> For it became him, for whom are all things, and by whom are all things, in bringing many sons unto glory, to make the captain of their salvation perfect through suffering.
>
> - Hebrews 2: 9-10.

Jesus could not taste death for every man in heaven. There were no sinful men in heaven. That act of love had to be done in the environment where sinful men were. The Word had to manifest as a human to enter the earth environment, to function as a man and to die; for it is appointed or mandated that every human should taste natural death at least once. When the seed of God entered the earth environment and became a man, it was subject to the laws that govern the existence of man; there is a time to be born and a time to die.

Death is the key to transformation from the natural to the spiritual. What made the death of Jesus on the cross the key to the liberation of mankind was the fact that Jesus was a sinless man. He became the first fruit of the resurrection, and was then able to reproduce in man eternal life.

> And being found in fashion as a man, he humbled himself, and became obedient unto death, even the death of the cross.
>
> - Philippians 2:8.

Bearing fruit is a divine truth. As long as the earth remains there will be seed time and harvest. The universe functions on the principle of the seed. The natural seed is of man, is corruptible and ends with death, but spiritual seed is incorruptible and produces life that endures.

The process can be called regeneration, transformation, metamorphosis, gestation, but it takes a period of time for the process to be completed. But when the set time is come the fruit manifest in the form of a harvest in the natural or in the spirit as a new creation, a born again individual.

The first directive God gave to man was "Be fruitful."

> And God blessed them and God said unto them, "Be fruitful, multiply, replenish the earth, and subdue it; and have dominion over the fish of the sea, and over the fowl of the air, and over every living thing that moves upon the earth."
>
> -Genesis 1: 28.

With this directive, God was speaking futuristically; He was positioning man for the future, because God thinks generationally. Adam could not have dominion without fruitfulness. This directive was to begin with Adam and it was to be incorporated into the generations to come. Fruitfulness will always produce dominion.

This directive was not just to the male, because he could not reproduce himself without the female. God blessed male and female, they got the same assignment, the exact same directive. Be fruitful, multiply, replenish the earth, subdue it and have dominion. Their respective reproductive apparatus has to work together to produce fruit.

The Directive is:
- Be fruitful
- Multiply your fruitfulness, by taking what you have and multiplying it in an area that doesn't have your fruitfulness.
- Replenish that area with your fruitfulness
- When you saturate an area with your fruitfulness, your fruitfulness will then subdue that area. And that whole area will then become subservient to your fruitfulness
- Then you will have dominion.

This was the strategy for the apostolic commission that Jesus gave to the church. Reproduce yourself by making disciples of all nations.

> "Go and make disciples of all nations, baptizing them in the name of the Father, the Son and the Holy Spirit, teaching them to obey everything I have commanded you."
>
> -Matthew 28: 19.

When the seed is first placed in the ground, the natural seed faces the earth forces, before it produces fruit. When spiritual seed is planted, it faces spiritual forces, before it begins to produce. The ground breaking process is often difficult. But persistent, diligence, and commitment pays off.

Jesus wanted His disciples to produce fruit that will endure from generation to generation; a generational harvest. One generation praising the works of the Lord to another generation and declaring His mighty works.

After man sinned, God began the process of recovery with Abraham. Once again He chose a man, and gave him an assignment to be fruitful.

> God told Abraham – I will make thee exceedingly fruitful, and I will make nations of thee, and kings shall come out of thee.
>
> And I will establish my covenant between me and thee and thy seed after thee in their generations for an everlasting covenant, to be a God unto thee, and to thy seed after thee.
>
> And I will give unto thee and to thy seed after thee, the land wherein thou art a stranger, all the land of

Canaan, for an everlasting possession, and I will be their God.

- Genesis 17: 6-9.

Abraham had to leave his country, his geographical location, to enter into the land of promise; the place where his generational seed would be planted. The land was not for Abraham; God promised the land to his descendants. Abraham had to occupy the land, walk the length and breadth of it, to establish a presence, to dig wells, and to build altars to the Lord. His seed, Isaac, was born there and he was fruitful in the land.

Divine Positioning: If a leader does not understand the concept of divine positioning, he or she would not understand why some geographical locations are more receptive for a kingdom harvest than others. Location is important, land is important, the people we do business with, those we are connected to, all these factors play an important part is being fruitful.

Too many chosen leaders are in the wrong environment, in the wrong position, doing the wrong thing, with the wrong people, in the wrong relationships, and they cannot understand even though they are praying and reading their word, paying tithes and offerings, and attending church regularly, why so many things in their life are out of balance.

I know God is dealing with many chosen ones in the Body of Christ to leave their "Ur of the Chaldees" and take a faith walk toward their divine destiny. But many who are under the yoke of fear, control, and manipulation, are afraid to quit their jobs or leave their geographical location to venture out into the unknown to take a faith walk, similar to Abraham. Some are ignorantly trying to be men pleasers, because people's opinion matter to them more than following the leading and promptings of the Holy Spirit.

When God is leading you to relocate, be careful, because the spirit of Fear, the spirit of Deception, and people who want you to invest in their destiny without considering the will of God for your life, will try to influence you to join their team instead. This is how many chosen ones have become a slave to another man's vision, and what God called them to do stays pending like seed fallen on the wayside, for the fowls of the air to devour.

When you get to where God is calling you to, everything will change. That is why the enemy will always try to disconnect you from your call. When God speaks to you about getting into position, you have to move, and where you go, and how to get there, is between you and your God. You cannot go to people to get their opinion, especially if God did not speak to them about your prophetic position.

When Abraham's feet touched the land of Canaan, God appeared unto Abraham and gave him a promise. Abraham marked the places where he communicated with God by building an altar. These places became generational landmarks and strategic positions; exit and entry portals for angels and the manifestation of God in the land.

> So Abram went up from Egypt to the Negev, with his wife and everything he had, and Lot went with him. Abram had become very wealthy in livestock and in silver and gold.
>
> From the Negev he went from place to place until he came to Bethel and Ai where his tent had been earlier, and where he had first built an altar. There Abram called on the name of the Lord.
>
> -Genesis 13:1-3.

> Jacob left Beersheba and set out for Haran. When he reached a certain place, he stopped for the night

because the sun had set. Taking one of the stones there, he put it under his head and lay down to sleep.

He had a dream in which he saw a stairway resting on the earth, with its top reaching to heaven, and the angels of God were ascending and descending on it. There above it stood the Lord, and he said; I am the Lord, the God of your father Abraham and the God of Isaac. I will give you and your descendants the land on which you are lying.

Your descendants will be like the dust of the earth, and you will spread out to the west and to the east, to the north and to the south.

All peoples of the earth will be blessed through you and your offspring. I am with you and will watch over you wherever you go, and I will bring you back to this land. I will not leave you until I have done what I have promised you.

When Jacob awoke from his sleep, he thought, surely the Lord is in this place, and I was not aware of it. He was afraid and said, "How awesome is this place! This is none other than the house of God; this is the gate of heaven."

Early the next morning Jacob took the stone he had placed under his head and set it up as a pillar and poured oil on top of it. He called that place Bethel, though the city used to be called Luz.

-Genesis 28:10-17.

God thinks generationally, and He renewed the Abrahamic covenant with every succeeding generation.

One generation will commend your works to another,
they will tell of your mighty acts.

-Psalm 145: 4.

Symbolic Language of the Text: Every fruit tree produces fruit after its kind. The Creator has programmed every seed with the ability to produce the next generation of fruit. This is an important principle in the kingdom of God.

When one is born again by the incorruptible seed of the word of God, the inner core of one's being is transformed by the word of God. Spiritually, one becomes a tree of righteousness, the planting of the Lord.

> To appoint unto them that mourn in Zion, to give unto them beauty for ashes, the oil of joy for mourning, the garment of praise for the spirit of heaviness that they might be called trees of righteousness, the planting of the Lord, that He might be glorified.
>
> -Isaiah 61: 3.

To Every Truth in the Natural There is a Parallel Truth in the Spirit.

- The natural tree bears natural fruit after its kind.
- The natural man that bears fruit [children] according to the will of his flesh, after his kind.
- Symbolically, trees represents mankind; they are trees of righteousness, the planting of the Lord which refer to the children of God, that produce the fruit of the Spirit.
- Then there are evil trees which produce corrupt fruit, this reference is made to the wicked. Jesus said, "By their fruit you shall know them."

- John the Baptist prophesied, "The axe is laid at the root of the tree" referring to the ungodly that shall not stand in the judgment of God.
- God put two trees in the center of the Garden of Eden, the tree of life and the tree of the knowledge of good and evil. Each one depicting the choice given to mankind; Obey God and live in the presence of God or disobey God and die by living outside the presence of God.

Psalm 1 gives the revelation of man symbolically referred to a tree.

Blessed is the man who walks not in the counsel of the wicked, nor stands in the way of sinners, nor sits in the seat of the scoffers; but his delight is in the law of the Lord, and on his law he meditates day and night.

He is like a tree planted by streams of water that yields its fruit in its season, and its leaf does not wither. In all that he does, he prospers. The wicked are not so, but are like the chaff that the wind drives away.

Therefore the wicked will not stand in the judgment, nor sinners in the congregation of the righteous; For the Lord knows the way of the righteous, but the way of the wicked will perish.

-Psalm 1:1- 3

In the natural, when the season of harvest comes there is a manifestation of fruit. Similarly, in the spirit the manifestation of a good harvest is souls; lives that have been transformed by the Spirit of God. In the kingdom, the way of the righteous is to be fruitful. The man that is fruitful thinks about his purpose.

Every man has a destiny, a purpose and a harvest, when he will reap what he has sown.

The question we must ask ourselves is, "What is God's plan for my life?" Am I producing fruit, am I productive, am I fruitful? As trees of righteousness, and branches of the true vine, if we become fruitful, then we can ask the father for whatsoever we desire, in Jesus name and He would give it to us.

John the Baptist also used symbolic language in his dissertation:

> Bear fruit in keeping with repentance.
> Even now the axe is laid to the root of the trees.
> Every tree therefore that does not bear good fruit is cut down and thrown into the fire.
>
> -Matthew 3:8, 10.

> Either make the tree good, and his fruit good; or else make the tree corrupt, and his fruit corrupt for the tree is known by his fruit.
>
> -Matthew 12: 33.

You cannot make a natural tree good or evil, so Jesus is not speaking about natural trees, they do not have the power of choice, they have to produce after their kind.

Fruit bearing trees are symbolically used to depict man, because man has a generational seed in his loins similar to fruit bearing trees.

Levi paid tithes when he was in the loins of Abraham, but Abraham had Isaac, and Isaac had Jacob, who produced Levi. Levi was Abraham's great grandson. Yet the Bible says that Levi paid tithes when he was in the loins of Abraham. When we pay tithes it is not just for the person paying the tithes, but tithes produce generational blessings.

Even though trees and man have similar purposes, the difference is - man has a spirit, and if a man is born again, his dual nature allows him to bear fruit naturally and spiritually.

- The axe being laid at the root of the tree speaks of impending judgment for man.

- The hewing down of the tree and casting it into the fire, speaks of final judgment of man.

Jesus said:
> I am the vine, ye are the branches; He that abides in me, and I in him, the same brings forth much fruit for without me ye can do nothing.
>
> If a man abides not in me, he is cast forth as a branch and is withered and men gather them, and cast them into the fire, and they are burned.
>
> -John 15: 5, 6.

His apostles were the first fruits of Jesus' ministry. Then His apostles had to reproduce the ministry of Jesus in others. Fruitfulness is a kingdom requisite, but seed must experience darkness before it reproduces; transformation takes place in darkness. This is the prescribed formula for seed to be fruitful. Darkness is the prescription for kingdom transformation and fruitfulness. When the harvest comes, the manifestation of the fruit will be a life seasoned by the word of God.

> I am the true vine, and my father is the gardener. He cuts off every branch in me that bears no fruit, while every branch that does bear fruit He prunes so that it will be even more fruitful.
>
> Remain in me, and I will remain in you. No branch can bear fruit by itself; it must remain in the vine. Neither can you bear fruit unless you remain in me.

I am the vine; you are the branches. If a man remains
in me and I in him, he will bear much fruit; apart
from me you can do nothing.

-John 15: 1-4.

There are two types of cutting, Jesus cuts the ones that do not
bear fruit, and He throws them into the fire because they are
unfruitful. But those that bear fruit, He says, I'll cut that one
too; I will prune it so that it can produce more fruit.

- Anytime a man or woman of God is striving for mastery
  or a higher level in the kingdom, the order of the
  kingdom demands that he receives a cutting mark.

- In the natural the sons of Abraham received the mark of
  circumcision but for the New Testament believer,
  circumcision is that of the heart in the spirit; the core of
  the man.

- Once the spirit of the world has been removed, the
  disciple of Christ is now qualified to bear the type of fruit
  that will last.

It takes a lifetime of commitment and consecration to Jesus
Christ, the true vine, for you to bear kingdom fruit. It takes
obedience to His word, our daily walk with God, our willingness
to take up our cross daily to follow Him, and to spend quality
time in prayer.

Prayer is the foundation for a successful life as a Christian. You
need to pray, and you need people around you who can pray.
Jesus said, "If ye abide in me and my words abide in you, then
you can ask the father in my name and He will give it to you."

When you are chosen of God, how you handle adversity qualifies
you or disqualifies you for promotion. Many have been replaced

or demoted for not bearing the quality of fruit the kingdom requires.

If you come out of a place of adversity and you are angry, rebellious, unforgiving, disobedient, full of resentment, hate, full of discord, confusion, blaming everybody, full of revenge, then you are bearing the wrong kind of fruit. That quality of fruit will not remain because it is not kingdom fruit; it is the works of the flesh.

Principles of Increase

How does increase occur? God has given us certain universal principles to tap into and utilize to produce increase. These principles need to be meaningfully applied in the emerging apostolic movement so that dynamic increase can come to the Church.

Increase Comes From Investment: Leaders have to invest their lives, their resources, and their time into the kingdom to be profitable. The kingdom is everlasting, and it is over and above all other kingdoms. It covers the realm of the man and the realm of the spirit; the rewards are not only received here on earth but there are also eternal rewards.

> "There is one who scatters, yet increases more; and there is one who withholds more than is right, but it leads to poverty."
> -Proverbs 11:24.

Increase Rises Through Faith: Leaders must move in faith for increase. They must teach faith to their people, knowing that this results in an extension of the scope of their ministries (2 Corinthians 10:15). "So the churches were strengthened in the faith, and increased in number daily" (Acts 16:5).

Increase Follows Effort: True Leaders are not afraid of hard work. "Wealth gained by dishonesty will be diminished, but he who gathers by labor will increase" [Proverbs 13:11]. A true leader is like a mighty ox that rarely gets tired and brings forth great increase.

Increase Comes Through Synergy: Leaders must understand the importance of unity; widespread and effective participation from the people of God. It took Paul and Apollos to water and plant. Every part of the Body must be active, contribute, and be in harmony for increase to occur.

Increase Is A Reward For Obedience: Leaders must understand the blessings of obedience to the heavenly vision. The blessing outlined for those who obey the Word of God is increase.

As the people of God we are all concerned about the times we are living in; we all desire to be positioned so that our future will be prosperous. What does the Biblical narrative say, to give us guidance, comfort, exhortation, reassurance, and wisdom for the days ahead?

> And there was famine in the land, beside the first famine that was in the days of Abraham. And Isaac went unto Abimelech, king of the Philistines unto Gerar.
>
> And the Lord appeared unto him, and said, "Go not down in to Egypt: dwell in the land which I shall tell thee of: Sojourn in this land, and I will be with thee, and will bless thee; for unto thee, and unto thy seed, I will give all these countries, and I will perform the oath which I swore unto Abraham thy father."
>
> Verse 6 - And Isaac dwelt in Gerar.

Verses 12-13 - Then Isaac sowed in the land, and received in the same year a hundredfold; and the Lord blessed him. And the man waxed great, and went forward, and grew until he became very great.

NIV- Isaac planted crops in that land and the same year reaped a hundredfold, because the Lord blessed him. The man became rich, and his wealth continued to grow until he became very wealthy. He had so many flocks and herds and the servants that the Philistines envied him.

-Genesis 26: 1-3.

What Can We Learn From This Lesson?

- Isaac was chosen by God
- There was a famine in the land affecting the economy of the land.
- The famine affected everyone.
- In the economy of the kingdom of heaven there is no famine, lack or drought.
- God told Isaac to dwell in the land, take your position in the land.
- Isaac obeyed God.
- It was in that place of drought, hardship, in the midst of famine and economic devastation for the Philistines that God ordained for Isaac who dwelt among the Philistines to be fruitful.
- Isaac believed and trusted the God of his father Abraham; he was not deterred by the earth forces that were attacking the land with barrenness.
- God proved once again that He is a God that keeps His part of a generational covenant by demonstrating His ability to make His chosen fruitful, regardless of the economy.

- Isaac sowed his seed in the land and reaped a hundredfold because God was with him.
- Isaac was blessed and continued to be fruitful because the Lord made room for him in the land.
- He was the envy of all the Philistines around him, because their Pagan gods could not do for them what Jehovah did for Isaac.

We conclude with this thought, fruit is the evidence of a person's accomplishments, the evidence of a person's life's work in the secular field or in the ministry of the kingdom of God. Fruit is also evidence of character. Jesus said, by their fruit you shall know them.

You will know who has been with Jesus by the evidence of a transformed life. An evil tree cannot produce good fruit, and a good tree cannot produce evil fruit.

Bibliography

English Standard Bible – Crossway, Wheaton, Illinois: www.EVS.org.
King James Version: (KJV) of the Bible. NIV. NKJV.

References:

Becoming a leader – Elmer L. Towns.
Spheres of Authority – C. Peter Wagner.
Apostles and the emerging apostolic movement – David Cannistraci.
God's leaders for tomorrow's world – Harold R. Eberle.
School of the Holy Spirit –https://theschooloftheholyspirit.org

ABOUT THE AUTHOR

Apostle Gemma Valentine was born in the Caribbean island nation of Trinidad and Tobago. Following in the footsteps of her parents she answered the call to the ministry when she was twenty three years old.

Her ministerial training began with the Church of God of Prophecy in Trinidad. After which she transferred to the Southern New England Diocese where she served as an Authorized Teacher, Regional Evangelist, Regional Director of Women ministries, Regional Director of the Sunday School Department and as a Pastor.

When her tenure with that institution ended, she began her apostolic training at St John's Full Gospel Deliverance Church, in Bloomfield Connecticut. She was ordained an Apostle in 2006 and was given a mandate by God to preach the gospel of the Kingdom of God.

Matthew 24:14 – And this gospel of the kingdom shall be preached in all the world for a witness unto all nations; and then shall the end come.

God changed the genre of her ministry from a 'Pastoral Ministry' to an Ambassadorial, Motivational apostle. Some of her accomplishments are:

She is the founder and chief executive of "The Apostolic Prophetic network of Watchman and Gatekeepers" headquartered in the nation island of Trinidad and Tobago.

She is the founder and president of Harbor Lights Associates, Inc. a nonprofit, [501©3] initiative.

She is the principal of "The School of the Holy Spirit." A teaching and discipleship program for believers and for those called into the ministry.

She is the founder of a fellowship, mentoring and counselling ministry called, "For Women Only." She has done extensive work with women in ministry, given spiritual counselling, prayer, and support.

Apostle Valentine writes a monthly column called "The Apostle's Corner" in the Power Pages newspaper serving Collin County in the state of Texas.

She is a published author and has published other books, entitled -The Purpose for Marriage, While Men Slept and Marriage, Myths and Divorce, and a workbook for with questions for discussion and deeper study.

She leads an Early Riser Intercessory prayer meeting Monday to Friday in McKinney, Texas.

She operates in the kingdom with an apostolic and prophetic mantle, and is known for the depth of her revelation, her wisdom, and for validating and authenticating the true calling of believers, to bring about prophetic alignment and clarity to the true nature of their call and purpose in the kingdom.

She is a graduate of the Church of God of Prophecy, Bible Training Institute, Cleveland Tennessee; she also holds a Doctor of Divinity degree from the Maryland Theological Seminary and College.

She currently resides in McKinney, Texas and is married to John Valentine.

Websites:

http//:Watchmen-Gatekeepers.org.
http//:theschooloftheholyspirit.org.

PayPal: eldergemma@msn.com

Email: eldergemma@msn.com

Apostle Gemma Valentine teaches a variety of workshops with various topics dealing with the development of people called to the ministry.

Workshops on Prayer
Seminars on Marriage
Understanding your Calling
Spiritual warfare
Leadership for God's people
The symbolic language of Dreams and Visions
The seven dimensions of water and the spirit.
Called and Commission
And many more topics

Her Books are sold at www.amazon.com; Barnes and Noble.com
Watchmen-gatekeepers.org

Made in the USA
Middletown, DE
28 August 2022

72551488R00195